LETTERS FROM MADRAS

Julia Maitland
artist unknown

JULIA MAITLAND

Letters from Madras
during the years 1836-1839

with introduction, notes and appendices by
Alyson Price

OTLEY
Woodstock Books
2003

Letters from Madras first published 1843

This edition published 2003 by
Woodstock Books
Otley, West Yorkshire
England LS21 3JP

ISBN 1 85477 267 8

New introduction, notes, and appendices
copyright © 2003
Alyson Price

British Library Cataloguing-in-Publication Data

A catalogue record for this book is available from the
British Library

Printed and bound in England by
Smith Settle Printing & Bookbinding Ltd
Ilkley Road, Otley LS21 3JP

Contents

Illustrations and maps, vii

Introduction, ix

Note on the Text, xxviii

Letters from Madras

Appendix 1
Response of the Company authorities to the building of a church in Black Town, 200

Appendix 2
Petition for Native Education, 201

Sources and References, 205

Acknowledgements, 207

Illustrations

Julia Maitland
facing title-page

'Harrington Gardens, Madras'
facing page 64

'Rajahmundry, View of the Courthouse'
facing page 65

'Rajahmundry, View of a Moorman's Bungalow'
facing page 88

'From our Verandah at Samuldavy'
facing page 89

Maps

Madras and the Coromandel coast
page xviii

Rajahmundry and surroundings
page xx

Endpapers

Letter dated Rajahmundry, 3 October 1837
Julia's letters were cross-written, making them difficult to read. This one is made the more troublesome by including a very faint ground plan of her house, showing a bedroom, dressing room, drawing room, dining room, entrance hall, spare room, baby room and three bathrooms.

Introduction

Julia Maitland was born on 21 October 1808, the daughter of Charlotte and Henry Barrett. Her grandmother Charlotte Francis Broome was a younger sister of the novelist Fanny Burney and daughter of the historian of music Dr Charles Burney. Julia and her younger sister and younger brothers grew up near London, in Richmond, until Henry Barrett's losses on his West Indian plantations obliged him to rent out his Richmond house and live on the continent or in rented accommodation lent by friends. The boys attended boarding schools, and the girls travelled with their parents to France and Belgium where the cost of living was lower and hiring masters for them was cheaper. Fanny Burney (who had married General Alexandre D'Arblay in 1793) wrote to her sister Esther Burney in 1826 that Julia was

a most lovely companion, without and within, for though well informed, and quite au fait in Botany, and Mineralogy, and Metalogy, and Shellalogy, and all the other ogies now requisite for les demoiselles comme il faut to dilate upon, she is simple, unaffected, affectionate, useful, and pleasing (Hemlow, xii, 672).[1]

Julia was the favourite of her grandmother, and spent some of her time as an adolescent and young woman living and travelling with her. Fanny D'Arblay wrote to her sister Charlotte in 1819:

I am truly glad you have got your favourite Julia with you. She is universally beloved, and seems to merit that high distinction by her modesty and good qualities, united with so much beauty (Hemlow, xi, 81).

Julia's beauty is frequently commented on within the family, and Sarah Harriet Burney, Fanny's half sister, wrote to Julia's mother in 1825:

---
[1] For an explanation of sources see p.205.

INTRODUCTION

I cannot tell you, my dearest, how I was struck ... with your Julia's beauty the day you brought her to Green Street. I saw my Sister d'Arblay that or the next evening, and she was as much impressed. Upon my word, such a fine creature as that, ought to marry the Duke of Devonshire – and I dare say she would, if he could but see her (Clark, p. 259).

There was even talk of Fanny's son, Alexander D'Arblay, taking an interest in Julia. Marianne Francis warned her sister Charlotte Barrett:

One word to you as a Mother, Alex d'Arblay has been most pointedly after sweet Ju at Raper's and here, and appearing to me deeply smitten. But I trust Ju will have the sense to let it all be on his side, as it would be a most dismal affair so to throw herself away, poor dr. Alex, with all his cleverness not being at all nice enough for Julia (Hemlow, xii, 672).

By the 1830s the family was settled in Brighton and it was here, some time in 1835, that Julia met James Thomas, probably among the congregation of the Rev. Charles David Maitland's St James's Chapel. James Thomas was on leave from India and his mother lived in Brighton; he was a widower with three small daughters. The couple were married in the summer of 1836.

Charlotte Barrett was not in favour of the match and wrote many letters to her mother on the subject:

I think she is throwing herself away on a very poor sly fellow – but he has a sweet temper – and he loves religion and religious people – And she is so tired of her home and of poor Governor [her father], and so desirous of a change that it may be for her happiness (Barrett Eg3702A, 139-40).

James Thomas promised Charlotte that he would bring Julia home after five years in India, and satisfied her on his circumstances:

All the probabilities are in favour of his having a good appointment soon after he gets to India – his rank is high and so is his character in India – he has a married brother who is now at Madras with a good house and income ... Julia seems quite angry if the least fault is found with him and his prospects (Barrett Eg3702A, 137-8).

Charlotte was not entirely sanguine about her daughter marrying a man with three children. There was the anxiety

INTRODUCTION

that her family money would find its way to Thomas's children, should 'the fatigue of the Voyage and Climate carry [Julia] off, poor thing' (Barrett EG3702A, 139-40). And she may have had the well-founded suspicion that the burden of the children would fall on her. Julia took her new charges very seriously but they were left behind in England and, as her letters show, she expected the assistance of her mother:

> Now, my dearest Mammy, what are we to do if you keep to this notion of never acting about the children! I would not say to anyone but you James really has not among his own relations, anyone whom he can thoroughly trust about managing for his children, and he always hoped that he had left them under your superintendence and as they should not be considered my children, it is more natural that you should have as much as possible the direction of them than anyone else (Berg Collection, 10 April 1839).[2]

Many in the family feared they would never see Julia again, and her grandmother wrote to her sister Fanny D'Arblay 'the distance of Madras seems like going from this world to the next.' Julia, by now twenty-eight years old, may well have 'long fretted inwardly under petty contradictions and constant disturbances from her poor Father's irritable humours' (Hemlow, xx, 895), but she had not been short of suitors and this was by no means a desperate choice on her part. Her mother and grandmother mention a local preacher, Langdon, and Julia herself gives her mother an account of the reaction of another suitor on being given the news of her marriage. 'He showed more disturbance than I expected, for I thought he would take it all coolly and pretend he did not care. He did begin so, but he could not keep it up' (Barrett Eg3704B, 103-4). She also knew the Rev. Maitland's son, Charles, who was to become her second husband in 1842 after her return from India.

Julia's grandmother described the wedding to her sister Fanny D'Arblay :

---

[2] See p. xv, note 4.

xi

INTRODUCTION

'Such an affecting wedding wrung our hearts, the thoughts of the parting that was to follow, that very day, embittering every part of it – deep sorrow clinging to every consideration … it was a beautiful wedding to look at, but almost insupportable, to her sweet Madre and myself … I am so dismantled, body and mind (Hemlow, xii, 903 and Berg 9 August 1836).

A few days after the wedding, Julia and James Thomas sailed for India.

By 1800 the East India Company had been trading in India for two hundred years. Initially a society of merchants and adventurers trading on even terms with the Indian population, its character was changing. The conquests of the eighteenth century and the decline of the Moghuls were early evidence of the imperialism that was to follow in the Victorian period, especially after 1858 when the Crown took control of India from Company hands. The India in which Julia arrived was governed by a powerful élite and with a large private army. The Company had become increasingly important to the British economy, so much so that any threat to its prosperity was a threat to the British state.

Other changes were taking place. The Company had always expressly forbidden missionary activity or any interference with local customs. But in 1813 it lost its commercial monopoly and, through the work of men like Wilberforce, it was forced to allow the entry of missionaries into its territories. In the parliamentary debate at the time, Wilberforce stated that Christianity was

beyond all other institutions that ever existed, favourable to the temporal interests and happiness of man: and never was there a country where there is greater need than in India for the diffusion of its genial influence (Stokes, p.33).

The growing numbers of European women in India in the late eighteenth century also changed relationships between Europeans and Indians. It is estimated that in the first two hundred years of the Company presence as many as ninety

INTRODUCTION

per cent of Company men in India had Indian mistresses or wives. Tolerance of these relationships was to end with the arrival of European women who, whether they were conscious of it or not, came to defend the national and religious identities of their countrymen. Many came looking for husbands. The boundaries between the races became more rigid and was reflected in the political topography of towns, in Madras, for example, where Julia writes in her *Letters* of going into 'Black Town.'

Julia's years in India reflect this period of change, and of a growing missionary fervour at odds with the traditional Company attitude of regard for Indian religion and customs. She does not question her belief in the rightness of British rule in India, in the superiority of the Christian religion and in progress through a European scientific education. Her own activities in India, concentrated as they were on education, were a response to Macaulay's *Minute on Indian Education* (1835), in which he advocated educating 'a class of persons, Indian in blood and colour, but English in taste, in opinions, in morals, and in intellect', adding to their dialects 'terms of science borrowed from Western nomenclature', and ensuring they were 'fit vehicles for conveying knowledge to the great mass of the population.'

Julia's husband, James Thomas, attended Haileybury College, the training ground for Company servants, where students learned three or more oriental languages, and studied the classics, mathematics, political economy and history. He entered the service of the East India Company in 1812 as a Writer, or clerk (Writers recorded the proceedings of the Company for forwarding to London). By the time he took Julia to India he had risen through the ranks of Writer, Factor and Junior Merchant and he was listed in the *Madras Almanac* as a Senior Merchant, the highest civil service grade. Before his leave in 1833, he had been the Principal Collector and Magistrate of Coimbatore, and Third Judge of the Provincial

INTRODUCTION

Court, Centre Division. He had two brothers in India, John and Edward Thomas, who began respectively as Writers in 1816 and 1824. Both were also Senior Merchants. Edward was on leave in England almost the entire time Julia was in India. Of the three brothers, it was John who rose highest in the service before resigning in 1855.

Seniority tended to place men in line for posts as they occurred. However, personal introduction to the Governor could play a role. Julia's mother had done what she could herself to introduce Julia and her husband to influential circles before their departure for India, but she also enlisted the support of Fanny D'Arblay:

Do you think it would be possible for you (without difficulty or inconvenience to your dear self – otherwise not) but could you, without difficulty ask Lady Keith for a line to introduce Julia (when she goes to Madras) to the acquaintance of Lord Elphinstone? [the new Governor of Madras](Berg 30 June 1836).

But Fanny D'Arblay's approach to Lady Keith came to nothing, for reasons perhaps explained in a letter Julia wrote to her mother in April 1837:

Your letter of October 30th enclosed Miss Elphinstone's note of introduction to Lord E. Many thanks for it, and for all the pains you took about it. There is nothing like any little private introduction for really making interest. It happens that Miss Elph's recommendation is a much better one than Lady Keith's would have been, for it seems there is some gossiping story afloat concerning Lady K's having wanted him to marry her daughter and his having shirked (Berg 25 April 1837).

Julia and James Thomas arrived in Madras in December 1836, and went immediately to stay with James Thomas's brother John and his wife Diana. The couple were in Madras for seven months until August 1837 when James Thomas took up his post both as Judge (dealing primarily with cases involving property) and as Criminal Judge, at Rajahmundry. They were to stay at Rajahmundry for a year and a half, some of the hottest months of which Julia spent on the coast at Samuldavee.

INTRODUCTION

A new posting in July 1839 meant first a transfer to Madras and then another to Bangalore in October. The sudden illness followed by the death of her husband on 6 January 1840, the very same day that her great-aunt Fanny D'Arblay died in London, brought Julia back to Madras and on to England with her children.

Letters from Madras ('by a Lady') was published by John Murray in 1843. It was anonymous at the request of Charlotte, who had a 'great objection' to her daughter publishing under her own name.[3] Julia insisted on reading and correcting the proofs herself. Three years later there was a second edition, published in Murray's Colonial Library, for the copyright of which Julia received forty guineas. It contains a few, very minor revisions.

By far the majority of the letters published in *Letters from Madras* were based on those written to her mother. Julia referred to them as 'journal letters'; they form part only of an extensive correspondence.[4] In addition, she used extracts from letters to her grandmother, her brothers Richard and Arthur, and her cousin and friend Minette Raper Kingston.

In editing *Letters from Madras* Julia cut almost all detail relating to her family – to her family at home in England (her grandmother and her cousin Alexander D'Arblay died in her absence, her brother Arthur got into debt and her brother Dick worried over his Cambridge exams), to her children born in India, and to James Thomas's children. She also cut details involving her husband's career in India, his family,

---

[3] Julia to John Murray, 9 July 1843 (Murray Archive).
[4] Julia's letters to her mother are preserved in the Berg Collection of the New York Public Library. With her letter of 11th January 1837, Julia began numbering them. She numbered that letter as three. In the Berg Collection there are letters numbered up to 64 (Bangalore, 24 October 1839), with the following numbers missing: 15 (June/July 1837), 17 (July/August 1837), 36 to 39 (May/June 1838), 43 (August/September 1838), 48 (October 1838), 56 (April/May 1839), 59 (June/July 1839), 63 (September/October 1839) and those that must have followed no.64. One of these missing letters, number 17, is in the Barrett Collection in the British Library.

INTRODUCTION

the friends she made and most of the reading she did (e.g. the *Life of Wilberforce*, Coleridge's *Table Talk*, Charles Lamb's *Letters* which she found 'delightful', and Dickens's *Nicholas Nickleby* which she 'greatly admired'). The result of all this cutting is that the dominant themes of the published *Letters* emerge as education and missionary activity, intentionally or not a contribution to the debates of the time.

Elizabeth Eastlake, reviewing *Letters from Madras* in John Murray's *Quarterly Review* in 1845, described it as 'the very lightest work that has ever appeared from India, yet it tells us more of what everybody cares to know than any other.' Today, though in a totally unselfconscious way, it probably tells us more about Julia's attitudes and opinions than it does about India. In Rajahmundry she believed she was seeing 'the real India' and every day saw 'something new and foreign.' To contemporary readers her interests may have mirrored their own when she described herself as 'longing to get into one of their native houses'; and when introduced to the Rajah's wife, 'I had been longing to see her,' 'I was very curious to see the ladies of the family. I peeped about in hopes of catching a glimpse of them.'

Julia arrived with firm assumptions about race. She believed Indians to be not only 'ignorant', but also 'lazy', 'servile', 'like babies', 'cheats'; and her female servants could be 'wicked' and 'foolish'. At the same time she is struck from the start by the treatment meted out to Indians by Europeans:

> these natives are a cringing set, and behave to us English as if they were dirt under our feet; and indeed we give them reason to suppose we consider them as such. Their servility is disagreeable, but the rudeness and contempt with which the English treat them are quite painful to witness. (Letter Five).

This aspect of English behaviour never leaves Julia while in India, and she was gratified to find her views reflected in John Shore's *Notes on Indian Affairs* (Letter Sixteen). Yet, while Julia was able to concur with Shore's views on the British treatment of Indians, she does not investigate her own prejudices and assumptions. What the Indians need is education and Christianity: 'at home we talk of ignorance and heathenism, but we have no idea of what the ignorance of heathenism really is'; 'It is very striking to see how completely want of education has blasted all their powers of intellect.' Indian religion could be undermined by education:

> that is the great difficulty with these poor natives; they have not the slightest idea of the value and advantage of *truth*. No one in England knows the difficulty of making any impression upon them. The best means seems to be education, because false notions of science form one great part of their religion. Every belief of theirs is interwoven with some matter of religion; and if once their scientific absurdities are overthrown, a large portion of their religion goes with them, and there seems more likelihood of shaking their faith in the remainder. (Letter Twenty).

With her curiosity and her commitment to leading a useful life, Julia did not like Madras very much. Twenty-eight years earlier, Maria Graham had recorded her impressions of a lady's life in the city, an eternal round of balls, flirtations, and lying about reading novels. To Julia, every creature was 'eaten up with laziness.' But she set herself to enjoy life in the city as much as she could, 'to try and see everything that I can while the bloom of my Orientalism is fresh upon me, and before this apathy and listlessness have laid hold on me.' She involved herself visiting schools, meeting Europeans and Indians, surviving her first pregnancy and childbirth, and observing the world around her.

She began learning Tamil on board ship, and continued with a moonshee (teacher) in Madras. She visited a caste school (one for high caste Hindus), where the Bible was used as a tool but Christianity not instructed, and the Female Orphan Asylum. Maria Graham had visited the same Asylum in 1810 and explained that such places were needed in India:

> where the numbers of half-caste, and therefore (if I may use the expression) half-parented children, exceed what one could imagine … I cannot

INTRODUCTION

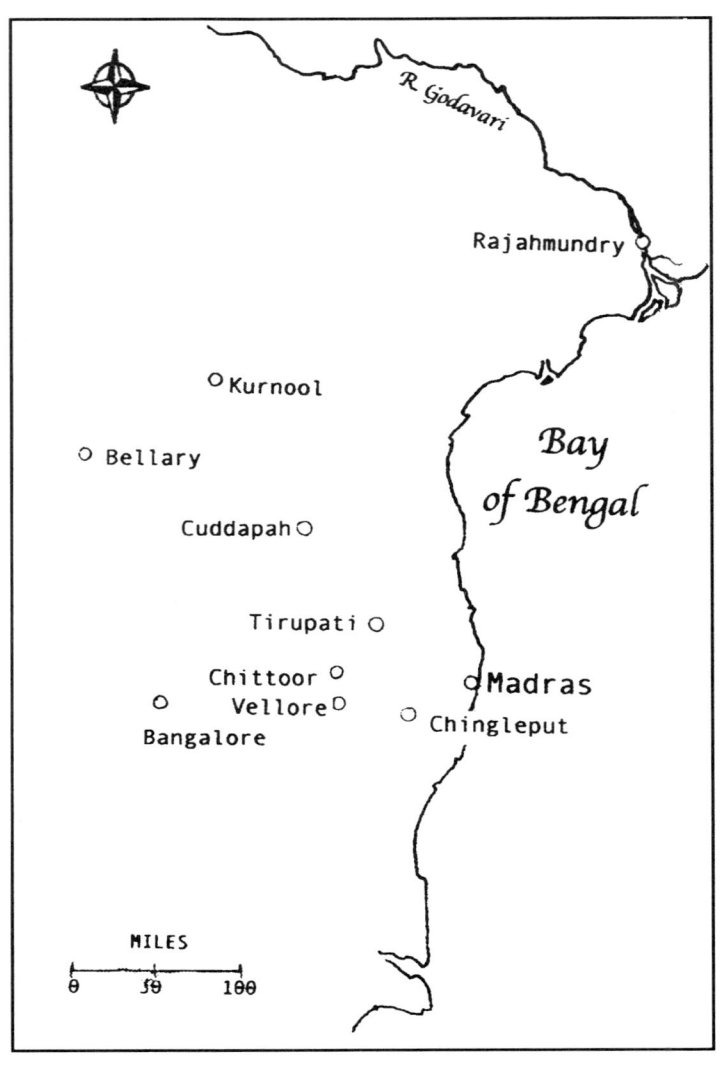

Madras and the Coromandel coast.

but think it a cruelty to send children of colour to Europe, where their complexion must subject them to perpetual mortification. Here, being in their own country, and associating with those in the same situation as themselves, they have a better chance of being happy (*Journal of a Residence in India*, p.128).

'Half-caste' was the term used at the time for people of mixed race, now more commonly called Anglo-Indian. In a letter to her brother Dick, Julia's views differ from Graham's:

the Half Caste people are the worst off of all – they are just half and half everything, and nobody cares so much for them as for the Heathen – they are looked down upon from all sides, and are puffed up in pride themselves accordingly (Berg 1 Mar 1837).

In elaborating on the two themes of missionary activity and education, Julia was particularly concerned with the kind of person suitable to be a missionary or a teacher. This is demonstrated in her very first letters to her mother from on board ship, and by December 1837 she writes:

I believe that the more educated and the more of a gentleman he is, the more influence he will have among the Hindoos. They are themselves most excellent judges of manners and standing in society, and invariably know a gentleman, and respect him accordingly. Their own priests are of the highest caste, and it lowers our religion in their eyes if they see that our Padres, as they call the Missionaries, are of what they consider low caste (Letter Fifteen).

Her impatience with 'John Company' and, as it appears to her, its support of native religious observance, reflects the transitional period in which she found herself. The case of a missionary building a chapel and thereby disturbing his Indian neighbours in Black Town, illustrative of this transition (see Appendix 1), was going on while Julia was in Madras and shows how the official Company view was changing.

Though clearly she was not impressed by rank Julia found herself moving in high circles, and in those with access to schools and church organisations. Her brother-in-law John Thomas was a subscribing member of the Incorporated Society for the Propagation of the Gospel in Foreign Parts, as

INTRODUCTION

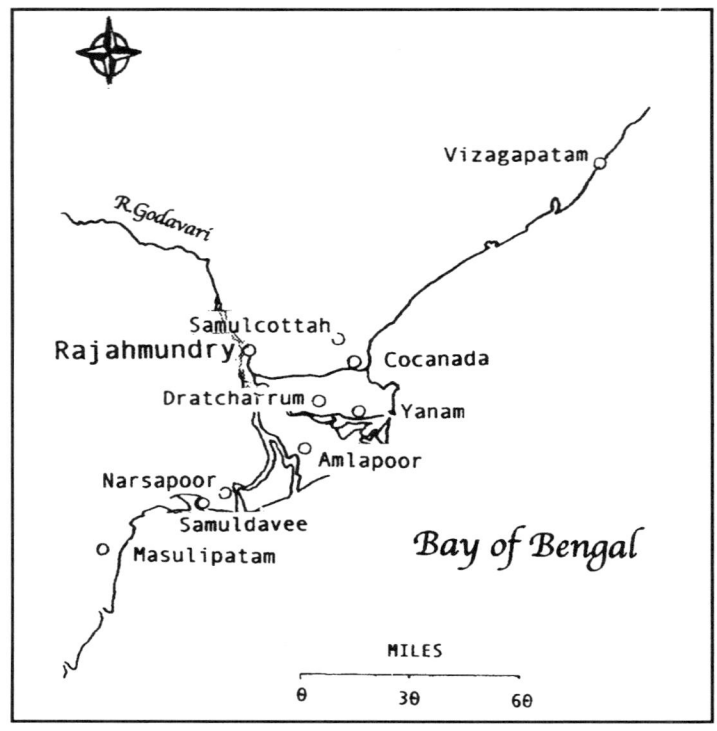

Rajahmundry and surroundings

was the Rev. J. Tucker whom Julia heard preach in Black Town. Tucker was the secretary of the Church Missionary Society, and his sister was on the Ladies' Committee for Native Female Education; Julia was to get to know them both. John Thomas was also on the Committee of the Indian Missionary Society and the Madras School Book Society, and he was a Governor of the Male Orphan Asylum. Tucker and the Rev. Vincent Shortland, whom Julia was to meet in Rajahmundry, were both patrons of the Hindoo Christians' Religious Book Society. Tucker and Thomas were on the

INTRODUCTION

Committee of both the Native Education Society and Bishop Corrie's Grammar School.

It was not until she was 'up country' in Rajahmundry, that Julia was able to put some of her ideas into practice. Rajahmundry, now in the state of Andrah Pradesh, is approximately 370 miles from Madras. It was the main town in the taluk, an administrative subdivision of the zillah, or district. It stands on the north bank of the Godavari river and was described in Murray's 1859 *Handbook* as consisting

> of one principal street half a mile in length, running nearly due N. and S., where is the chief bazaar. The houses on each side are generally of mud, one storey high, and tiled. Several narrow lanes run E. and W. from the principal street. Those to the W. proceed to the bank of the river, and consist of mean houses, with here and there large two-storied dwellings, belonging to the Zamindars of the district, or wealthy brahmans. The streets on the E. side are more narrow and irregular, and have fewer houses of the respectable classes.

Rajahmundry was of importance to Hindus, who were advised that anyone travelling to the holy city of Varanasi (Benares) from the area should also bathe in the Godavari at Rajahmundry. In the 1825 *Survey* of the district, Rajahmundry was described as having 5,008 inhabitants, 'of which a considerable proportion are Mohammedans.' There was a 'mosque of some antiquity as also several pagodas.' The surrounding land was considered very fertile and a good trade was carried out with the Nizam's Hyderabad territories.

By the time James Thomas was appointed Judge and Criminal Judge of Rajahmundry the Zillah Court had been in place there for about thirty-five years. The Judge, in his civil capacity, was assisted by a pundit ('very much of a mountebank') and a moofti ('in his shabby magnificence looking like a beggarly king'), respectively the expounders of Hindu and Mohammedan Law. The Judge dealt largely with property disputes, in which he was assisted by a Registrar, or Register. As a Criminal Judge, local judges were supported by

INTRODUCTION

a system of circuit judges and courts. During their residence in Rajahmundry there was no Chaplain in the town, and Thomas held Sunday services for the English residents in their own home.

Julia took an interest in her husband's work and reported on a few cases that came before him, but her main focus in *Letters from Madras* is on the school for caste boys that she and her husband set up:

> we have no immediate hope of making Christians of these boys by our teaching, but we wish to 'do what we can': this kind of school is all we can do for them, and I fully believe that, if schools were set up all over the country, it would go far towards shaking their Heathenism (Letter Thirteen).

Yet Julia was sensitive to some degree when considering educational method. There was 'no objection made to the use of our books', so long as no overt teaching of Christianity was taking place. She complained that many elementary books were 'translated from English lesson-books, and are altogether out of the comprehension of the natives – not so much *above* them as *different* from them.' It is perhaps the case that while Julia at first adopted many of the prejudices of her husband (her complaints of Indian laziness occur so soon on her arrival that she could barely have had time to make her own judgement), but she could nevertheless make fair assessments of her own from experience.

Her concern that the 'right' kind of person came to India as missionary or educator was amply justified by an incident in Rajahmundry itself. The school appeared to be thriving with up to forty-five boys in attendance when it was visited, without the knowledge of Julia and her husband, by the dissenting missionary Mr Gordon, 'a conceited, show-off sort of person.' The response to Gordon's activities meant that the school was 'almost broken up' with boys saying they would never attend the school again. Numbers went down to twenty, and 'they are all petitioning to use their own Heathen books, instead of ours, and we have no more requests for admittance.' Julia had observed enough to understand the value of subtlety.

Along with her entomologising, caring for her children (a daughter born in Madras and a son in Rajahmundry), her reading, her sketching (the Berg Collection has ten of Julia's water colours and two etchings done from her drawings) and music-making, the school and missionary activity, Julia took a general interest in things Indian. She was instrumental in ensuring there was a visit to the Rajah Puntooloo; her husband had no real interest in going, but 'I wished to "see a little of life".' She continued her language studies – 'I have not learnt much. No Moonshee has any idea of teaching' – and reports her conversations with various moonshees. She made more than one attempt to appreciate south Indian music, describing a Brahmin as 'too stupid' to repeat a 'pretty Hindostanee song', but she dismisses Indian learning and Indian religions and is appalled at what she sees as Company support for 'idol worship.'

The Indians she meets are diplomatic in their response to both her and her husband. Puntooloo, for example, when given a lecture by Thomas on the importance of girls' education, responds that 'he thought it was a very fine thing to teach girls, but that his people were "too much stupid," and did not like it, and he would not go contrary to their prejudices.' The general Indian attitude shown in *Letters from Madras* is one of curiosity, patience and a degree of self-protection.

It is noticeable, both in the published *Letters* and even more so in sections left out of publication, that Julia did not suffer fools gladly and that she was not entirely welcoming to strangers. She makes it clear how little she enjoyed being subject to the custom of offering hospitality to any European strangers who passed through Rajahmundry. But accompanying this natural reserve is a humour and courage that assist her in periods of isolation. As is shown by her transfer to

INTRODUCTION

Rajahmundry, and even more by her two periods of four to five months' solitude on the coast at Samuldavee, she is self-sufficient; in Rajahmundry she is happy without the 'troublesome company' of Madras and she confronts the loneliness of Samuldavee with industry.

Letters from Madras gives her daughter's health as the reason for Julia's sudden return to England. Unpublished letters show that the original plan had been to send Etta home with her brother-in-law, to be cared for by her mother. But James Thomas died, and with that any reason for Julia to be in India also died, 'home always means England; nobody calls India home.' In the Berg Collection is Julia's account of her husband's illness and death, written not as a letter but as a way of documenting events lest she forget, 'no one could know what he was to me — of late more precious even than before.' He became ill in Bangalore; he was given emetics, calomel, and had leeches applied to his stomach. He complained little but, she wrote, suffered greatly on the journey from Bangalore to Madras. In Madras he was told to return immediately to England, and the family booked passages on the *Wellington*. 'The disease increased rapidly and frightfully', and was diagnosed as a tumour or as an abscess of the liver so painful that morphine could not dull his agony. He died, she wrote, with his children in the room next door, so that he could hear them play.

Letters from Madras ends in a rather rushed and unsatisfactory way. From the summer of 1839 Julia was clearly troubled by her daughter's state of health and confused by the national and international events unfolding, the British invasion of Afghanistan especially.

She returned to England on the *Duke of Argyll*, with her children and her brother-in-law and, coincidentally, the Rev. Vincent Shortland whom she had met in Rajahmundry. Letters show that once she returned to England she stayed with her mother, and with her cousin Minette (who reported that Julia seemed to look better than when she had left for India), and settled in Richmond until she married Charles Maitland in 1842. 'Now do you not think,' she wrote to her mother, 'that I shall be much pleasanter with Charles than all alone by myself?' (Barrett, Eg3704B, 127-8). With Minette, she assisted her mother in editing Fanny D'Arblay's *Journals*.

Three years after the appearance of *Letters from Madras* in 1843 Charles Maitland's *The Church in the Catacombs: a Description of the Primitive Church of Rome, illustrated by its Sepulchral Remains* was published by John Murray. Charles Maitland had trained as a doctor but at some point in the late 1830s he decided to become a clergyman, and the family, by now with the addition of their child Julia Caroline, moved to Oxford where Julia attended lectures by those lecturers who admitted women.

Reading Julia's descriptions of animals in the *Letters*, and her delightful descriptions of her daughter, it is really no surprise that she went on to write for children. In 1847 she published *Historical Charades*, in 1852 *The Doll and her Friends; or, Memoirs of Lady Seraphina*, and in 1854, *Cat and Dog: or, Memoirs of Puss and the Captain* (with a French edition in 1863). None of these was published under her own name. Her intention in writing *The Doll and her Friends* was to 'inculcate a few such minor morals as my little plot might be strong enough to carry; chiefly the domestic happiness produced by kind tempers and consideration for others.' And in writing *Cat and Dog* she wanted to show 'the advantage of making the best of untoward circumstances, and of cultivating kindness and goodwill in place of prejudice and dislike.'

In the last years of his life Charles Maitland became estranged from his family. Julia may have been living with her mother and her brother Richard, rector of St Michael's, Stour Provost, Dorset, where she died in 1864. Her death certificate describes the cause of death as phthisis, from which she had

INTRODUCTION

suffered for seven years. 'Phthisis' meant severe coughing and other problems of the chest; many of the cases so described would now be considered as due to tuberculosis. She is buried in the churchyard between her mother Charlotte, who died in 1870, and her brother Richard, who died in 1881. Her three children survived her; Henrietta Thomas married the Rev. Eldon Vaughan Chappell, James Thomas became a Navigating Lieutenant in the Royal Navy, and Julia Caroline married the Rev. David Wauchope.

In 1843 George Borrow, sitting next to Julia at a John Murray dinner party,

asked particularly after Don and my snakes and scorpions and the Rajah. He particularly likes the account of Madras ladies because it puts him in mind of the English ladies he had seen in Russia, who never knew anything about what was curious and characteristic (to her mother, Barrett Eg 3704B, 129-31).

Apart from the insight Julia's letters can provide into one privileged woman's experience of early nineteenth century British India, the *Letters* are quite simply an enjoyable read, witty expressions of what was 'curious and characteristic.' Her letters certainly draw us into that contradictory world she saw as 'a compound of mud and magnificence, filth and finery.' From her recorded conversations with Brahmins and moonshees, Rajahs and servants, to her descriptions of people and animals, Julia interprets the world around her in her efforts to understand the 'strange habits and ways of the Natives.' She scolds her 'plenty sick' tailor as she tries to flush out what she sees as his lies; she employs 'beggar-boys ... crumpled up and looking like tadpoles', to look for insects; they soon tire, of course, and 'will not give themselves the trouble even to put out their paws to take an insect if he crosses their path;' she discusses religion with her moonshees:

Then I would ask your honour, suppose any Europe lady or gentleman make such wickedness – never repent ... what will become of them?' 'They will go to hell.' 'What! Europe lady or gentleman?' 'Certainly'.

INTRODUCTION

Her visit to the Rajah's town is vividly described, from the entertainment provided, 'I was quite unprepared for the uproar he had provided for us', to the food, 'a different little conundrum on each leaf', from the decoration of their rooms, 'two French looking-glasses in fine frames, fastened to the wall in their packing-cases, the lids being removed for the occasion', to a temple visit, 'a wonderful, dreamy, light-headed sort of place ... an interminable perspective of rows of massive, grotesque pillars, vanishing in darkness ... here and there a strange, white-turbaned figure, just glancing out for a moment, and disappearing again in the darkness.'

Julia's descriptions extend to the animal world, to the 'first-caste monkeys' which 'sat there like gentlemen taking the breeze and talking politics', to the Madras 'screaming, and not singing, birds', the 'formidable scorpions ... creeping about the room', the snakes with their 'great deal of countenance', and to the elephant she meets at festival time

with his face painted in crimson and gold half way down his trunk, and his little cunning eyes peering through his finery, such an object that his own mother could not have known him ... floundering along, shaking his ears and waving his trunk, and never dreaming what a figure they had made of him.

Alyson Price

Note on the Text

Letters from Madras was first published by John Murray in 1843, and in 1846 reissued in Murray's Colonial Library. This edition follows 1846. A few minor variations from the 1843 text are commented upon in the notes.

LETTERS

FROM

M A D R A S,

DURING THE YEARS 1836-1839.

BY A LADY.

LONDON:
JOHN MURRAY, ALBEMARLE STREET.
1846.

Introduction [to 1843 edition]

The public attention has of late been so much directed to our East Indian possessions, that any particulars concerning that part of the globe may probably find a welcome from the general reader. It is under this impression that the following Letters are offered to the public. They were written during the years 1836, 37, 38, and 39, by a young married lady, who had accompanied her husband to Madras for the first time, and they are (with the necessary omission of family details) printed verbatim from the originals. This will account for some abruptness of transition, and also for a colloquial familiarity of style, which might easily have been remedied if it had not been thought more advisable to give the correspondence in its genuine unsophisticated state.

Those who open the volume with an expectation of finding details relative to the wars and vicissitudes which have lately excited universal interest will be disappointed, as the writer quitted India in 1840. Neither did she devote much attention to public affairs, though she occasionally notices the apprehensions and opinions that were prevalent at the time. But first impressions, when they occur incidentally in a familiar narrative, are amusing, and may sometimes be useful: such, indeed, constitute the chief feature in these Letters. The reader will also find in them many traits of national character; and some descriptions of the Author's intercourse with the natives of Hindostan, and of the endeavours in which she shared to improve their condition.

It is proper to observe that, whenever European individuals are mentioned, fictitious names have been assigned to them, and other precautions taken to prevent the personal application of such passages.

INTRODUCTION [1843]

Notes

printed verbatim from the originals : not strictly true. The omissions are more than those concerning 'family details', and there are some additions.

Unless otherwise stated, the originals of the letters as published were written to her mother. The same applies to those unpublished letters quoted from in these notes. All letters are housed in the Berg Collection of the New York Public Library unless indicated differently. See p. xv, note 4.

wars and vicissitudes: Julia refers to the British invasion and subsequent war in Afghanistan, 1839-42. See also Letter Twenty-Seven.

individuals ... fictitious names: not always: some people appear under their true names. Identification of those with pseudonyms is made in the notes where possible.

Contents

Letter the First   7
Outward passage – Bay of Biscay – Combination of noises – Cure for sea-sickness – Passengers – Land at Madeira – Visit to a convent – Re-embarkation

Letter the Second   12
Letters for England – Amusements on board – The Tropics – The "Wave" emigrant vessel – Cape Verd – Fire-works – slave-brig – Whales

Letter the Third   16
A Triton – Letter from Neptune – Ceremonies on crossing the Line – Catching albatrosses

Letter the Fourth   21
Tristan d'Acunha – Governor Glass – Land at the Cape – Cape Town – Boa constrictor – English Church-Expenses – Society – Political Parties – Schools – View from the Kloof – Return on board

Letter the Fifth   27
Gales of wind – Passengers from the Cape – Landing at Madras – Catamarans – Witch of Fife's voyage – Curiosities – Snake-charmers – Native servants – "Griffins" – Visitors – A native's advice – Native servility – Treatment of servants – Jargon spoken by the English to the natives

Letter the Sixth   34
Bishop Corrie – Schools – A Moonshee – Lessons in Tamul – Dinner-parties – General laziness – Letters from Natives

Letter the Seventh   41
Native entertainment – Mohammedan dancing girls – Concert – Hindoo dancing-girl – Conjurer – Supper – Hindoo speech

Letter the Eighth   47
Anxiety for despatches – Madras scenery – Moonshee's letter – Native ignorance – Religion – Death of the Bishop – Dishonesty of native servants – Trial of a thief – Reasons for submitting to a false charge

CONTENTS

Letter the Ninth   54
Entomologising – St Thomé – Temperature – Wedding – Tamul translation – The tailor – Mohurrum – Excessive heat

Letter the Tenth   60
Preparing for a journey – Sail for Coringa – Land at Vizagapatam – Arrive at Rajahmundry – Law-officers – Cholera – Domestic arrangements – Peons – A traveller

Letter the Eleventh   69
Residents – Snakes – Hyænas – Thugs – Employment of time – Schemes – Fishing for wood – The Barrack-sergeant – Poor travellers – Visit from a Rajah – A Cobra capello – Snake-charmer

Letter the Twelfth   78
Domestic expenses – An amah – The butler's bills – Indian mode of visiting – Religious service – Visit from "Penny Whistle Row" – A dialogue

Letter the Thirteenth   85
Native school – Female education – Leopards – Hyænas – Letter from the Moonshee – M. d'Arzel – French adventures – An ensign and his pony – School opened – Utility of Schools

Letter the Fourteenth   92
Visit to "Penny-Whistle" – Dratcharrum – The Rajah's palace – Method of dismissing visitors – Dinner – Procession – Pagoda – Amusements – The Rajah's Wife – A new tribe

Letter the Fifteenth   101
Instance of faithfulness – Progress of the school – "Curry-and-rice" Christians – Want of missionaries – Topics of conversation – Visit to Narsapoor – The missionaries and their wives – Palanquin travelling – Return home

Letter the Sixteenth   111
Discussion on divinity – Interruption to the school – Shore's 'Notes on Indian affairs' – English incivility to natives – Magazines and reviews – Pagoda service – Progress of the school – Snake-poison – Remedies for snake-bites – Dexterity of snake-charmers

CONTENTS

Letter the Seventeenth 118
Indian toy – Rule against accepting presents – Dishonesty of rich natives – Company – Military and civilians – Hindoo tradition – A Moonshee translator – Lending-library – School lectures – Indian spring

Letter the Eighteenth 125
Religious discussion – Parables – Fondness of natives for metaphysical subtleties – Heads and tails – A native's notion of "charity" – Government circular – Salutes in honour of the native religions – Presents to idols by Government – Offerings to idols – Tricks of the Bramins – Idolatry encouraged by Government – School-prizes – Motives for learning English – A "tame boy" – Invitations to officers

Letter the Nineteenth 132
Samuldavee – Native dialects – Moonshee's method of reading the Church Prayer-book – "First-caste" monkeys – Jackals – Bramins' reasons for preserving idols – A dishonest Zemindar – "Don" and the monkey

Letter the Twentieth 136
Filling of the rivers – Native indifference to truth on religious subjects – Progress of the school – Moonshee's definition of idolatry – Quaint translations – Land-wind – Moonshee's conscience – Boasting of natives – Notions of honesty – Devotedness to employers – A false alarm

Letter the Twenty-First 142
Snakes – Green bugs – Thugs – Trial of a Moonsiff – Dutch settlement – Black bugs – Return to Rajahmundry – A cool visitor – Captain and Mrs C – – Exchange of presents – Instance of encouragement given to idolatry – Emigration of Hill Coolies – Proposed "Europe" shop – The Dussera – Prospect of war – Visitors – An eclipse – Importance attached to employment in a Government office – Indian "hospitality" – Misgovernment – Moonshee's account of the eclipse – Cause of superior progress of some of the scholars – National music – News from Europe

Letter the Twenty-Second 154
Delay of the post – Distress of natives – Sale of grain – Captain and Mrs Kelly – Anxiety for letters – A lazy Moorman – The

CONTENTS

Hakeem and the idol – State of the country – Shipwreck – Female education – Robbers – Scarcity – Major C–'s drawings – Bone-stones – Method of teaching – Visit from "Penny-Whistle" – Progress of the school – Management of children

Letter the Twenty-Third   162
Decrease of the famine – Mode of distributing charity – Proposed native reading-room – Gentoo newspaper – A ball – Narsapoor missionaries – Reading-room opened – School-rewards – A Sunnyassee – Circulating library

Letter the Twenty-Fourth   167
Arrive at Samuldavee – Magic lantern – Schools – The Collector and the Swamy – Christenings – A proxy – Abolition of the pilgrim-tax – Decline of idolatry – Want of elementary books – Schools – Letter to the editor of a Madras newspaper on native education – Return of plenty – Monsoon – A new school – Rajah Twelfth-cake – Society for protecting the natives – Native manner of ending letters

Letter the Twenty-Fifth   179
Birthday feast – School at Samuldavee – Converts – Rule of promotion – Appointment – Chittoor – Masulipatam – Ramiahpatam – Arrive at Madras – Native love of finery – Female Orphan Asylum – Education – The "Caste" question – Addictedness of natives to perjury – Death of Runjeet Singh – Suttee – English encouragement of idolatry – Rebellions – "Chit"-writing – Etiquette of visiting

Letter the Twenty-Sixth   189
Indian fever – Employment of a thorough Madras lady – Chittoor – An unwelcome arrival – Bangalore – The Pettah – Inhabitants – A Moorish horseman – Architecture – Hindoo mythology – Reported conversion of a Hindoo tribe

Letter the Twenty-Seventh   195
Climate – European ladies in Bangalore – Conspiracy at Kurnool – Unjust proceeding at Rajahmundry – Storm on the coast – Poverty of the people – A "crack" Collector – End of the conspiracy – Return of the troops – Expectations of a war with China – Conclusion

Letter the First

Bay of Biscay, August 17*th*

I begin now, in hopes of meeting a ship, to tell you our histories. This is the first day I have been well enough to write; and I am not very steady yet, as you may perceive, but still we are all exceedingly well – *for the Bay of Biscay*.

We have persuaded my brother Frank to go with us as far as Madeira, and take his chance of finding a homeward-bound ship.

The Captain says he never had so smooth a passage, but there is a good deal of swell here. The wind allows of our passing outside the roughest part of this unfortunate Bay, which is a very great advantage.

Mrs M— was quite right in advising us to take the round-house. There is much more air than in the lower cabins, and the noises do not annoy me at all. We all go to bed at nine o'clock, so that it is no hardship to be awakened at five. Certainly, the first morning, when I woke, there did seem to be as quaint a combination and succession of noises as could well be imagined. Pigs, dogs, poultry, cow, cats, sheep, all in concert at sunrise. Then the nursery noises: Major O'Brien twittering to his baby – the baby squealing – the nurse singing and squalling to it – the mamma cooing to it. Then the cuddy noises: all the servants quarrelling for their clothes, &c. &c So on till breakfast-time.

I was too sick to laugh then, and I am used to it now. Then, when I was as sick and cross as possible, in came my Irish maid Freeman with a great plate of beefsteak and potatoes. I exclaimed in despair at the very sight of it, "Oh, what is all that for? O dear me!" – "Sure, it's for you to ate, ma'am." – "Eat! I can't eat." – "Oh, you must ate it all, ma'am: you've no notion how well you would be if you would only ate hearty!" Her cramming was a great bore, but she cured me by it. Frank is nearly mad: he is in such raptures with everything on board, I think he will end by turning ship's surgeon. The first night his hammock was slung under the doctor's. The poor doctor complained to me in the morning how very odd it was he could not keep his cot steady – he had been swinging about, he said, all night. Frank confided to me privately the reason, viz. that the doctor looked so tempting over his head, he could not resist swinging him at every opportunity. However, next night he was found out, for the doctor peeped over the top of his cot and caught him in the fact; and when Mr Darke, the second mate, came into the cabin poor Dr Lowe exclaimed, "Here, Darke! I could not imagine why I could not keep my cot steady all night, and at last looked over the top, when I found this precious fellow swinging me!"

Our passengers are Mr and Mrs Wilde (he is going to St Helena as Chief Justice: they go with us to the Cape, and there wait for a homeward-bound ship to take them to St Helena); – the O'Briens; – Miss Shields, good humoured and lively, going out as a missionary; – Miss Knight, sick and solemn; – several Irish girls apparently on their promotion; – Captain Faulkner, very good humoured and civil, and rather original and clever, but the most incessant talker I ever did meet with in all my life: he can talk down the whole ship's company, and be quite fresh to begin his rounds again: he is the universal adviser to the whole company on every subject: I suspect he teaches the captain to sail; – Mr Harvey, who plays chess, and takes care of his flowers; he has them in an hermetically sealed glass case, which he is taking to the Cape; – a number of hitherto unnamed gentlemen, who sit down to eat and drink, and rise up to play; – one or two pretty boys, who saunter about with Lord Byron in hand; – and Mr Stevens, the missionary, who is good and gentle, but so sick that we have not yet made much acquaintance: he is getting better, and talks of reading the service next Sunday.

August 23rd Funchal. – Here we are on shore again, in this beautiful Madeira, and all excessively thankful and happy to be out of our ship, though it is very hot on shore, compared with the real sea air: it has been quite cold at sea. Our chief employment just now is eating figs and grapes, and planning our excursions for tomorrow. We have been landed about an hour, and are to remain here till Thursday. Frank is gone to the consul to get a passport, and inquire about a ship to take him home. We are grown pretty well used to the life on board ship. Everybody is good-natured and civil. Captain Faulkner is our chief crony, but we are all good friends. I am beginning greatly to enjoy some parts of our sea-life, especially the bright blue water, and the bright yellow moonlight, – such colours as no shoregoing people ever saw.

August 25th – Madeira is very lively, very like Lucca: the country, and the heat, and the people, are Italy over again. We have just been to visit a convent here. There is not much to be seen. The nuns spoke to us through a double grating and sold us flowers. Nobody is allowed to see the inside of the convent. They spoke nothing but Portuguese. They came to me, chirping, and asking me to talk to them, and to tell them something; but, unluckily, though I could understand what they said to me, I could not answer a word; so we were obliged to be content with nodding and bobbing, and looking friendly at each other. We have taken some beautiful rides and gathered nosegays of wild flowers – heliotropes, roses, fuchsias, and every variety of geraniums. Tonight we go on board again, leaving Frank here to find his way home by the first ship. We shall be very anxious to hear his adventures: I am afraid he may be obliged to go round by Lisbon, for no English ship is expected just at present. The Captain has sent his summons for us, so I must say "Good-bye".

LETTER ONE

Notes

my brother Frank: Julia had written to her mother earlier than 17 August. An undated letter was sent to her mother from 'just off Cowes'. Her brothers, Dick and Arthur, were still on board ship with her and she sends her mother the news that Dick (i.e. 'Frank') is to sail with them, while Arthur returns to land. Her parents had also accompanied her to the ship. 'I watched your boat till I could distinguish the sail no longer.'

Mrs M ... the roundhouse: a Mrs Mortlock advised Julia to take this cabin, or set of cabins, on the after-part of the quarter-deck. In a passage deleted from the letter printed as Letter Five, Julia explains that the cabin is a couple of degrees warmer than elsewhere, 'but is far more than compensated for by the great convenience of that Bath with sea water pouring upon me as long as ever one chooses to stand under it' (14 November). The cuddy was situated underneath the roundhouse.

Fellow passengers mentioned in this letter are not all given fictitious names. The Wildes and Mr Harvey, later mentioned as entomologists, keep their own. Julia is a little dismissive of Mr Wilde who fails to teach her much about his collection of butterflies as he doesn't appear to have known their names (6 October). Major Dyce, whom Julia is to see again in Madras, twitters to his baby, while 'our chief crony' is Captain Maitland. Captain Maitland, who was to die in Madras the following year, was another member of the Maitland family known to Julia. The missionary, a Mr Thomas rather than Stevens, was, explained Julia, 'a good man but not very wise I think − he does things which set people laughing to no purpose − viz: sitting on deck among all the people singing to himself as loud as he can with his eyes shut' (6 October). Julia mentions two women going out as missionaries, a Miss Spiers and a Miss Craven. The former became Assistant Governess at the Female Orphan Asylum in Madras, but at this stage the pair are setting out to find some kind of work in education. Julia complains that they are not fit to set up a school, 'they have visited all the principal schools in London without having an idea of the plan of one of them, or the manner of teaching any of the lessons ... at present they can only chirp about "the interesting undertakings of our sosahety"' (6 October). Julia later learns to respect Miss Spiers but on board ship finds her 'a horrid bore − so meddlesome, and interfering and impertinent.' The Irish girls 'on their promotion' could be a reference to young women seeking husbands in India.

like Lucca: in 1829, not long after the death of her youngest son Henry, Charlotte Barrett took her daughters to Italy in the vain hope that Henrietta's consumption would be cured. The three women spent their summers in Bagni di Lucca and their winters in Rome. 'Taken up' by Lady Caroline Morrison, who as a child had been educated for a year by Mary

AUGUST 1836

Wollstonecraft, Julia spent one summer at Castellamare near Naples. Henrietta died on 31 January 1833, aged 21, and was buried in the Protestant Cemetery in Rome. The time Julia spent in Italy accounts for her references to that country, and for the smattering of Italian punctuating her letters.

Julia deletes a passage at the end of her 23 August letter. She was offered the following diversion. 'The Captain says, if I like, he will send me to the masthead in a chair – that the people on deck can keep the ropes from twisting, and it is quite safe – I should like very much to go, if I were not afraid of being laughed at.'

Mr Faulkner ... teaches the captain to sail: this passage in the 1843 edition was dropped in 1846.

Letter the Second

August 29th, Lat. 22°N., Lon. 23.5°W.

The Captain has just told us that he expects to pass a ship every day, so we are all setting to work getting our letters ready, as he only allows five minutes for sealing and sending off. I hope, by the time you receive this letter, Frank will have arrived safely at home, and not the worse for his journey. Pray make him write to me directly; I shall be quite uneasy till I hear from him, for we left him at Madeira quite ignorant of what his plans might be. Everybody on board was very sorry to lose him, and they all sing his praises with much good taste.

We are now entering the Tropics, and the weather is still cool, owing to the constant breeze. We have had no calms, but on an average have made about one hundred and fifty miles in the twenty-four hours. I suspect I shall never get over the sea-sickness in rough weather, and I almost give up the hope of employing myself, for I really can do nothing; but as long as I keep quiet, and do not interrupt my idleness, I am much better. Towards evening, like all other sea-sick people, I grow very brisk, and can walk the quarter-deck, and chirp with anybody. Our chief adventures since we left Madeira have been the sight of flying-fish and porpoises. I made a good many sketches at Madeira, but cannot work much towards finishing them. I have learnt two or three Tamul verbs, and read different bits of different books – made the Captain teach me now and then a little geography, and the first mate a little astronomy – finished Melville's 'University Sermons' – chatted with our fellow-passengers – and that is all I have done; and in fact that is the way most of the ladies spend their time on board ship. We are too uncomfortable to be industrious, and too much interrupted and unsettled to be busy.

September 3rd – We are beginning to be aware of our latitude. The trade-winds have left us, and we have a strong suspicion of a calm coming on; but, unluckily, calm does not mean smooth, for the rocking and rolling are just as bad as when we had plenty of wind. The thermometer now stands at 78° in the day, and higher, I should think, in the night; but our cabin is certainly the coolest of any, and I have not yet found the heat unbearable. The gentlemen are all "rigged Tropical", with their collars turned down, and small matters of neckcloths; – grisly Guys some of them turn out! The very sea looks tepid, and goes past with a lazy roll, as if it was too languid to carry us on.

We live in hopes of catching a shark: one was seen this morning, but he was too cunning for us. We are also on the look-out for an albatross. When we first sailed, all the gentlemen protested against the horror of ever shooting an albatross, and quoted the Ancient Mariner at every opportunity ; but since the 1st of September, the recollections of the shooting season have greatly softened down the sentiment, and they are now ready for all the albatrosses that may make their appearance. They say "they think that old fellow of Coleridge's must have been a horrid bore." We passed the Cape de Verd Islands the day before yesterday, but did not go on shore. They are not much of a sight.

September 9th – Yesterday we overtook a ship going to New South Wales, filled with settlers and live stock. A good many of our gentlemen went on board, and brought back miserable accounts of the discomforts of the ship compared with ours. This ship (the "Wave") left England before us, but we overtake all the ships. Mr Kenrick, our first mate, says he thinks he should feel quite mortified at being in a ship which let others pass her, but he supposes it is all habit! The "Wave" had felt a good deal of bad weather from going inside the Cape de Verd Islands, instead of outside, as we did. Captain — says he never settles his course till he sees how the weather promises; and this time he thought the outside would be best – which we all consider very clever of our skipper. At night we had a show of fireworks, that the two ships might know each other's places: it was really very pretty. We, being magnificent, sent up two blue-lights and two skyrockets: the blue-lights were the best; it looked as if the whole concern – ship, sails, and sea – were playing at snap-dragon: altogether it was the best adventure we have had. I contrived to creep forward to see it, but I have been ill and keeping to my cabin lately. I sit with the door open, which gives me plenty of air: and if I spy any of the ladies looking neighbourly, as if they thought of "sitting with me", I just shut my eyes, which answers as well as "sporting my oak", and does not exclude my air; but they must think I get plenty of sleep!

September 24th – Yesterday, at three o'clock in the morning, we came up with a French brig bound from Madagascar to Rio. She was, as the sailors said, "A most beautiful little craft!", and looked to great advantage in the moonlight: I put my head out of the port to admire her and listen to the conversation, little suspecting her real character; but next morning the skipper told us there was no doubt she was a piratical slaver, and that, if we had been a ship of war, we would have stopped and examined her; but we were not strong enough for such adventures, so she and her poor slaves are gone on. Next morning we saw two whales playing in the waters, swimming, blowing, jumping, turning head over heels, and pleasuring themselves, as if they had been minnows.

October 1st – News of a homeward-bound ship in the distance, so I must get ready.

Notes
Melville's University Sermons: Henry Melvill (1798-1871) had the reputation of being one of the great evangelical preachers of his time. By this date, 1836, his only published work was *Sermons preached before the University of Cambridge*, published in that year. It is possible her brothers had heard Melvill preach these sermons at Cambridge, or Julia herself could

have heard him in London where he was the incumbent of Camden Chapel, Camberwell from 1829 to 1843, or while staying with her friends the Jenyns (see note to Letter 21) who lived near Cambridge.

chatted with our fellow passengers: deleted from the published letter is more on the 'chief crony', Captain Maitland: 'he talks Politics and History to Thomas, and Poetry and Painting to me.' Julia refers to her husband as Thomas only in her first few letters home; he soon becomes James.

grisly Guys: the first recorded reference to the effigy of Guy Fawkes burnt on 5 November being called a 'Guy' is early nineteenth century. This phrase of Julia's is used in the OED to illustrate its use to describe just the 'grotesqueries' in dress she sees here.

playing at snap-dragon: the game in which raisins in burning brandy are snatched out by the players.

Letter the Third

To her younger brother

Herewith you will receive a full, true, and particular account of the Ceremony of shaving on crossing the Line, which you are requested to communicate to "Master Frank", whose absence was most particularly regretted on the occasion. The night before, we heard some one call out that a sail was in sight, upon which I scrambled out on deck in the greatest possible hurry, in hopes of an opportunity of sending a letter to Mamma. When I got out, all the officers began to laugh at me, and I found that the announcement was merely some of the Tritons informing Neptune of the arrival of our ship. About an hour afterwards, a Triton suddenly appeared on the quarter-deck, dressed up in oil-cloth and rags, and bits of rope, &c. &c., bringing a letter from Neptune to the Captain, and waiting for an answer.

The Captain read the letter aloud: it was very civil, saying how happy Neptune was to see the Captain again, and that he would come on board at one o'clock next day, and have the pleasure of introducing any of the youngsters to his dominions: he condoled with the ladies who had been suffering from sea-sickness, and hoped to have the honour of seeing them all in the morning.

The Captain sent his compliments in return, with a cordial invitation to Neptune for the next day, only begging that he would use the youngsters very civilly.

Triton then took a glass of grog and made his bow. Then a lighted tar-barrel was sent off from the ship, supposed to be Triton's boat going off, and the first mate lighted him home with blue-lights and skyrockets. Altogether it had a very fine effect. Next morning the usual tricks were played on the novices. One young midshipman was up before light "to look out for the Line." Another saw it, as well he might, a hair having been put inside his telescope. Another declared he felt the bunt of the Line at the moment we crossed it. When I came out I beheld a great sail stretched across the deck, just in front of the main-mast, so that we could see nothing, except that on the other side of it there was an immense slop oozing out from something, and in front was written "Neptune's original easy shaving-shop." At the appointed time the sail was hauled away, and we saw all the contrivances. At the starboard gangway there was a sail hung across two masts, stretched from the bulwark to the long-boat, so as to make a great bag, filled about four or five feet deep with water: there was also a ladder by which to help the victims in on one side, but nothing to help them out on the other. On the other side of the ship were all Neptune's party, hallooing and bawling with speaking-trumpets. Neptune himself was not a bad figure. Face and legs painted black and white, and dressed up *à la* Guy, with oil-cloth and bits of rope and yarn hanging on each side of his head. He sat in his car with his wife and daughter, who were merely dressed up in gowns and bonnets begged of the maids. The car was drawn by eight Tritons with painted legs, and black horns on their heads. Neptune was accompanied by his secretary, his doctor, and his *bear*, who was, by far, the best of the set, dressed in sheep-skins, and held by two Tritons.

We were all on the poop, to be out of the way of the mess; and all the gentlemen who had not crossed the Line before had taken care to dress conformably, in jerseys and trowsers, and no stockings. Presently all the party came aft, and Neptune and the Captain had a conversation concerning the news of the ship and Neptune's own private history. "How are you off for fish, Mr Neptune?" "Very badly, indeed, sir; I've had nothing these two months but a bit of an old soldier who was thrown overboard; and he was so tough I could not eat him." Bear began to growl. "Can't you keep that beast

LETTER THREE

quiet?" said Neptune. Tritons tugged at bear. Bear sprawled and flounced, knocked down two men, all rolling in the slop together; at last Tritons tugged bear into order. The Captain desired Neptune to proceed to business: so the bear got into the sail, that being his domain, in order to duck the victims. The barber brought out his razor and shaving-pot, which were an old saw and a tar-brush, and established himself on the top of the ladder; the doctor at the bottom, with a box of tar-pills and a smelling-bottle, with the cork stuck full of pins; and all the Tritons with buckets of water in their hands. The two first mates went upon deck "*to see fair play*", as I was told. Of course, fair play is always a jewel, but in the present case it proved rather a rough diamond; for before many minutes were over Mr Darke had a bucket of water in his hands, as hard at work as anybody; and Mr Kenrick was mounted on the top of the hay, working a water-pipe in full play. Then a Triton came on the poop to summon down the passengers, and began with Captain Faulkner.

As soon as he got on deck they received him with buckets of water, and hunted him up the ladder and into the bear's dominions. They had orders not to shave the gentlemen, only to duck them, which hurt nobody. Then came a scuffle between gentleman and bear, which ended by both going under water together. Then bear's work was done, and gentleman had to scramble out how he could, people being stationed on the other side with buckets of water, "a dissuading of the victim": however, he got free at last, and was quite ready to help drown all the others, as their turn came round. Young Temple managed best: he was so strong and active that the great bear (who was the most powerful man in the ship) could not get him under the water at all; but he kicked the barber down the ladder, and then, in spite of the water-pipe playing in his face, sprang on to the bear's back, like a monkey, and with one more leap cleared bear, bath, and buckets, and was in the midst of the liberated party, ready to take his share of the fun without having been touched by anybody. After they had settled all the stranger gentlemen, they took the midhipmen, and then the sailors. The gentlemen and midshipmen were all very good sport, but the sailors grew rather savage with each other, and especially when they came to shaving, with tar and their rusty saw. The end of all was Samson: Samson is very little boy, who had a name of his own when he came on board, but it is quite forgotten now, and he is always called Samson, because he is so small and weak. They shaved him very gently and good-naturedly, holding him on their knees, as the monkey did Gulliver, and then bathed him, and handed him over from one to another just like a baby: the poor little thing, partly frightened and partly amused, looked as if he scarcely knew whether to laugh or to cry; so he did both. This was the whole concern, I think.

We have seen plenty of whales and shoals of porpoises, and caught four albatrosses. They catch them by fishing with a line and a bait: the albatross comes peering at the bait in hopes of its being a fish, entangles itself in the line, and is drawn on deck quite easily, unhurt : when they are on deck they look about them and squall: they are rather stupid: they will not eat, but snap at anybody who is civil to them. They patter about with their great web feet, and seem to like to watch what is going on, but they are not really tame, only stupid: they are about the size of a large turkey, and have very long bills; some are all grey, but the largest are white and grey: they are rather handsome birds. Three of those we caught were set at liberty, but one was killed, to be stuffed. I am trying to get some of his feathers for Frank. Do not forget you promised to write to me. Be sure and send me off a letter as soon as ever you have taken your degree, for I shall be most particularly anxious to hear of that grand event.

Tell me everything you can about all at home. The more trifles and the less worth telling they seem to you, the more valuable to me at such a distance.

LETTER THREE

Notes

to her younger brother: this letter was addressed to Arthur, the brother who had relinquished the last-minute opportunity to accompany his sister for part of the voyage, anxious as all three siblings were not to leave their parents alone.

crossing the line: the ceremony taking place on crossing the equator. Julia's description of events is particularly vivid. Another can be found in Fanny Parkes, *Wanderings of a Pilgrim in Search of the Picturesque*, first published in London in 1850.

taken your degree: Arthur was not to graduate until 1838, and took his MA in 1841. This was not without attendant difficulties. Arthur appears to have lacked application and to have succumbed to the temptations of gambling; in 1838 Julia was to send money home to help with 'Snip' (Arthur) – her father had paid his 'Play debt'. After taking his degree, Arthur tutored privately for a time in Cambridge and London, adopted teaching as a career, and wrote several textbooks, including *Propositions in Mechanics* (1847).

Letter the Fourth
October 6th

Yesterday we arrived at Tristan d'Acunha: very few ships touch there, on account of its being out of the way; but occasionally, as was the case with us, the wind allows of it, and good-natured skippers are glad when it so happens, on account of the poor Robinson Crusoes who live there.

Tristan d'Acunha is an extinct volcano, so steep that it seems to rise perpendicularly from the sea: the Captain told me it was eight thousand feet high. It is almost a bare rock, but here and there are patches of ground which can be cultivated. In Bonaparte's time Lord Castlereagh took a fancy that the French might make it useful as an intermediate point of communication with St Helena: sailors say it was an absurd notion, for that the winds and currents make it impossible for any ship to sail from the one island to the other. However, Lord C. established a corporal and party of soldiers to take care of the island. When all fear of Boney was over, they were sent for home; but some of them had grown so fond of their desert island, that they begged leave to remain, and here they have been these twenty years – Corporal Glass, now styled the Governor, and five of his men, with their six wives, and among them thirty-two children. It was not possible for us to go on shore, but Glass and four of his men came off to see us. They looked very healthy and comfortable – cared not a *sous* for anything out of their island – and did not ask one question concerning anything outside their own little rock. The Captain gave them a good supper and plenty of valuable presents, and everybody made up a parcel of clothes or some little oddments. They said what they most wanted was nails, as the wind had lately blown down their houses. They have fifty head of cattle and a hundred sheep; a little corn, twelve acres of potatoes, plenty of apples and pears, and "*ecco tutto!*" I was curious to know whether old Glass was master, and whether the others minded him; but he said no one was master; that the men never quarrel, but the women do; that they have no laws nor rules, and are all very happy together; and that no one ever interferes with another. Old Glass does a great deal of extra work; he is schoolmaster to the children, and says many of his scholars can read the Bible "quite pretty." He is also chaplain, – buries and christens, and reads the service every Sunday, "all according to the Church of England, Sir." They had only Blair's Sermons, which they have read every Sunday for the last ten years, ever since they have possessed them; but the old man said, very innocently, "We do not understand them yet: I suppose they are too good for us." Of course they were well supplied with books before they left us. They make all their own clothes out of canvas given them by the whalers; they sew them with twine, and they looked very respectable: but they said it was not so easy to dress the ladies, and they were exceedingly glad of any old clothes we could rummage out for them. Their shoes are made of seal-skin: they put their feet into the skin while it is moist, and let it dry to the shape of the foot, and it turns out a very tidy shoe.

After they had collected all the "incoherent odds and ends" we could find for them, and finished their supper, they went off again in a beautiful little boat given them by a whaler. The Skipper gave the Governor a salute of one gun, two bluelights, and two rockets; and they treated us with a bonfire from the shore. I was sorry for several things I had left behind, which would have been treasures to Mrs Glass, especially worsted for knitting.

These South Seas are much worse than the Bay of Biscay; nothing but rolling by day and by night: but we are all looking forward to a week at the Cape to set us right again.

October 19th. Cape of Good Hope – We landed here on Sunday morning, and were very happy to find ourselves on shore. We are to stay a week, and have hired horses, and mean to ride every day.

Cape Town is just like the Dutch toy-towns — straight streets; white houses of only two stories, with flat roofs; trees in almost every street. The place is filled with English, Dutch, Hottentots, Malays, Parsees, fleas, and bugs; the last appear to be the principal inhabitants and the oldest settlers. At first we got into a Dutch boarding-house, which Frank would have called the "Hotel de Bugs"; now we are in an English lodging, much cleaner; only we have to wait on ourselves a good deal.

On leaving the ship we all divided into separate parties, as at Madeira: ours consists of ourselves, Misses Shields and Knight, Captain Faulkner, and Mr Temple. Mr Temple is a tame boy, whom Captain F. looks after, for fear he should get into scrapes on shore — going out as a cadet. He is very merry, good-natured, and hungry; and his company and pretty fresh face come very natural to me, and remind me of my brothers. I especially like him when he is very hungry.

We all went yesterday to see a live boa constrictor: he was the most horrible creature I ever saw; thirty-three feet long, greenish and brownish, and with a few silver scales, but the most detestable countenance you can imagine. If the Lady Geraldine's eye were like his when they shrunk in her head, I do not wonder at anything that happened to Christabel.

I hear there is a Hottentot infant-school here, which I mean to go and see; but we make all our distant excursions first; we have been about fifteen miles into the country. It is not so pretty as Madeira, but there are one or two magnificent views: the chief characteristics of the scenery are high rocks, green grass, and white sand, but the white sand is entirely covered with flowers — English hothouse flowers, growing wild.

We went to the English church twice on Sunday — a pretty church, built by the English residents, with a respectable High-church clergyman — somewhat dull. There is a Sunday-

LETTER FOUR

school belonging to the church, and taught principally by English ladies. Here are plenty of Methodist chapels; the Wesleyans are said to be the best.

There is a very poor museum; but I bought at it a couple of ugly shells for the C—s. I hope they will not break in coming. Mr Harvey, who is very scientific, says they are curious, and "right to have": they are land-shells — Achatina.

Papa always likes to know how a place would answer to live at; so tell him that here there are three prices: one cheap, for Dutch; one dear, for English; and one dearest, for visitors: we pay the dearest, of course; and we get six mutton-chops for fourpence halfpenny, and everything else in proportion. Houses are dear, and society baddish — second-rate — with a great deal of quarrelling concerning Colonial politics. Instead of Whigs and Tories, they have the Caffre party and the Government party, who will scarcely speak to each other.

We dined yesterday with some people named Wilderspin — queer, and good, and civil: they have been many years at the Cape, and are most curiously adrift as to English matters. They asked whether O'Connell was still "celebrated in England?" whether he was received in good society? whether party-spirit ran high? whether there were many disputes among Church-people and Dissenters? &c.

I saw at the Wilderspins' a Miss Bazacot, who is here superintending the schools: she seems really clever, and minding her schools well. The Hottentots are very willing to come, both to week-day and Sunday schools. English, Malay, and Hottentot children are all taught together. At one of the schools there was a little Malay girl, who had learned to read, but was very dull at learning her tasks by heart, when suddenly she grew uncommonly bright, and knew all her texts, chapter and verse, better than any child in the school: when the mistress made inquiries into the cause of this great improvement, she found that the creature had taught her old Malay father to read, and he in return used to take immense pains in teaching the child her texts, till they were thoroughly driven into her head: she taught him to read and to pray; and now, every night before he goes to bed, he repeats his prayers and *the rules of the school*! I think the innocence of repeating the rules is very pretty.

I have got a Malay cap, for Frank's private admiration: they are high pointed things, made of straw and wicker-work, very uncouth, but picturesque-looking, especially on the boatmen.

We have been up the Kloof. I long to go up Table Mountain, but it is thought unsafe. When the cloud that they call the Table-cloth comes down, people are often lost in the fog. There is a magnificent view from the top of the Kloof – Cape Town, and the plain, and the hills on one side; and on the other only the sea and the rocks – but such sea, and such rocks, that anything else would be but an interruption, frittering away their grandeur. It is a sort of Chine, as they call the openings between the hills in the Isle of Wight: the side on which we stood, covered with the beautiful silver-tree; and, directly opposite, the immense rock of Table Mountain overhung by its cloud, and the sea at its base, so far below, that the roar of the breakers round Green Point is only a murmur that just softens the silence. To-morrow we go on board again, leaving here our fellow-passengers, Mr and Mrs Wilde and Mr Harvey. We shall all be sorry to part with them: their cabins are taken by people returning from the Cape to Madras, and we shall think ourselves very fortunate if our new companions are as agreeable and friendly as those we lose.

Notes
Tristan d'Acunah: one of a group of three volcanic islands, now a dependency of the British colony of St Helena. Tristan da Cunah is the only inhabited island of the three. Attempts at settlement had been made before the stationing of a British garrison on the island in 1816. When the garrison was withdrawn in 1817 Corporal Glass elected to stay on the island and by 1886 there were 97 inhabitants.

LETTER FOUR

Lord Castlereagh: Viscount Castlereagh (1769-1822) was Foreign Secretary and Tory leader of the House of Commons from 1812 until his death.

these South Seas: Julia adds here in the original, 'I am wretchedly seasick again every day till evening', and that, having alluded to learning two or three Tamil verbs in Letter Two, 'I have given up the idea of learning Tamul till I get on shore, on account of the sickness weakening my brains too much.'

Blair's Sermons: Hugh Blair (1718-1800), Scottish divine, was one of the distinguished literary circle flourishing in Edinburgh throughout the eighteenth century and was on very friendly terms with Hume. His sermons enjoyed extraordinary popularity, went through many editions and were translated into many languages. Johnson wrote of one, 'to say it is good is to say too little.'

Lady Geraldine's eyes: in Coleridge's 'Christabel' the heroine is possessed by the lamia-snake Geraldine, 'So deeply had she drunken in/That look,/those shrunken serpent eyes,/That all her features were resigned/To this sole image in her mind.'

the C—s: these are the Fieldings in the original. It is possible that Julia is sending the shells to Antony Vandyke Copley Fielding (1787-1855) and his wife. Fielding had taught Julia painting in water-colour.

the Wilderspins were the out-of-touch Rutherfords, while Miss Bazacot retains her own name. This passage on the Malay schoolgirl is taken from a letter to her grandmother, Charlotte Burney Francis Broome, 19 October 1836.

O'Connell: Daniel O'Connell (1775-1847) founded the Catholic Association in 1823 and became the first Catholic in modern history to sit in the House of Commons. He concentrated the rest of his life on winning repeal of the Act of Union and getting an Irish parliament for the Irish people, but failed in his great goal.

Letter the Fifth

Madras, December 19th

Here we are at last, in our cousin Staunton's house, safe and well. He and his wife very kind and friendly, and I like all that I have seen of the place and the people. We are most happy and thankful to be on shore. The latter part of our voyage was very wearisome. After leaving the Cape we had a constant succession of gales of wind, very often contrary, and what the sailors called "a chopping sea", pitching and tossing us every way at once; and whenever we asked whether there was any hope of a change, the sailors answered, "No, there seems a fresh hand at the bellows." Then we had calms where we did not expect them, and the Captain said there had been a hurricane somewhere, which had "upset all the winds." Then many of the passengers grew tired of one another, and squabbled a little for amusement, as it is said they always do after passing the Cape; and though the skipper used to harangue concerning the affecting scenes he always witnessed on the passengers leaving the ship, nobody seemed to agree with him. The passengers we took in at the Cape were chiefly officers in the Indian army, who went out as cadets before they had learnt much, and since that time had pretty well forgotten the little they knew. They might have been divided into two classes – those who knew their declensions, and those who did not. They were particularly fond of grammatical discussions, and quite eager about them, – such as whether any English words were really derived from the Latin; whether *regiment* is to be considered as a word of three syllables or two; whether *lunatic* comes from the French, because "*loon*" is French for moon, &c. They used also to extend their acquirements by the study of navigation. After

LETTER FIVE

breakfast the captain and officers always took an observation of the sun, technically called "taking a *sight*." Then the passengers all began doing the same, privately called "taking a look." They were a capital set in their attitudes, with their glasses, all peering up into the sky, *à la chasse* for the sun and moon. However, they were all very civil, and inoffensive, and unobjectionable; and I hope they are all as happy on shore as we are.

We had a beautiful day for landing – no surf at all. In England I have often bathed in a worse sea. It is very curious that the Madras surf should be so formidable: it generally looks nothing, not to compare to a Brighton rough sea; but in reality its force is irresistible. I sometimes see the great lumbering Masoolah boats as nearly as possible upset by waves which look so gentle and quiet that one longs to bathe in them. We landed in a great boat with twelve boatmen, all singing a queer kind of howl, and with very small matters of clothes on, but their black skins prevent them from looking so very uncomfortable as Europeans would in the same *minus* state.

The scene in the Madras Roads is the brightest and liveliest possible. The sea is completely studded with ships and boats of every size and shape, and the boats filled with crews even more quaint and picturesque than themselves. But none can compare to the catamarans, and the wonderful people that manage them. Fancy a raft of only three logs of wood, tied together at each end when they go out to sea, and untied and left to dry on the beach when they come in again. Each catamaran has one, two, or three men to manage it: they sit crouched upon their heels, throwing their paddles about very dexterously, but remarkably unlike rowing. In one of the early Indian voyagers' log-books there is an entry concerning a catamaran: "This morning, six a.m., saw distinctly two black devils playing at single-stick. We watched these infernal imps above an hour, when they were lost in the distance. Surely

DECEMBER 1836

this doth portend some great tempest." It is very curious to watch these catamarans putting out to sea. They get through the fiercest surf, sometimes dancing at their ease on the top of the waves, sometimes hidden under the waters; sometimes the man completely washed off his catamaran, and man floating one way and catamaran another, till they seem to catch each other again by magic. They put me in mind of the witch of Fife's voyage in her cockle-shell:

> And aye we mountit the sea-green hillis,
>   Till we brushed through the clouds of the hevin;
> Then sousit downright, like the star-shot light
>   Frae the liftis blue casement driven.
>
> But our taickil stood, and our bark was good,
>   And sae pang was our pearly prowe,
> Whan we could not climb the brow of the waves,
>   We needlit them through below.

December 27th – I think I shall like Madras very much, and I am greatly amused with all I see and hear. The heat now is not at all oppressive, this being the cool season. The houses are so airy and large, and the air so light, that one does not feel the heat as much as one would in Italy when the temperature is the same. At present the thermometer is at 78°, but it feels so much cooler, from the thorough draughts they keep up in every room, that I would not believe it to be more than 70°, till I looked with my own eyes. The rooms are as large as chapels, and made up of doors and windows, open day and night. I have seen so many curiosities already, that I do not know which to describe to you first – jugglers, tumblers, snake-charmers, native visitors, &c.&c.; for the last few days we have been in a constant bustle. Those snake-charmers are most wonderful. One day we had eight cobras and three other snakes all dancing round us at once, and the snake-men singing and playing to them on a kind of bagpipes. The venomous snakes they call good snakes: one, the Braminee cobra, they said was so good, his bite would kill a man in three hours; but of course all these had their fangs extracted. I was told that they had their teeth drawn once a month, but I suppose in fact they have the venom extracted from their teeth. The men bring them in covered baskets. They set the baskets on the ground, and play their bagpipes for a while; then they blow at the snakes through the baskets; then play a little more : at last they take off the lid of the basket, and the snake rises up very grand, arching his neck like a swan, and with his hood spread, looking very handsome, but very wicked.

There is one great convenience in visiting at an Indian house, viz. – every visitor keeps his own establishment of servants, so as to give no trouble to those of the house. The servants provide for themselves in a most curious way. They seem to me to sleep nowhere, and eat nothing, – that is to say, in our houses, or of our goods. They have mats on the steps, and live upon rice. But they do very little, and every one has his separate work. I have an ayah (or lady's maid), and a tailor (for the ayahs cannot work); and A— has a boy: also two muddles – one to sweep my room, and another to bring water. There is one man to lay the cloth, another to bring in dinner, another to light the candles, and others to wait at table. Every horse has a man and a maid to himself – the maid cuts grass for him; and every dog has a boy. I inquired whether the cat had any servants, but I found that she was allowed to wait upon herself; and, as she seemed the only person in the establishment capable of so doing, I respected her accordingly. Besides all these acknowledged and ostensible attendants, each servant has a kind of muddle or double of his own, who does all the work that can be put off upon him without being found out by the master and mistress. Notwithstanding their numbers, they are dreadfully slow. I often tire myself with doing things for myself rather than wait for their dawdling; but Mrs Staunton laughs at me, and calls me a "griffin", and says I must learn to have patience and save my strength. (N.B.

DECEMBER 1836

Griffin means a freshman or freshwoman in India.) The real Indian ladies lie on a sofa, and, if they drop their handkerchief, they just lower their voices and say, "Boy!" in a very gentle tone, and then creeps in, perhaps, some old wizen, skinny brownie, looking like a superannuated thread-paper, who twiddles after them for a little while, and then creeps out as softly as a black cat, and sits down cross-legged in the verandah till "Mistress please to call again."

We have had a great many visits from natives to welcome A— back again, or, as they say, "to see the light of Master's countenance, and bless God for the honour!" One – a gentleman, in his black way – called at six in the morning: he left his carriage at the gate, and his slippers under a tree; and then, finding we were going out riding, he walked barefoot in the dust by the side of our horses till "our Honours" were pleased to dismiss him. Another met us, got out of his carriage, kicked off his shoes, and stood bowing in the dirt while we passed; then drove on to the house, and waited humbly under the verandah for an hour and a half, till we were pleased to finish our ride. One paid me a visit alone, and took the opportunity to give me a great deal of friendly advice concerning managing A—. He especially counselled me to persuade him "*to tell a few lies*". He said he had often advised "Master" to do so; but that he would not mind him, but "perhaps Mistress persuade Master. Master very good – very upright man; he always good: but Master say all same way what he think. Much better not! Mistress please tell Master. Anybody say wrong, Master's mind different: that quite right – Master keep his own mind; his mind always good: but let Master say all same what others say; that much better, and they give him fine appointment, and plenty much rupees!" I said that that was not English fashion, but my visitor assured me that there were "plenty many" Englishmen who told as many lies as the natives, and were all rich in consequence: so then I could only say it was very wrong, and not Master's fashion nor mine; to which he agreed, but thought it "plenty great pity!"

These natives are a cringing set, and behave to us English as if they were the dirt under our feet; and indeed we give them reason to suppose we consider them as such. Their servility is disagreeable, but the rudeness and contempt with which the English treat them are quite painful to witness. Civility to servants especially seems a complete characteristic of *griffinage*. One day I said to my ayah (a very elegant lady in white muslin), "Ayah, bring me a glass of toast-and-water, if you please." She crept to the door, and then came back again, looking extremely perplexed, and whined out, "What Mistress tell? I don't know." "I told you to bring me some toast-and-water." "Toast-water I know very well, but mistress tell if you please; I don't know if you please." I believe the phrase had never before been addressed to her. Everything seems to be done by means of constantly finding fault: if one lets the people suppose they have given a moment's satisfaction, they begin to reason, "Master tell very good; try a little more than worse; perhaps Master like plenty as well." One day I gave some embroidery to be done by a Moorman recommended by my tailor: the Moorman did not bring his work home on time; I asked Mrs Staunton what was to be done. "Oh," she said, "of course stop the tailor's pay." "But it is no fault of the poor tailor's." "Oh, never mind that: he is the Moorman's particular friend, and he will go and beat him every day till he brings the work home."

They are like babies in their ways: fancy my great fat ayah, forty years old, amusing herself with puffing the wind in and out of my air-cushion till she has broken the screw! The jargon that the English speak to the natives is most absurd. I call it "John Company's English," which rather affronts Mrs Staunton. It seems so silly and childish, that I really cannot yet bring myself to make use of it; but I fancy I must in time, for the King's English is another characteristic of griffinage, and the servants seem unable to understand the commonest direction till it is translated into gibberish.

My letter is called for, as a ship sails this evening; so I must say Good-bye.

Notes

our cousin Staunton's house: on their arrival the couple went immediately to Julia's brother-in-law and his wife, John and Diana Thomas, 'until we see what turns up in the way of appointments' (28 December 1836).

a beautiful day for landing: landing in the Madras surf was a much illustrated and described event. Julia's description is taken partly from a letter to her mother and partly from a letter to her brother, Dick (26 May 1837). There may have been additions at the time of editing since nowhere in the surviving letters does she mention James Hogg's 'Witch of Fife'.

griffin: there is no use of this word in her letters, likewise the discussion of 'John Company's English' does not appear in any surviving original. Julia herself is reduced to using this mode of speech and it is perhaps for this reason that she explains it here. A griffin was, as Julia explains, a newcomer to the Indian scene. The burlesque poem, *Tom Raw, the griffin*, was published in London in 1828 and it gives an account of the experiences of a young Company cadet in India.

Letter the Sixth

January 11th, 1837

Bishop Corrie called on us the other day, to my great delight, for I had so long revered his character, that it was a very great pleasure to me to see and make acquaintance with him. He is a most noble-looking old man, with a very fine countenance, and a gentle, benevolent manner – a pattern for a bishop in appearance as well as everything else. On Sunday morning we went to the cathedral, but the good bishop did not preach, and we had but an indifferent sermon, on Virtue and Vice. In the evening we went to a chapel in Black Town, some miles from the place where we live, and so crowded that we were obliged to be there three-quarters of an hour before the time, in order to secure seats; but we were well repaid for our labour and trouble. We heard a most delightful preacher: his sermon was clear, and striking. He is said to be doing an immense deal of good here. His chapel was originally intended for *half-castes*, but he is so popular that the Europeans will go there too. People complain, and perhaps justly, that those for whom the chapel was built are kept out in consequence; but I do not see why the English should not have a good sermon once on a Sunday, as well as the blackies.

We went yesterday to the examination of a native school of *Caste* boys – not Christians, but they learn to read the Bible for the sake of the education they receive in other respects. They looked very intelligent, and very picturesque in their turbans and jewels. They answered extremely well, in English, questions on Scripture, on geography, and history, and wrote English from dictation. However, they gave one or two queer, heathenish answers, such as: *Query*. "What is meant by God's *resting* from his work on the seventh day? Did God require

JANUARY 1837

rest?" *Answer.* "In the night time he did." This school was established by some English gentlemen for the more respectable class of natives. Most of the English schools admit Caste boys and Pariahs without any distinction, which is really almost like expecting young gentlemen and chimney-sweepers to learn together in England. The real Madras schools, which taught Dr Bell his system, are native hedge-schools, held under a shed. The industry of the poor little scholars is wonderful: from six in the morning till eight at night (with the exception of a short time in the middle of the day to go to sleep and eat rice) they are hard at work, bawling their hearts out; our infant-school noise is nothing to theirs. It is very curious – such a lazy, inert race as the Hindoos are – what pains and trouble they will take for a little learning; and little enough they get (poor things!) with all their labour.

A *Moonshee* seems to be a component part of most English establishments, so I have set up one also. He comes three times a week to teach me Tamul. He is a very solemn sort of person, with long mustachios, and numbers of beautiful shawls which he twists round his waist till they stand out half a yard in front of him, and come into the room before his face appears. When we hired him he made many salams, and said he preferred our friendship to any remuneration we could give; but he condescends to accept five pagodas a month besides. He comes when I choose, and goes away when I bid him. If I am not ready, he sits on his heels in the verandah for a couple of hours doing nothing, till I call him. If I am tired in the course of my lesson, I walk away, and bid him write a little; and there he sits, scribbling very slowly, and very intently, till I please to come back again. He is President of a Hindoo Literary Society, and at its first opening delivered a lecture in English, of which he is very proud. He brought it to me to-day to read. The whole was capital; and it concluded with a hope "that this respectable institution, so happily begun in smoke, might end in blaze!" This Tamul that he is to

LETTER SIX

teach me is a fearfully ugly language – clattering, twittering, chirping, sputtering – like a whole poultry-yard let loose upon one, and not a singing-bird, not a melodious sound among them. I suspect I shall soon grow tired of it, but meanwhile it is a little amusement. I read stories to Moonshee, and then he writes down the roots of the words for me to learn by heart. One day I was reading about a "hero who ate kicks"; but Moonshee looked a little coy, and said he would not write down "kicks", because that was a word that would be of no use to me. A Tamul-writer came to-day to copy some document on cadjan-leaf for Mr Staunton. He held the leaf in one hand, and a sharp steel-pointed style for a pen in the other. He had the nail of his little finger as long as a bird's claw, which I thought was for untidiness, but I find it is for ornament. He wrote very fast, and seemed quite at his ease, though sitting on his heels, and writing on his hand in this inconvenient manner.

We have been to one or two large dinner-parties, rather grand, dull, and silent. The company are generally tired out with the heat and the office-work all day before they assemble at seven o'clock, and the houses are greatly infested by musquitos, which are in themselves enough to lower one's spirits and stop conversation. People talk a little in a very low voice to those next to them, but one scarcely ever hears any topic of general interest started except steam navigation. To be sure, "few changes can be rung on few bells"; but these good folks do ring on "the changes in the service", till I cannot help sometimes wishing all their appointments were permanent. At an Indian dinner all the guests bring their own servants to wait upon them, so there is a turbaned sultan-like creature behind every chair. A great fan is going over our heads the whole time, and every window and door open; so that, notwithstanding the number of people in the room, it is in reality cooler than an English dining-room. What would grandmamma say to the wastefulness of an Indian dinner?

JANUARY 1837

Everybody dines at luncheon, or, as it is here called, tiffin-time, so that there is next to nothing eaten, but about four times as much food put upon the table as would serve for an English party. Geese and turkeys and joints of mutton for side-dishes, and everything else in proportion. All the fruit in India is not worth one visit to your strawberry-beds. The ingenious French at Pondicherry have contrived to cultivate vines; but the English say nothing will grow, and they remain content to waste their substance and their stomach-aches on spongy shaddocks and sour oranges, unless they send to Pondicherry for grapes, which the French are so obliging as to sell at a rupee a bunch. After dinner the company all sit round in the middle of the great gallery-like rooms, talk in whispers, and scratch their musquito-bites. Sometimes there is a little music, as languid as everything else. Concerning the company themselves, the ladies are all young and wizen, and the gentlemen are all old and wizen. Somebody says France is the paradise of married women, and England of girls: I am sure India is the paradise of middle-aged gentlemen. While they are young, they are thought nothing of — just supposed to be making or marring their fortunes, as the case may be; but at about forty, when they are "high in the service", rather yellow, and somewhat grey, they begin to be taken notice of, and called "young men". These respectable persons do all the flirtation too in a solemn sort of way, while the young ones sit by, looking on, and listening to the elderly gentlefolks discussing their livers instead of their hearts.

Every creature seems eaten up with laziness. Even my horse pretends he is too fine to switch off his own flies with his own long tail, but turns his head round to order the horse-keeper to wipe them off for him. Some old Anglo-Indians think themselves too grand to walk in their gardens without servants behind them; and one may really see them, skinny and straw-coloured, and withered like old stubble, creeping along their gravel walks, with a couple of beautiful barefooted

LETTER SIX

peons, with handsome turbans, strutting behind them, and looking like bronze casts of the Apollo in attendance upon Frank's caricature of our old dancing-master.

Few things amuse me more than the letters we daily receive from natives, underlings in office, who knew A— before he went to England. One apologises for troubling him with "looking at the handwriting of such a remote individual", but begs leave humbly to congratulate him on the safe arrival in India of himself and "his respectable family", meaning me! Another hopes soon to have the honour of throwing himself "at your goodness's philanthropic feet." Is not this the true Fudge style?

>   ——The place where our Louis Dixhuit
>   Set the first of his own dear legitimate feet.

Notes

Bishop Corrie: Daniel Corrie (1777-1837) worked in India from 1806 when he was appointed to a chaplaincy in Bengal. In 1817 he was promoted to the senior chaplaincy at Calcutta. He also served the missionary cause as secretary to the local committee of the Church Missionary Society and later as president of the Church Missionary Association. In 1823 he became archdeacon of Calcutta, and in October 1835 bishop of Madras. He was memorialized in Madras with the establishment of the Corrie scholarships in Bishop Corrie's grammar school.

Bishop Corrie called with his sister (his wife had died a few months earlier) and Julia wrote to her mother, 'I like them the best of my acquaintances I have yet made ... she a simple sensible good girl, working at her schools, and being as useful as ever she can – in a little innocent pottering sort of way' (11 January 1837).

Black Town was the name given to the area of town where the majority population was Indian. It is now known as George Town. The Thomas house was approximately four miles from the centre of Madras. The preacher Julia went to hear was a Mr Tucker. In 1837, as listed in the *Madras Almanac* a year later (and confirmed by the *Gazette*), there were 20 Church of England chaplains in the Madras Presidency, with 24 assistants. The chaplains served in the 21 Presidency stations (in 1837 the Masulipatam station, which included Rajahmundry, did not have a chaplain), 4 of which were in Madras. In addition there were six ministers of the Church of England, an Armenian priest, and an approximate number of Catholic priests given as 38. There were a number of Missionary Societies

JANUARY 1837

represented in Madras, and there were approximately 12 listed missionaries in the Presidency over the period of Julia's stay.

The native school Julia visits is, she explains, 'John Thomas' own especial pet' (4 January 1837). She asks her mother to ask Mr Langdon (the Brighton preacher) to recommend a Master for the school; he should have a European education, teach Christianity but 'without insisting on their being professed Christians. A superior Master, a religious man with a university education' (February 1837). Julia's mother, as others in the family, had a great interest in charitable work and particularly in education. Julia's reference to chimney-sweepers is apposite. Her mother's charitable work included contributing to an evening school for 'poor Chimney Sweep boys.'

While in Madras, Julia also took an interest in the Female Orphan Asylum, of which Lady Sarah Maitland was patron and of which Diana Thomas had been made a Directress. After her first visit to the Asylum she wrote to her mother, 'The mistress is a dirty, proud half-caste' and the residents were 'dirty and unwholesome looking – and 24 were in the Hospital with the itch' (February 1837). In late March she reported to her mother that Miss Spiers had been appointed Assistant Governess: 'Lady Sarah is managing matters very well, and getting it all into a decent condition.' The Asylum was founded in 1787 on the initiative of Lady Campbell, distressed to see girl orphans of European parentage neglected.

Caste boys and Pariahs: pariahs were the lowest of the low in Indian society, people without caste. For a note on caste see Letter Fifteen.

taught Dr. Bell his system: Andrew Bell (1753-1852) went to India in 1787 and in 1789 became superintendent of the Madras Male Orphan Asylum, founded in that year by the East India Company for the education of the sons of military men (usually half-caste children). The system he adopted at the school made use of monitors, the older pupils teaching the younger. In 1796 Bell returned to England and in 1797 published a report on his system. In 1798 the system was introduced into the protestant charity school of St Botolph's, Aldgate. The quaker Joseph Lancaster (1778-1838) evolved a similar system and while each initially paid compliments to the other, a row developed over who was the true originator of the system and which elements of it were valid or not. The church took the side of Bell, and those supporting a religious but non-sectarian education supported Lancaster. The poet Robert Southey was one who took the side of Bell, supporting him in an essay in the *Quarterly Review* in November 1811.

a *moonshee* was a teacher, particularly of Indian languages to foreigners.

pagoda was a term used to describe either a gold or silver coin, or a temple. A coin in use in south India had a temple tower, or gopura, stamped upon it. Julia uses the term to describe a temple in Letter Eight.

LETTER SIX

cadjan-leaf: coca-palm leaf prepared for writing on.

dinner parties: the party described here was one given by Sir Peregrine and Lady Maitland. Sir Peregrine, the new Commander-in-Chief, was the brother of the Rev. Maitland, described by Mrs Broome in a letter to her sister, Fanny d'Arblay, as 'Julia's favourite preacher' (August 1836).

Steam navigation is not mentioned as a subject of dinner party conversation in the original letters. These were the early years of steam navigation (the Peninsular and Oriental Steam Navigation Company, P & O, was founded in 1837) and Julia does mention it frequently when instructing her mother on the posting of letters. If her mother paid an extra shilling she could send mail overland via Alexandria and by steamer. Information gleaned from Julia's letters shows that mail could take up to six months. The new overland and steamer passage could cut this down to two months, and perhaps as little as 45 days.

All the fruit in India: this passage does not appear in any of the existing letters. The shaddock is a large form of grapefruit.

Pondicherry was settled by the French in the early eighteenth century. French power in India ended with the siege of Pondicherry in 1761 and the Treaty of Paris signed in 1763. The treaty allowed the Compagnie des Indes to keep its trading stations but its bases were to be unfortified and its garrisons limited. Apart from a scare in the late 1790s, the French never threatened British interests in India again.

true Fudge style: the lines are from Thomas Moore's comic poem, 'The Fudge Family in Paris'.

Letter the Seventh

January 31st

The other day a very rich native, an old protégé of A—'s, came to say that he and his son wished to make a feast for me, if I would come to their house. I was extremely glad, for I was longing to get into one of their native houses; so last night we all went to him by appointment – Mr and Mrs Staunton, A—, and I. It was a most curious entertainment; but I was surprised to find that the Stauntons, who have been so long in the country, had never seen anything of the kind before. It is wonderful how little interested most of the English ladies seem by all the strange habits and ways of the natives; and it is not merely that they have grown used to it all, but that, by their own accounts, they never cared more about what goes on around them than they do now. I can only suppose they have forgotten their first impressions. But this makes me wish to try and see everything that I can while the bloom of my Orientalism is fresh upon me, and before this apathy and listlessness have laid hold on me, as no doubt they will.

I asked one lady what she had seen of the country and the natives since she had been in India. "Oh, nothing!" said she: "thank goodness, I know nothing at all about them, nor I don't wish to: really I think the less one sees and knows of them the better!"

Armogum and Sooboo, our two entertainers, met us at their garden-gate, with numbers of lanterns, and rows of natives, some of them friends and some servants, all the way up to the house. The whole house was lighted up like a show, with chandeliers, lamps, and lustres in every possible corner, and hung from the ceiling and festooned to the walls besides: it looked very bright and pretty. The house consisted of one

LETTER SEVEN

very large verandah, in which stood the native company; that opened into a large drawing-room, with a smaller room at each end, and sleeping-rooms beyond; and on the other side of the drawing-room another verandah leading into another garden. The house was furnished very much like a French lodging-house, only with more comfortable ottomans and sofas; but the general effect was very French: quantities of French nicknacks set out upon different tables, and the walls quite covered with looking-glasses.

We were led into the great drawing-room, and placed upon sofas, and servants stationed at our side to fan us: then Armagum and Sooboo brought us each a nosegay of roses, and poured rose-water over them and over our hands; and they gave me a queer kind of sprig made of rice and beads, like a twelfth-cake ornament; then they gave us each a garland of scented flowers, so powerful that even now, at the end of the next day, I cannot get rid of the perfume on my hands and arms. Then the entertainment began: they had procured the musicians, dancers, and cooks belonging to the Nabob, in order that I might see all the Mussulman amusements, as well as those of the Hindoos. First, then, came in an old man with a long white beard to play and sing to the vina, an instrument like a large mandoline, very pretty and antique to look at, but not much to hear. His music was miserable, just a mixture of twang and whine, and quite monotonous, without even a pretence to a tune. When we were quite tired of him, he was dismissed, and the Nabob's dancing girls came in: most graceful creatures, walking, or rather sailing about, like queens, with long muslin robes from their throats to their feet. They were covered with gold and jewels, earrings, nose-rings, bracelets, armlets, anklets, bands round their heads, sévignés, and rings on all their fingers and all their toes. Their dancing consisted of sailing about, waving their hands, turning slowly round and round, and bending from side to side: there were neither steps nor figure, as far as I could make

JANUARY 1837

out. The prettiest of their performances was their beautiful swan-like march. Then they sang, bawling like bad street-singers – a most fearful noise, and no tune. Then we had a concert of orchestra music, with different-looking instruments, but in tone like every modification of bagpipes – every variety of drone and squeak: you can form no idea of such sounds under the name of music: the chimney-sweeper's clatter on May-day would be harmonious in comparison. Imagine a succession of unresolved discords, selected at random, and played on twenty or thirty loud instruments, all out of tune in themselves and with each other, and you will have a fair idea of Hindoo music and its effect on the nerves.

When my teeth had been set on edge till I could really bear it no longer, I was obliged to beg A— to give the musicians a hint to stop. Then there came in a man to imitate the notes of various birds: this sounded promising, but unfortunately the Madras birds are screaming, and not singing, birds; and my ears were assailed by screech-owls, crows, parrots, peacocks, &c, so well imitated that I was again obliged to beg relief from such torture. Than we had a Hindoo dancing-girl, with the most magnificent jewellery I ever saw: her dancing was very much like that of the Mahometans, only a little more difficult. There was a good deal of running backwards and forwards upon her heels, and shaking her silver bangles or armlets, which jingled like bells: then glissading up to me, waving her pretty little hands, and making a number of graceful, unmeaning antics, with her eyes fixed on mine in a strange unnatural stare, like animal magnetism. I think those magnetic actings and starings must first have been imitated from some Indian dancing-girl, and in fact the effect is much the same; for I defy any one to have watched this girl's dull, unvarying dance long, without going to sleep. The natives I believe can sit quite contented for hours without any more enlivening amusement; but then they are always half asleep by nature, and like to be quite asleep by choice at any opportunity.

After her performance was ended we had a conjurer, some of whose tricks were quite marvellous. He had on a turban and cummerbund (or piece of muslin wrapped round him), but no jacket, so that one could not imagine a possibility of his concealing any of his apparatus about him; but, among other tricks, he took a small twig of a tree, ran his fingers down it to strip the leaves off – small leaves, like those of a sensitive-plant – and showered down among us, with the leaves, five or six great live scorpions; not little things like Italian scorpions, but formidable animals, almost as long as my hand: I did not admire their company, creeping about the room, so he crumpled them up in his hand, and they disappeared; then he waved his bare arms in the air, and threw a live cobra into the midst of us. Most of his other tricks were juggling with cups and balls, &c., like any English conjuror; but the scorpions and cobra were quite beyond my comprehension.

Our gentlemen were surprised at seeing the string which is always worn by Brahmins round this man's neck, and said that twenty years ago no Brahmin could possibly have so degraded himself as to show off before us as a common juggler. After he was dismissed we had another gold and silver girl, to dance upon sharp swords, to music as sharp; then a fire-eater; and last of all a great supper laid out in the back verandah. The first course consisted of all the nabob's favourite dishes of meat, and curries and pillaws set out in China plates; the second course, all Hindoo cookery, set out in cups and saucers. A— whispered to me that I must eat as much as I could, to please poor old Armagum; so I did my best, till I was almost choked with cayenne-pepper. The Moorman pillaws were very good; but among the Hindoo messes I at last came to something so queer, slimy, and oily, that I was obliged to stop.

JANUARY 1837

After supper Armagum made me a speech, to inform me that he was aware that the Hindoos did not know how to treat ladies: that he had therefore been that morning to consult an English friend of his, Mr Tracey, concerning the proper mode of showing me the respect that was my due; and that Mr Tracey had informed him that English ladies are accustomed to exactly the same respect as if they were gentlemen, and that he had better behave to me accordingly. He begged I would consider that, if there had been any deficiency, it was owing to ignorance, and not to want of affection; for that he looked upon me as his mother! Then he perfumed us all with attar of roses, and we came away after thanking him very cordially for his hospitality and all the amusement he had given us. I was very curious to see the ladies of the family, but they could not appear before English gentlemen. I peeped about in hopes of catching a glimpse of them, and I did descry some black eyes and white dresses through one of the half-open doors, but I could not see them distinctly.

Notes

had never seen anything of the kind before: Julia's interest in things Indian was unusual. Her curiosity and her commitment to useful activity make her impatient with life in Madras. This entire passage on her 'Orientalism' has the ring of a later addition and is not to be found in any of the existing letters.

very French: wealthy Indians often adopted elements of the style of the occupier, whether French, British or Dutch. Architecture and interiors absorbed the foreign and an Indo-European style developed.

twelfth-cake: a decorated cake eaten during twelfth-night festivities.

play and sing to the vina: song is at the heart of south Indian music, and the majority of the texts are religious. The vina is not unlike the sitar but is without the sympathetic strings of that instrument. It has seven strings and gourds at either end and is plucked. Julia, despite other attempts later described, is unable to appreciate Indian music. She came from a musical family, her great-great-uncle being Charles Burney (1726-1814) the historian of music; she brought a guitar on board ship; and she had an organ sent out to Madras. The organist of Madras came to see the instrument

LETTER SEVEN

when it arrived and declared, 'it is the best instrument that was ever sent to India' (January 1837). What appears to have been the most obvious difficulty in Indian music for Julia was the absence of harmony as developed in the western tradition.

sévignés: a bandeau, particularly for the hair, and probably named after Mme de Sévigné (1627-96).

chimney-sweepers' clatter: in England the first of May each year was a holiday for chimney-sweeps and the boys, with whitened faces and hair and decorated with flowers, ribbons or foil, paraded the streets, banging their cleaning and climbing tools.

Hindoo dancing-girl: again, as with music, Julia is unable to interpret the movements and meaning of Indian classical dance.

Brahmin: a member of the highest, or priestly, caste. See Letter Fifteen for a note on caste.

Moorman pillaws: Julia refers to a Muslim rice dish, the pilao, rice boiled with meat or fish and spices.

Mr Tracey: Armagum, who I have been unable to identify further, had consulted Mr John Turnbull. Turnbull was the Accountant General and later in the year married Sir Peregrine Maitland's daughter, Lady Caroline.

Letter the Eighth

Madras, February 9th

We have just received all your letters, which were more welcome than ever letters were before. In England, with your daily post, you little know the eagerness with which we poor Indians look out for our monthly despatch, nor the delight with which we receive it. For some days before the mail is expected all Madras is in a fever, speculating, calculating, hoping, almost praying, that it may arrive a few days, or even a few hours, before the usual time; and when it is known to be "in", the news travels like wildfire in all directions; peons are despatched from every compound to wait at the post-office and bring the letters the instant they are given out, in order to gain an hour upon the general postmen; all other interests and occupations are forgotten; and many people will receive no visits, if there should chance to be any unfortunate beings so letterless as to be able to pay them.

You ask what kind of scenery we have round Madras. Flat plains of sandy ground, covered with a little harsh dry grass; half-cultivated gardens with high hedges; and large dilapidated-looking houses. Here and there we see very curious and picturesque native buildings, chiefly pagodas; but in general there is very little beauty either of architecture or scenery. Indian colouring is not for a moment to be compared with Italian for lightness, softness, or brilliancy. The sunsets are sometimes exceedingly beautiful, but in general I think the colouring is rather heavy and glaring. However, Madras is not considered a good specimen; people tell me that when I go up the country I shall be "surprised and delighted." The number of open fields and gardens must be healthy, but there is never any fresh feeling in the air: it is all as

LETTER EIGHT

dead and close as the air of a street. The flowers have no perfume, except the pagoda-flowers, and those are sickly, like withered jessamine; and at every turn in the road one meets with the smell of native cookery, fried cocoa-nut oil, and nasty messes of the same kind.

Moonshee has just sent me a plate of cakes, with a letter to say that he feels convinced I will not disdain the offer on account of its futility, but accept it as a token of the filial affection with which he regards my benignity; hoping I will foster him with the milk of my kindness, and regard him as my own son! This is really word for word his composition.

This morning I had a visit from Armagum and Sooboo to ask leave to borrow Mrs C—'s beautiful Landscape Annual, which they had peeped into and admired as it lay on the drawing-room table. They promised to "make cover up, and plenty take care, if Mistress would lend", which of course Mistress was very happy to do. Armagum said that all the books about England were so long and big that it frightened anybody to look at them, and yet he wanted very much to know something about what Europe was like; and that this "little book, with very good yellow cover, plenty pictures, and very little read", was exactly what he wanted. So pray tell Mrs C— that it is probably at this moment making grand show, with a party of natives solemnly looking over and wondering at it. They wonder at everything European, particularly children's toys. They admire our dolls so much, that they are almost ready to make Swamies* of them. At home we talk of ignorance and heathenism, but we have no idea of what the ignorance of heathenism really is. They think it a most marvellous piece of learning for a boy to be able to find Europe on a map of the world, and they are almost as ignorant of the history of their own country as of ours. They think they already know everything that is at all deep or dry and requires study.

---

* Inferior gods.

FEBRUARY 1837

A Mr N— has established a sort of conversazione once a-week at his own house, for the better class of natives to meet and discuss subjects of general interest and information, in hopes of leading them to think of something a little beyond their monthly salaries and diamond earrings. One of our visitors had been there last night, so we asked him how he liked it, and what was the subject of conversation. It was some branch of political economy connected with Indian government and taxation; but as to how he liked it, he said, "What use hear all that? I know everything Master make talk. Now and then I look, just see other people there too, and then I make slumber!" And that is just the way with them in everything but money-getting: they seem awake and alive to nothing else. This man is a sort of half-heathen, half-deist, like most of those who have associated much with Europeans; but he declares that his religion is just the same as ours, only that there are four grades of religion, suited to different orders of minds — idolatry being the lowest, and proper for the common people, but more educated persons see what the idols are intended to represent, and they progress through all the different grades till they arrive at the highest, when they understand everything, and find all religions alike, and all true, only different ways of representing the same thing. A— says he has argued with him till he is tired, but that it is of no use: he always answers "Yes, sar; that all same what I say."

February 12th — Everybody in Madras has been in real sorrow of late for the death of Bishop Corrie. They say he was the most useful person in all India, and the most beloved. He was thought to have more judgment, experience, and knowledge of the native character, than any one else. Everybody of every class looked up to his wisdom and firmness: yet he was so gentle, benevolent, and courteous, that it was impossible to know him without becoming really attached to him. I used always to think I had never seen such a pattern of "the meekness of wisdom." Like most good and active men here, he fell

LETTER EIGHT

a victim to over-exertion of mind and body. He went on too long at the highest possible stretch, and was suddenly paralysed – carried home insensible from a public meeting at which he was presiding on Tuesday, and was buried on the Sunday following.

The weather is now fast changing and growing very oppressive: the thermometer stands at 87°. The other day we had a storm, which lowered it to 82°, and a native wrote us word that he was very sorry he could not keep an appointment with us, because the weather was so cold he was afraid to venture out!

As you say you like to hear all about our domestic economy, servants, &c., I must tell you of a thievery which took place last week. We lost a pair of sheets, and the loss was laid to the horse-keeper, who was fined two rupees, it being the custom to punish the servants for every misdemeanor just as if they were children. But the purloiner of our sheets was in reality A—'s dress-boy, who had stolen them to make his own jackets. To avoid the expense of paying for making, he took them to a Coolie tailor, which you may understand to mean a cobbling tailor, who sometimes cobbles for us, and is therefore obliged to do the servants' needle-work for nothing, for fear of having lies told of him to "Master", and so losing Master's favour. Coolie tailor lives near *my* tailor, who is a grandee in comparison; and Coolie, being very glad to have some good European materials to boast of, and extremely proud of his job, showed them off to my tailor. Grandee tailor was more used to the ways of Europeans, and knew that they did not give their good sheets for the servants to make jackets of; so he guessed they had been stolen, and told my ayah, and she told me, not out of any pretence of conscience or care of my goods, but because, as she said, Mrs Staunton had told her, on hiring her, that she was to take care of my things, and that, if anything was lost, I would "take away her bread", meaning, dismiss her; and then she must "eat up her own money". It was hopeless for any of us to attempt to find out the truth, because the chances were even as to the dress-boy's being a thief, or the ayah and tailor liars; so the only way was to give orders that two of the other servants should search into the matter: one alone would have just told a lie on whichever side suited him, but two were supposed to be a check on each other. Accordingly, there was a regular form of trial held under a mango-tree in the compound*: I watched them from the window, and a capital group they made. The butler, as judge, waving his arms in the air like the leaves of a cocoa-nut tree; the criminal standing in the midst, looking more mean and crestfallen than any European could manage to look under any possible circumstances; the ayah, smoothing down her oily hair with her fingers as she told her story; and the rest of the servants standing round to make a kind of jury, assisted by all their retainers of hags and imps in the shape of old women and naked black children. A verdict of Guilty was brought in, and the thief, Chelapa by name, was of course dismissed from our service. There followed a variety of queer scenes. Chelapa would not go, but remained on his knees in A—'s dressing room, his turban in his hand, stroking his shaven poll, and kissing the floor, in hopes of being forgiven. When he was sent "out of that", the butler came back with him to bespeak compassion: "Sar! Master boy, cry Sar!" Chelapa took the hint and began to cry accordingly, till, finding nothing would do, he consoled himself by abusing the ayah, telling her he would "walk round the house" every day till he could find out some "rogue business" of her doing: to which, she says, she "made compliments"; but she was in reality so frightened at the threat, that she cried for three days. Then the tailor began to cry, for fear some harm should happen to him in the scuffle, and looked up in my face so piteously every time I went up and down stairs that I could

---

* Field, or garden, round the house.

LETTER EIGHT

not pass him without laughing. A— asked the horse-keeper why he had submitted to a false accusation, and to be fined for stealing, when he knew he had done no such thing; he answered, "What for make trouble? Master tell horse-keeper thief; what use horse-keeper tell? Horse-keeper make trouble, Master tell 'Go away!'" The probability is, that he was paid by the thief to take the blame. See what a set they are!

Notes

The letters that make up Letter Eight were written in February, March and April. In a letter dated 1 March, Julia told her mother of her suspected pregnancy. 'The rest of them all will persist in thinking that you have a grandson or granddaughter coming, but I do not believe it myself at all, but they have made me leave off riding' (1 March). She adds that she has had an 'obstruction' for the past five months (this may have been a way of explaining an absence of menstruation). 'I would rather believe it to be obstruction or dropsy, or anything rather than a baby, because an illness might be cured, and I am sure a baby would kill me . . . I should not mind it so much, only that I think I should never live to come home and see you again.' Julia tried to restrain her fears in her letters over the following months. On 28 March she wrote of working with her tailor, 'who sits crumpled upon a mat at my bedroom door, sewing for the bare life . . . I feel all the time as if I were making my shroud. However I am very well and must hope for the best.' On 12 April, 'I am still needling away for the bare life.' Diana Thomas complains that all the patterns Julia uses are for boys' clothes, 'but I like them best, and if by any unfortunate accident, the creature should turn out to be a girl, why she must wear boys [clothes] ... I wish with all my heart she was nothing at all, for I get more horrified and frightened every day.' On 19 May she writes, 'Everybody tells me I am looking uncommonly well – but I look to myself very wizen and green.' In June she gives her mother an account of her Ayah's misunderstanding on the question of an Amah (wet-nurse) – the very idea of which she loathes as she believes children come to look like their native nurses: 'Ayah sometime Mrs may want Amah. Sometime don't want. Can't tell – understand? Mrs plenty strong don't want – Mrs plenty weak, shall want – by bye time know – now you make enquire for Amah.' The next day when going to her bathroom, Julia stumbles over a bundle, 'a little black woman no bigger than my thumb, with a little black baby in her arms, the size of my thumbnail.' The Amah is dismissed, Mrs not yet being 'plenty weak'.

On 8 March, Julia noted the arrival of Lord Elphinstone: he 'is quite a pretty young slip not much like a solemn Governor of a Country.'

FEBRUARY 1837

There were family preoccupations at the time. Towards the end of April Julia received news of Alex D'Arblay's death. He had died in January and she hears of his death from a Mr Halliwell who saw it in the January papers. Julia's brother Arthur was in trouble but Julia was finding it hard to get information out of her mother: 'I wish you would tell me ... you may depend upon our never breathing a word in any way to any body of what you tell us – and James never expects to read my letters – only I generally show them to him' (31 May 1837).

Mrs C— 's beautiful Landscape Annual: this Annual belonged to Archdeacon Cambridge. George Owen Cambridge (1756-1841) was Rector of Elme, Cambridgeshire, prebendary of Ely, and Archdeacon of Middlesex. In the 1780s there had been rumours of a mutual attraction between himself and the young Fanny Burney. It came to nothing but he remained a friend to the family for the rest of his life. Julia knew him well and often stayed at the Archdeacon's home, and it was the Archdeacon who officiated at her marriage to James Thomas.

Swamies: in the original letter Julia writes of dolls, 'they want them to make Gods of', and she quotes an Indian as asking, 'to make sawmee [sic] Missy please to give!' (28 March 1837). The word could mean either a Hindu idol, or a Hindu religious teacher.

Bishop Corrie's expertise was in fact thought to be more than the Bishop of Calcutta's, not of 'any one else.'

coolie tailor...cobbling tailor: a cobbling tailor would be one who mended clothes. Coolie was a word loosely used to describe a hired labourer and its use here is uncommon.

Letter the Ninth

August 16th

I have been trying to entomologize, as there are abundance of curious insects. Mr Spence himself told me, before I left home, that the insects of India were very little known; and that I could not fail to find many new specimens, especially among the smaller Coleoptera. It is impossible to go "*à la chasse*" oneself, so I employed the beggar-boys, who at first liked the amusement and brought me a great many, but they gradually grew tired of it, and are now too lazy to find me any more at all. I raised my price, but all in vain. These naked imps prefer sitting on the grass all day with nothing to do, crumpled up and looking like tadpoles, and will not give themselves the trouble even to put out their paws to take an insect if he crosses their path. They are indeed a lazy race. The servants lie on their mats, strewing the floor like cats and dogs, and begin to puff and whine whenever one gives them any employment. The truest account of their occupations was given me in her blundering English by my muddle. I said, "Ellen, what are you doing? why don't you come when I call you?" "No, ma'am." "What are you doing, I say?" "Ma'am, I never do", meaning, "I am doing nothing." However, sometimes they contrive to do mischief. I found my watch stopped: I said, "Ayah, how did you break my watch? did you knock it?" – "Ma'am, a little I knock, not too much!"

We are now living at St Thomé, a sort of suburb of Madras, close by the sea-side, and comparatively cool. We are really now not oppressed by heat; I could not have supposed such a short distance could have made so much difference: the thermometer is at 84°, which is quite bearable after one has tried 92°. But St Thomé is not thought healthy the whole year through, because the "long-shore winds", as they are called, are more felt here than inland. This long-shore wind is very disagreeable – a sort of sham sea-breeze blowing from the south; whereas the real sea-breeze blows from the east: it is a regular cheat upon the new-comers, feeling damp and fresh as if it were going to cool one, but in reality keeping up a constant cold perspiration, which is more weakening and relaxing than even the heat; and yet one cannot shut the wind out, for the moment one is out of its influence the heavy dead heat is insupportable. It only blows at particular times of the year, and is now going off.

This St Thomé is said to be a thievish place: we have two Sepoys to guard the house at night. When we first came we were awakened at intervals by a most horrible yelling and screaming: we thought it must be drunken men, and scolded the Sepoys for not keeping them off, but we found it was the Sepoys themselves, yelling for their own security, to frighten the hobgoblins. Yesterday I saw a slim young black creeping up my back-stairs outside the house, peering about in a sneaking, suspicious sort of way; and as soon as he saw me he ran off and hid himself. I thought he might be a thief, so I turned out all the servants to catch him, but he proved to be nothing but the dog-boy looking for shoes to clean. I asked him why he ran away in that foolish fright, if he was only employed in his proper business; and I was told that he could not help it, for he had never seen the Mistress so close before, and she frightened him.

Mr and Mrs Staunton are gone today to the wedding of their young friend Miss L—. She has married a lieutenant in the army with nothing but his pay, and I am afraid they will be very poor. It seems to me that in this country a small income must be wretched indeed, for what would be luxuries in England, such as large airy houses, carriages, plenty of servants, &c. &c., are here necessaries indispensable to the preservation of health, independently of comfort. The

LETTER NINE

real luxury here, and for which one would gladly pay any price, would be the power of doing without such matters.

A— is busily employed in translating into Tamul a book which we hope may be useful. The Moonshee transcribes it for him, and is a complete baby about it. I think he must spend all his time in copying it over and over. One day he brings "to show Mistress a fair copy", and the next day "if Mistress please to look, a more fairer copy", and he will stand for a quarter of an hour at a time in the middle of the room, making salaam, and twirling his mustachios, and stroking his manuscript. A- works with the Moonshee while I scold the tailor. I scold him from the "best of motives", and here are my reasons: he is hired by the month, and paid a great deal more than he is worth, – dawdle that he is! – but it is the only way of getting needlework done at all here. He often asks for a day's leave of absence, and often takes it without asking. I used to be compassionate to him at first, believing his excuses; but when I repeated them to Mrs Staunton, she said they were all lies. One day he told me that his mother was sick, and that she would soon be dead, and he would "put her out of the way"; but Mrs Staunton said that his mother had already died three times to her certain knowledge, and that I must forbid her ever being sick again without my permission; so I gave my orders accordingly, and she has been quite well ever since. Sometimes he sits on his mat crying, and saying he is "plenty sick" himself, so then I send him away for half a day, with orders to come back quite well next morning, or I shall get another tailor; and this always cures him. One day he asked me for five days' leave "to paint his face": this did puzzle me, but I found it was on account of the Mohurrum, a kind af Mussulman carnival, when they all dress up, and paint not only their own faces, but those of all their animals. The cows' horns were all painted green and red, and sometimes one horn green and one red; and I met an elephant with his face painted in crimson and gold half way down his trunk, and his little cunning eyes peering through his finery, such an object that his own mother could not have known him; but he evidently thought himself dressed in a wonderfully becoming costume, and was floundering along, shaking his ears and waving his trunk, and never dreaming what a figure they had made of him.

June 1st – To-day we have the first specimen I have felt of real Indian heat; hitherto it has been an unusually cool season, but to-day there is a regular land-wind, and plenty of it. I can only compare it to a blast from a furnace, withering one as it passes by. I have a tatt, or thick mat, at my window, which excludes the sun, and men sit outside pouring water on it all day, so that the wind, which is extremely violent, blows always cooled through the water. This keeps the temperature of the room down at 90°, but it is dreadfully feverish, and far more distressing than a higher degree of the thermometer with the sea-breeze.

Just close under the tatt it is more tolerable, but the old Indians have a notion that it is unwholesome to sit in the damp: so it may be for them, but nothing will make me believe that I, just fresh from Europe, can catch cold with the thermometer at 90°: so I creep as close to the tatt as possible, and sit with my hands in a basin of water besides. This is a heat quite different from anything you ever felt in Europe, making one quite giddy; but they say it is only as bad as this for about ten days, after which the sea-breeze rises regularly at eleven or twelve o'clock, and restores one to life again. Now, the leaves of the trees are all curled up, and the grass crackles under our feet like snow, the sea is a dead yellow colour, and the air and light a sort of buff, as if the elements had the jaundice; and we are all *so* cross! creeping about and whining, and then lying down and growling – I hope it will not last long.

June 6th – Weather better: the sea-breeze comes in the middle of the day, and one can breathe without crying; but

LETTER NINE

the nights are hotter than the days. One contrives to sleep as well as one can, but Indian sleep is very unlike English – poor restless work! However, the musquitoes are not so bad here as in Italy: witness my sleeping without a musquito-net, rather than bear the additional heat of the gauze.

Notes
August 16: error for May.

I have been trying to entomologise: Julia had discovered in January that her Ayah had lived with 'an Entomological mistress once before, and understands catching and killing of insects – "Puscil" she calls them – she sits on her heels in my bath room with a brazier and a kettle always before her, in case the bigger boys should bring in a "Puscil"'(11 January 1837). Julia complains to her mother that she has no books from which to identify her prey and that there are no 'scientific people' of any kind in Madras ('Mr Macaulay, a very "amytor" entomologist – knows more than I, not so much as you'), though there are 'plenty at Calcutta.'. She says she has 'Newman but I want a more classifying book.' The naturalist Edward Newman (1801-76) published his *Grammar of Entomology* in 1835. Julia also lets her mother know here that she is sending some samples back with Edward Thomas, her brother-in-law.

busily employed in translating into Tamul: James Thomas had work as Deputy Accountant General by April as Turnbull was going on leave. Julia tells her mother that they are not concerned with the prestige and money attached to the post, but for the time being it serves their purpose and keeps them in Madras with the ability to contribute to household expenses. She indicates that at this time Turnbull would like James Thomas to succeed him. Ever busy, James Thomas carried on with his Grammar and in January the following year Julia, responding to her mother's question, tells her that the Tamul book was finished. 'Not exactly a Grammar, but an interlined translation of the common Tamul stories that everybody learns from, in Tamul and English with a grammatical analysis.' Julia herself was busy, 'writing a story book for the Asylum girls – I have done a great deal of it, more than I ever expected to do of a book in my life ... It is the history of an Asylum girl.' James Thomas also employed his time visiting native schools, 'inducing Hindoo gentlemen to become subscribers and members of the Committee – he is teaching the boys true Indian History, of which they are as ignorant as dirt, believing all sorts of absurd legends' (28 March 1837). The couple also continue to concern themselves with the work of missionaries. A Mr Groves is 'doing mischief ... unsettling and confusing people – calling himself a <u>Missionary</u>, but in reality not going among the Natives, nor doing any missionary work at all, but argufying and puzzling young unsteady Europeans'; and having added that the more sober types ignore Mr Groves she writes, 'I think in general there is more harmony and party spirit than in England, but less general interest and intelligence' (16 May 1837).

the Mohurrum: this is the first month of the Islamic calendar, and ceremonies commemorating the martyrdom of the Prophet's grandson take place over the first ten days of the month.

Letter the Tenth

Madras, July 10th

At last I am able to resume my journal to you, and I hope to continue it regularly. A— wrote to you constantly and circumstantially during my confinement, but till now I have not been able to sit up and write myself. How I long to show baby to you! She is a very fine creature, and as strong and healthy as if she had been born in Old England. She will be christened next week, and then, as soon as we are strong enough to travel, we are to set out on a long journey. A— has obtained the appointment of Zillah (or Distrlct) Judge of Rajahmundry, which makes us all very happy. He has never been in that part of the country before, and we are very busy, making all possible inquiries and preparations. Rajahmundry is in the Northern Circars (or Districts), and everyone who has been there tells us that it is a pretty place, and has the grand recommendation of two months of really cool weather. They say the thermometer falls to 58°, and we are advised to take warm clothing with us. It is also a cheap place. There is very little European society, but that is a much less privation here than at home; for in this climate it is almost more trouble than pleasure to keep up the necessary civilities, and there will be plenty of amusement in seeing the really Indian part of India, which Rajahmundry will be.

We must take with us stores of everything that we are likely to want for six months, – furniture, clothes, and even great part of our food – for nothing is to be procured there, except meat, bread, and vegetables; and even our vegetables we must grow ourselves, and take the seeds with us from Madras. Anything we forget we must wait for till we can send to Madras. We have not yet decided whether to go by land or by sea, but

AUGUST 1837

I am afraid it will be wisest to go by sea, though I should much like to see the country; but a long land-journey at this time of the year would be very fatiguing, and perhaps dangerous, on account of the cholera, which is now very prevalent. At Rajahmundry they speak Gentoo, or Teloogoo, which is a much prettier language than Tamul. There is no Chaplain, nor even a Missionary, I am sorry to say; but that is the case at eight stations out of ten, and one cannot choose one's station.

Rajahmundry, August 6th — I was prevented from finishing this letter at Madras, by take-leave visits, &c., so that I had not a moment to myself; but it was just as well, for now I can tell you of our safe arrival here. We embarked on Saturday night, July 29th, ourselves, baby, and servants, with almost a shipload of goods, on board a small Liverpool vessel which happened to be in the roads on its way to Calcutta. We had a beautiful evening, and no surf. We found the Captain in a fume at our being rather later than he expected: but it did not really signify, for, after all his fretting, he could not get his anchor up, owing to his having bad tackle, so there we were detained at anchor till one o'clock on Sunday afternoon. It was a pretty specimen of sea comfort; — ship rolling, captain growling; sailors singing, or rather bawling, some chorus about being "Off in a hurry; fare ye well, for she must go!" while they were dragging up the anchor; tackle breaking, and chain cable all flying to the bottom of the sea, as soon as ever the song was done; things in our cabin not "cleated down", but all "fetching way" with every roll of the ship, shuffling about, and taking their pleasure, like the dancing furniture in Washington Irving's dream; ayahs squatted on the floor, half-sick; baby squalling; A— turning round and round in the little cabin, like a tiger in his den, dancing her to keep her quiet, but quiet she would not be; I, ready to cry with sickness and despair, crouched up in a corner unable to move, — and all for nothing, during eighteen hours!

LETTER TEN

At last we were off. We had a pretty good voyage on the whole, but one violent storm on Sunday night; the thunder ringing like a gong, and the air all around us white with lightning. In the midst of it all, some Italian Capuchins who were on board amused themselves with singing to their guitar. While the sea and wind together were roaring their loudest, twang, twang went that wretched guitar! The mixture was so absurd that I could not help laughing, in the midst of all my sickness and fright.

On Tuesday morning our stupid Captain passed by Coringa, which was the port for which we were bound, and, when he took his observation at twelve o'olock, found himself half way to Vizagapatam. It was extremely inconvenient. All our letters of introduction were for the Coringa people, and the land-journey from Vizagapatam to Rajahmundry three times as long as from Coringa. Ths other passengers were very good-natured and obliging, said the delay was of no consequence to them, and begged us to go back to Coringa, if we liked. Accordingly, we did have the ship put about, but there was a strong wind right in our teeth; we were likely to be five or six days putting back; and the pitching and tossing such, that every minute of it settled our minds as it unsettled our stomachs: so we determined to go on to Vizagapatam, where we arrlved on Tuesday night.

Before we landed, a catamaran brought us off a note from Mr R., the Assistant Judge of the station, inviting us to his house. He has a little bungalow on the top of a rock, surrounded by bushes among which the hyænas walk about at their pleasure; but they never attack human beings, and the place is delightfully cool. Mr R. received us most hospitably, supplied us with everything we wanted for our journey, and treated us just as if we had had been old and intimate friends, though we had never seen nor heard of each other before. We spent Wednesday with him, and began our journey on Wednesday night, regular Indian fashion, in palanquins –

AUGUST 1837

A——, baby, I, and the ayahs; leaving the other servants to follow at leisure, with the luggage, in carts. We had fifty-two men to carry us, our provisions, clothes, plates, knives and forks, &c., for all the accommodations prepared for travellers are public bungalows, containing one table and six chairs, – and sometimes not those, only bare walls for shelter. An old Sepoy lives at each bungalow, to fetch water, and cook curry and rice; so one can get on comfortably enough.

It is all pleasant to me: baby has borne the journey quite well, and I enjoyed it very much. We travelled sometimes all night, sometimes part of the night, according to my strength, and rested at the bungalows during the day, and arrived here on Saturday night. We passed through a great deal of pretty country, and some notorious tiger-jungles; but we saw no tigers – they are always afraid of the lights and noise of travellers. (N.B. A jungle is a tract of uncultivated ground, covered with thick brushwood, and trees here and there, and inhabited by tigers, hyænas, leopards – or cheetahs as they are called – monkeys, wild hogs, snakes, and quantities of beautiful birds.) Rajahmundry itself is a most lovely spot, on the banks of a magnificent river, the Godavery, with fine hills in the distance.

We have a good house, a capital garden, and are most uncommonly great grandees. I am very much amused with all the natives who come to pay their respects to the "Judge Doory". (Doory means gentleman.) My favourite, hitherto, is the Moofti, or principal Mahometan law expounder. He is one of the handsomest and most elegant creatures I ever saw, – somewhat dirty perhaps, – with beautiful Cashmere shawls worn threadbare, and in his shabby magnificence looking like a beggarly king. Then there is the Pundit, or principal Hindoo law expounder – a Bramin, very much of a mountebank, and something of a cheat, I should guess, by his face and manner. There are plenty of underlings, but these are the two principal men. They always come accompanied by

LETTER TEN

their Vakeels, a kind of secretaries, or interpreters, or flappers – their muddles, in short: everybody here has a muddle, high or low. The Vakeels stand behind their masters during all the visit, and discuss with them all that A— says. Sometimes they tell him some barefaced lie, and, when they find he does not believe it, they turn to me grinning, and say, "Ma'am, the Doory plenty cunning gentlyman."

The cholera is raging here, – and no wonder! a hundred thousand people assembled twenty days ago, for a grand native festival which only takes place once in twelve years. Many of them are too poor to afford to buy proper food, and most of them are dirty; and the accumulation of dirt and filth, with all the wretchedness and starvation to work upon, has bred a pestilence. When I arrived in the town I was fast asleep in my palanquin, and was literally awakened by the horrible stench. A—'s predecessor was entirely occupied in making a road through the jungle to drive his tandem on, and never thought of taking any measures to lessen the sickness, which has gained ground fearfully. A— has set the prisoners at work immediately to clean the streets, and the heavy rains are to be expected soon, which always clears away diseases. There is little fear of cholera among Europeans, except in travelling. It is caused among the poor natives by bad feeding, dirt, and exposure to the climate. We always keep the cholera medicines in the house, in case any of the servants should be attacked; but that is very unlikely, as they are well fed and sheltered. The poor natives go on beating their tom-toms, or drums, all night, in hopes of driving it away; and the want of rest weakens them, and makes them still more liable to catch it.

August 11th – We get on very comfortably, and are beginning to feel a little settled, though still rather in confusion. A— is excessively busy with his Court work, having to get through long arrears of his predecessors. Our furniture is not yet arrived, so we are dependent upon a table and six chairs

'Harrington Gardens, Madras. John Thomas's house. The three upper windows in the right hand wing are those of my room.'

'Rajahmundry. View of the Courthouse, river Godavery and Goomsoor hills — taken from my drawing-room window. September 1837.'

lent to us for the present: however, a clear house at first arrival was rather a convenience with regard to cleaning the rooms, which I have been very busy about, as A— is in clearing out all the old "cases" accumulated in his Cutcherry. (N.B. Cutcherry means office.)

I fancy our predecessor was content with the same accommodation as the spiders, and thought sweeping unnecessary, so he kept no sweeping-woman, and, as may be supposed, the dirt crunched under our feet as we walked. I have had all the palanquin-boys, who are the best housemaids here, hard at work, taking away the old mats, hunting for scorpions and centipedes, dislodging the dirt-pies, disturbing the spiders, and clearing out every corner, – and now we are growing quite decent. We are planting vegetables, clipping hedges, and arranging all things to our own taste; and I think we shall soon be so comfortable, that when a better appointment offers, we shall not like to move.

Some of our arrangements are queer wild work. We have a hunting Peon, or "shoot-man", as he is called, who goes into the jungle every day to catch us half our dinner according to his taste or his luck. He brings hares, wild ducks, pigeons, &c., and yesterday he brought a magnificent peacock. It went to my heart to have such a beautiful creature cooked; but there was no help for it, and he was dead when he arrived. There are pretty spotted deer and antelopes wild about the country, and I am going to have some caught to keep in the compound: they soon grow quite tame, and come and eat out of one's hand.

"John Company" allows us nine Peons, to look grand with. Their business is to stand about, go on messages, walk after us (which, by the bye, we cannot endure), do odd jobs, and "help Bill" in various ways. The other day I sent the baby and nurse out for a walk in our garden, not supposing that she required any escort, but a great Peon immediately stepped forward to march after her. She crowed at his dagger and red belt, and

LETTER TEN

much approved of his attendance. A— has given me two of the Peons for my particular service: I have nothing on earth for them to do, so I mean to set them collecting the pebbles found in the river here, which are very beautiful onyxes and agates. When they have got over their surprise, and are a little broken in to the "Dooresany's" (lady's) ways, I mean to set them catching insects; but I must wait a little first, for fear they should think me mad.

We have had a travelling gentleman staying with us for the last two days: we never saw him before, but he asked for shelter on his arrival, so, India-fashion, we took him in to do the best we could for him. I am obliged to make him carry a chair about with him like a snail-shell – take it into his room at night, and bring it out again to breakfast the next morning. He is a good-humoured, simple sort of person, but most oddly fearful. He took such alarm at hearing the cholera was in one village at which he slept on his journey, that he lost his appetite, ate nothing for twenty-four hours, and came to us really ill with starvation and fright. Then he was exceedingly afraid of robbers on the road, and had a great mind to take a guard of Peons on with him to Vizagapatam, only we laughed him out of it. There was some excuse for his fears, because he was just come from a very wild part of the country, but here we are as quiet and safe as at home. Home always means England; nobody calls India home – not even those who have been here thirty years or more, and are never likely to return to Europe; even they still always speak of England as home.

Notes

during my confinement: Julia gave birth to her daughter on 8 June 1837 after a relatively easy labour of eight hours. On 26 July the baby was christened in St George's Cathedral in Madras. She was named Henrietta Anne, after Julia's sister, and her sponsors were John Thomas, Charlotte Barrett and Minette Raper Kingston. Julia tells her mother that the baby was born 'roaring' and was told she was hungry. When Julia suggested the baby be given something to eat, the doctor said, 'Eat! No! Give her a little castor oil.' 'Now' writes Julia, 'that I did think hard – for her first breakfast.' Ayah

AUGUST 1837

frightens her 'by the way in which she lumps her [Henrietta] about to wash and dress her,' and she has an Amah, 'who performs the part of Cow.' The baby has a large number of servants who have to be watched very closely as they are 'so lazy' and sometimes disappear all at once (6 July 1837).

A— has obtained the appointment of Zillah: Julia predicts that her husband will not be in this post for long as his 'natural place' in the service is as Collector or Circuit Judge, a post he will 'fall into' when it becomes vacant. This particular posting to Rajahmundry is, she believes, 'one of the first permanent employments Lord Elphinstone has had it in his power to give.' The pay is 2,300 rupees a month (about £2,500 a year), 'but that has a considerable reduction, like all the Indian salaries, for those annuity funds.' She added, in a note to a letter sent to her mother by James Thomas on 1 July, 'It is beneath him in Rank but he takes it rather than remain longer out of employ, and in the hopes of soon obtaining one more suitable. The pay will I hope, enable us with care to lay by £1500 a year.'

Gentoo, or Teloogoo: Telugu is a Dravidian language spoken on the Coromandel coast and now in Andhra Pradesh. Gentoo was the name given to Telugu-speaking Hindus and their language.

no Chaplain, nor even a Missionary: but she is told by her Madras doctor that 'there is a clever medical man there.'

in Washington Irving's dream: the dancing furniture appears in 'The Bold Dragoon or the Adventures of my Grandfather' in *Tales of a Traveller* (1824).

Italian Capuchins: the Franciscan friars of the new rule of 1528.

palanquin: a box-litter, with a pole projecting at front and back, carried by four men.

public bungalows: new regulations for the management of public bungalows had been published in the autumn of 1836 and indicate that there may have been abuse in their use in the past. The local Collector was responsible for the bungalows; no traveller was to stay more than two days unless sick; the first to arrive got the choice of rooms but was to make room for later arrivals; there was to be no defacing of walls; no European soldier or sepoy was permitted to stay in the bungalows; 'the maltreatment of the Invalid Sepoys or Peons attached to the Public Bungalows is expressly prohibited' (*Fort St George Gazette*, 12 October 1836).

a grand native festival: the Pushkaram, a festival for spiritual purification, is the Telugu equivalent of the Mahamakha of Tamil Nadu and the Kumbh Mela of the north of India.

LETTER TEN

our predecessor: James Thomas's immediate predecessor, acting in the post, was William Dowdeswell, who returns to the post in 1839 after Thomas's promotion. William Dowdeswell began his career as a Writer in India in 1826. After taking on James Thomas's position in Rajahmundry, he moved to Madura in the same role. By 1860 he was Collector and Magistrate in Trichinopoly.

peon: a footman.

travelling gentleman....India fashion: putting up travellers is a custom that causes some aggravation to Julia, who clearly loves her privacy.

Letter the Eleventh

Rajahmundry, August 14*th*

OUR goods arrived last week. They had all been wetted through in the journey, and very much spoiled, but, by dint of keeping the sun and the palanquin-boys at work upon them, they are coming round again.

Captain Price, the commanding officer here, has just called. He seems very civil, nothing else particularly. He has a wife, whom I have not seen yet, as they were away till yesterday. The commanding officers are generally changed every three months. There is a Scotch Dr Stewart, and a Mr Macdonald, the sub-collector, but he is not here now. There will also be in time a Registrar, or, as they spell it here, "Register", but none is appointed yet. These and ourselves are all the residents; but there are continually travellers passing through, as this place is on the high road from the north to the south of Madras. I fancy the civilians all expect to come to us on their journey; and the militaries go to Captain Price: and whichever of us receives the visitor must make a dinner-party.

Last night I was awakened by a great uproar: I found it was on account of a snake who had crept into the house and hidden himself under a box. The maty had found him out, and the servants were all hunting and fighting him with sticks. He was caught and killed. A— thought he was not of a venomous kind, but they are not pleasant visitors. I often hear the hyænas at night howling about the country. They are horrid spiteful-looking creatures, but so cowardly that they never attack any but weak animals. They do mischief in the poultry-yard, and sometimes carry off a small dog, and, if very hungry, now and then a young donkey; but one is no more afraid of them than of foxes in England.

LETTER ELEVEN

Did you ever hear of the Thugs ? They are a tribe of Hindoos whose business and trade is murder. They are brought up to it from childhood, choose their victim by omen, consider themselves and their vocation under the especial patronage and direction of one of their goddesses, Kalee, and set about their murdering work in the most cool and business-like manner. You will find a long account of them, and quite true, in Wolff's last volume of his Journal. There is a great sensation about them just now, and we are hunting them out everywhere. One has been brought to A— for trial to-day, and I am very curious to hear about him.

I left off writing just now for my "tiffin", and could not imagine what they were bringing me to eat. Some bran, which I had been boiling to season a new tin kettle, and which the maty supposed to be some particular Europe cookie I was making for myself; and, thinking I was provided for, he has eaten up all my meat!

August 15th – The Thug turned out to be an accuser instead of a criminal. A Peon had caught him, and he pretended that the Peon had offered to release him on his paying a certain sum, and that he had paid it, but the Peon still kept him prisoner. On investigation it turned out to be all a lie from beginning to end; so the Peon is released and the Thug sent to prison.

I was hard at work to-day unpacking books, sitting on the ground all over dust, sorting and putting them on the shelves, when Mrs Price called to pay her first devoirs with all her best clothes on, worked muslin and yellow gloves. I thought the only way to prevent her being ashamed of me was to make her as dirty and dusty as myself; therefore, under pretence that it would be so nice for her to have some new books to read, I made her sit down by me and look them over too, and we got on very well. She is very young, pretty, and unaffected, and I like the thought of having her for a neighbour. It is pleasant to have some Englishwoman within reach as a companion.

August 29th – Your packet, sent by private opportunity, has just arrived, to my great delight. I had received, a fortnight ago, letters from home of a later date, but private-hand letters are always slow. People never seem to be able to lay their private hands upon them till after they have finished all their unpacking.

We like our station better and better; it is far pleasanter than Madras, which was like England in a perspiration: here we have fresh, sweet country air, and no troublesome company, yet always enough to prevent us from feeling lonely.

I thoroughly enjoy the quiet, and I have plenty to do, more than I can ever get through in the day, so that I am never dull. In fact, one has less time at one's command here than at home, although the very early rising seems to give so many hours. But we are obliged to go out in the early morning; it is indispensable to lie down for some time in the middle of the day; we go out again in the cool of the evening, and come home again too tired to employ ourselves much at night. One's time seems to be spent in tiring and resting oneself.

I have caught a number of most beautiful butterflies: Coleoptera are more scarce, as I cannot grub for them myself, for fear of centipedes. This morning, I took a fancy for gardening myself, and while I was removing some dry leaves a large centipede showed his horrid pincers within an inch of my hand. He did not hurt me, but he has cured me of gardening. I have a number of schemes in hand; one is to make butter: the natives make it with rennet, shaking it in a bottle, and it is rather a nasty mess; but after a week's hard work and much scolding, the old carpenter has produced a churn: a fine, heavy, awkward concern it is, but the natives admire it greatly, and stand looking at it and calling it "Missis Dub" (meaning Mistress's tub). However, the butter is still waiting for pans to set the milk in, and they had to be made on purpose, from description, and have not yet appeared. When I inquired for them this morning, I was told "Potman

LETTER ELEVEN

done fetch mud, chatties done make, but mud not done dry yet."

The other day I wanted some book-shelves made, and I sent for the carpenter. They told me they thought I should be wanting wood, so he was gone *fishing*, which seemed rather, as Johnny M. would say, a "*non sequitur*"; but it was quite true, for they really do fish for all the wood they use. It is washed down by the river; and when any is wanted, they just swim out, and catch the first piece that suits them.

There is an old Englishman living here as barrack-sergeant, – a sinecure for long service. He has been in the place these ten years, and is a very respectable old man. He has a half-caste, dropsical wife, and a sickly nigger-looking child, but seems quiet and contented. A— lends him books and the newspaper, and lets him come every Monday to change his books, and chat a little, which he likes best of all. He sits and proses for about half an hour, and is very happy at having a little intercourse with Europeans again. He takes particular interest in the young Queen, thinking she has a troublesome life before her. Yesterday he said to me, "Only think, ma'am, of such a young person for to be Queen of the realm! And in these times too, when the oldest hand could hardly keep them in order. She'll have a tough job of it, poor young lady! I pity her from my heart, indeed I do! This paper says Lord Durham is to be called to Her Majesty's counsels. I hope his Lordship is a fatherly kind of gentleman, ma'am, who will help her Majesty in some of her difficulties."

A— is very kind in hunting out poor travellers who happen to be passing. The rich ones, who want for nothing, come to us as a matter of course, but the poor ones would pitch their tents under a tree during the hot hours, and go away again unnoticed, if he did not go and find them out. The other day he discovered seven English soldiers travelling to join their regiment: they were not in want of absolute necessaries, but, on his trying to find out what he could do for them, they told him at last, confidentially, that the greatest treat he could possibly give them would be a little tea and sugar to make themselves "a cup of English tea", which was a thing "they had not tasted they did not know when": of course we sent them plenty, and books and tracts for the tea to wash down. They had a Bible among them, but they said "they set such store by it, they seldom let it see the light"; so we gave them another for use. A— is very anxious to set up an English school for the natives, if he can persuade Sergeant Keeling to be schoolmaster; but the Sergeant thinks himself "not scholar enough." We think he is, and he speaks Teloogoo very well.

To-day a great Zemindar, or Rajah, came to pay us a visit: he is a proprietor of large estates in this district, and pays a rent to the Government of ten thousand a year, — quite a grandee; but he has some lawsuit going on at this court, so he said he was come to ask A— to "protect a poor little man". He stayed an immense time, and talked a great deal of nonsense, as they all do. It is very striking to see how completely want of education has blasted all their powers of intellect. They talk for hours and hours, without ever by any chance bringing out an original idea or a generous sentiment. Their conversation is never anything but wearisome twaddle. I suppose extremes meet. Do you remember Mr J. once telling us that some celebrated person was "too well informed" — that he had "lost his originality"? These people, from being too ill informed, have never found theirs.

September 16th — A day or two ago the Maty bolted into the breakfast-room, exclaiming, "Sar! one snake, sar! One big snake in godown! He very good snake, sar!" They call the venomous snakes "good" by way of propitiating them: they consider them as a species of evil-disposed gods, and pay them some kind of worship, though they kill them too whenever they can. This brute was a large deadly cobra capello: it had hidden itself behind some bottles in a recess under the

LETTER ELEVEN

steps where the water is cooled. A— went directly to load his gun, and I peeped out, but could not go near enough to see the creature on account of the sun, and I calculate I should not have gone any nearer if it had been ever so shady. There stood all the palanquin-boys with bamboos in their hands, ready to beat it if it came out, and all the Peons peeping over their shoulders, array enough to attack a tiger. A— forbade their killing it in that way, on account of the danger of their getting bitten if they missed a blow, and he shot it dead himself, after which they all dragged it out, and beat it to their hearts' content. Two days afterwards we were told of another cobra in a hole of a tree at the bottom of the garden; but while A— was preparing his gun, one of the snake-conjurers came and charmed it out of its hole, and brought it into the garden to show us: it was quite fresh, its teeth not extracted, and its bite certain death; but this man had it perfectly under command: he set it up and made it dance, and, when it tried to strike, he just whisked the tail of his gown in its face, and quieted it again. I offered to buy it, and pay him for killing and bottling it, but I could not persuade him to sell it at any price: he thought its possession would bring him good luck. In answer to my offers, the butler, who was interpreter, told me, "if Missis put snake in bottle of rack, snake dead." "I know that", said I, "I like it dead." "Yes, ma'am, but that man like 'live." "What is the use of his keeping it alive? sometime snake bite." "No, ma'am, no can bite; that man make conjure." However, to-day the conjurer came to say that he had found another cobra, so he was willing to sell me one if I liked it. Accordingly, he took it with his bare hands out of a brass pan which he brought with him, set it up, made it show its hood and dance a little, and then put it into a bottle of spirits, which soon killed it, and I have it now on my table corked up. It is a magnificent specimen, four feet long, and quite uninjured.

The snakes have very much confirmed my belief in physiognomy. They certainly have a great deal of countenance; a cunning, cruel, spiteful look that tells at once that they are capable of any mischief; in short, "*beaucoup de caractère*", and the more venomous the snake, the worse his expression. The harmless ones *look* harmless; I think I should almost know a "too much good snake" by his too much bad countenance. The Cobra is the worst, his eyes are quite hideous; and that boa constrictor at the Cape was very disgusting: but after all I do not know that there is anything more horrid in the way of physiognomy than a shark; there is a coldblooded, fishy malignity in his eyes that quite makes one shudder.

September 26th – There was a hyæna killed to-day about half a mile from the town: it had attacked a poor old Bramin, and wounded him severely, which is very extraordinary, as they almost always run away from men. I have ordered the tail to be kept as a trophy for Frank. Also I have a beautiful leopard's skin for him, to be sent by the first opportunity.

Notes
Captain Price: the commanding officer at the time was called Harrison, and Julia notes that the C.O. was changed every three months. The doctor was a Mr Lyell and 'Mr Binny or Binning, or some such name, sub-collector.' Lyell, she records, is 'a relation of the Geologist's but not a scientific man himself.' Sir Charles Lyell (1797-1875) had published his *Principles of Geology* in three volumes between 1830 and 1833. Binning is listed in the *Fort St George Gazette* for 1836 as the acting head assistant to the Collector and Magistrate of Rajahmundry. 'These and ourselves,' writes Julia in the same letter, 'are all the residents.'

Did you ever hear of the Thugs?: thuggee and suttee (see Letter Fifteen) were two issues that concerned the British in this period. The non-interference of earlier years had given way to a desire to eliminate what were considered 'barbaric' practices. The British need to 'know India' in order to exploit it meant the creation of detailed revenue maps, gazetteers for the various districts, efforts such as the Rajahmundry Survey (APAC) carried out in the 1820s and which collected and classified down to the finest detail (the number of potters' wheels, the numbers of trees and their type, the head of cattle, the numbers adhering to a particular religion, their caste). These details 'fixed' India for the British, and for Indians as well in the sense of reflecting back a static picture of themselves. In this way, representations and modes of perception were used as weapons of colonial rule. The classification of types (you only have to see Julia's passion for the new sciences to understand how far this obsession reached) emphasized caste (and occupation), religion and tradition, and showed that the British saw them in everything.

Thugs gained the confidence of travellers, murdered them by strangulation, robbed them and buried them. Thuggee, suppressed by law in 1836, was associated in the British mind with the worship of Kali (the Hindu mother-goddess, consort of Shiva the Destroyer). Julia's understanding of Thugs (see the note on Wolff below), and her desire to see the practice as deep-rooted in religious tradition, is typical of the time. It is less likely however that the Thugs were organized as a religious sect, than that poor migrants or laid-off soldiers stole from and murdered others on the road for their survival. In reality, hunting out Thugs enabled the British to gain further control over the native princes who were accused of harbouring them. Sir William Henry Sleeman (1788-1856), appointed general superintendent for the suppression of Thuggee in 1835, had a group of young men working for him, usually soldiers. In the *Fort St George Gazette* for 1836 it was announced that Captains P.A. Reynolds and F.C. Elwall would be in the Madras Presidency charged with the suppression of Thuggee. The records of the Madras Proceedings (Judicial) show Elwall reporting in 1837 that the majority of murders by Thuggee were taking place in the territories of the Nizam and Rajah of Mysore, and around the British-controlled area of Bellary.

The confession of over seven hundred murders by one Thug became the basis of Philip Meadows Taylor's popular novel, *Confessions of a Thug* (1839).

Wolff's last volume of his Journal: Julia refers to the *Journals* of Joseph Wolff (1795-1862). Wolff was born in Bamberg the son of a rabbi, studied oriental languages at Tübingen and Cambridge, became a member of the Church of England and began his nomadic career as a missionary in 1821. He travelled extensively in India in the early 1830s: Calcutta, Simla, Kashmir, Madras, Pondicherry, Tinneveli, Goa and Bombay. Of the various volumes of his *Journal*, the volume containing his report on the Thugs is *Researches and Missionary Labours among the Jews, Mohammedans and other Sects*, published in 1835. His report, which Julia believes to be 'quite true' details the 'several peculiarities in the customs of the Thugs.' He outlines a secretive cabal, worshipping Kali, made up of Hindus of every caste and Muslims of every sect. They move about the country in large groups, 'all subject to the same regulations', and are 'slaves to superstition, and as much directed by the observation of omens in the commission of their murders, as the most inoffensive of the natives of India are in the ordinary affairs of life.' The *khoddee* (pick-axe) is their chief symbol of worship and Wolff describes in detail the religious ceremonies involving the *khoddee* made in advance of any murderous expedition. Equally important ceremonies

SEPTEMBER 1837

attach to the strip of knotted cloth used to strangle victims. Wolff credits the Thugs with their own 'technical language,' naming the various positions held by individuals within the bands and the vocabulary employed to describe place. He also claims that many assist the Thugs by taking messages or by leaving markers. He ends, 'The impunity with which the Thugs have heretofore carried on their merciless proceedings, the ease with which they recruit their numbers, which are restricted to no particular caste or sect, and the facility with which they have purchased their release, when seized by the officers of the weak native Governments, in whose dominions they have usually committed their greatest depredations, have altogether tended to confirm the system, and spread it to such a fearful extent, that the life of no traveller in this country has been safe; and it seemed only by some happy chance that even large parties have ever escaped the fangs of these blood-thirsty demons.'

There is an old Englishman: Sergeant Keeling keeps his own name. John Keeling died in 1840 aged 49 and was buried in the Rajahmundry cemetery, near the old Civil Court. His son, the 'sickly nigger-looking child,' was buried with him in 1856: 'John Keeling, Head Draughtsman in the Civil Engineer's Department at Dowlaisweram, and son of John Keeling, Barrack Sergeant of Rajahmundry, aged 22 years, 2 months and 8 days' (Le Fanu).

the young Queen: Princess Victoria became Queen in June 1837. John George Lambton, first Earl of Durham (1792-1840), one of the architects of the first Reform Bill, was able but tactless and with a bad temper, and Melbourne did not admit him to the government in 1837.

zemindar: a landowner, by this time paying revenue direct to the government.

Do you remember Mr.J: the original letter has this as George Jelf referring to the geologist, Lyell. George Jelf (1796-1859) was a barrister, and son of Sir James Jelf. The Jelfs were friends of the Burney extended family through the Cambridges.

godown: storage area.

Letter the Twelfth

Rajahmundry, October 3rd

In your last letter you ask for particulars of living, servants, house-rent, and such-like domestic matters. We have a house unfurnished, and a garden of more than two acres, for which we pay about 60l. per annum. Provisions are cheap, but there is great waste, because nothing will keep on account of the heat, and we are obliged to take much larger quantities of meat than we can consume, in order to make it worth the butcher's while to supply us at all. We send for potatoes from Madras, as they will not grow here; other vegetables we have from our own garden, and we keep our own poultry. Servants are expensive altogether, though cheap individually; but we are obliged to have such a number of them that their pay mounts up. We keep fewer than many people, because we wish to be economical. Here is our establishment: one butler, one dress-boy*, one matee†, two ayahs, one amah**, one cook, one tunnicutchy††, two gardeners, six bearers, one water-carrier, two horse-keepers, two grass-cutters, one dog-boy, one poultry-man, one washerman, one tailor, one hunter, and one amah's cook – altogether twenty-seven: and this is reckoned few; and it is as much as ever they can do to get through their little work in their lazy dawdling way. If anybody comes to dinner, the cook sits down and cries for a cook's maty or helper, and I am obliged to hire one for him. They all find their own food themselves, and the caste people

---
*Valet.
† The matee cleans plate, washes china, and lights candles.
** Wet-nurse.
†† Housemaid.

would not touch any of our food; but the maties and under-servants are generally Pariahs, and are very glad to eat up anything they can lay their hands on. The amah is a caste woman, and her whims are the plague of my life : I am obliged to keep a cook on purpose for her, because her food must all be dressed by a person of her own caste; and even then she will sometimes starve all day rather than eat it, if she fancies anybody else has been near it: she has a house built of cocoa-nut leaves in the compound, on purpose to cook her food in. I am also obliged to keep a separate nurse for her baby, and see after it regularly myself, because they are so careless about their own children when they are nursing other people's, that she and her husband would let the poor little creature die from neglect, and then curse us as the cause of it.

Think of the amah's being caught drinking rack and eating opium! She used to go out and howl so that the servants were afraid to come near her, saying she made "one pishashi (devil) noise." When she had cleared the coast with her pishashi-ing, her own people crept out from their hiding-holes, and brought her rack and bang (that is, spirits and opium).

You ask what shops we have. None at all: the butler buys everything in the bazaar or market, and brings in his bill every day. One of the Court native writers translates it into English, and very queer articles they concoct together! such as "one beef of rump for biled"; "one mutton of line beef for *alamoor estoo*", meaning *à la mode stew*; "mutton for curry pups" (puffs); "durkey for stups" (stuffing for turkey); "eggs for saps, snobs, tips, and pups" (chops, snipes, tipsycake, and puffs); "mediation (medicine) for ducks"; and at the end "ghirand totell" (grand total), and "howl balance."

October 15th — Of late I have been hindered from letter-writing and everything else by relays of stranger-company — true Indian-fashion. People say this custom of receiving everybody without previous notice, and being received in return, is "so very delightful," "hospitable," &c. &c.; and so it

LETTER TWELVE

may be, – but it is also extremely inconvenient and disagreeable. I cannot get over the dislike to intrude myself upon people whom I never saw, and who must receive me whether they like it or not; neither do I enjoy being put out of my way and obliged to turn the house out of windows, for chance travellers whom I never heard of before, and never shall see again. However, such is the mode here. One of our visitors, Mrs S., was a very pleasing person, and I should have much liked to see more of her ; but she was on her way to England, and only stayed with us two days. Two of our visitors are with us still, and will remain till they have found a bungalow to suit them, as they are coming to live here: they are Mr and Mrs Hamilton, the new registrar and his wife.

We have had the English service now for the last month, and mean to continue it regularly; A—officiates, as is the custom when there is no clergyman; all the English residents attend very regularly, and some half-caste Protestants. There is a Roman Catholic half-caste dresser, or surgeon's assistant, named Rozer, father to Sergeant Keeling's wife: there is a little Roman Catholic chapel under his care, and he takes a great deal of pains about it, poor soul! keeping it clean, lighting the candles, and putting flowers before the images, though there is no priest living here, nor any one to notice him. When our service was announced, he sent a message to ask if he might be present at it, but when the day arrived he never appeared; and on making inquiry, we found from the Sergeant that poor Rozer himself was very anxious to attend, but was afraid of a reprimand from some distant priest who occasionally comes here in the course of his travels.

October 27th – I continue to like "up country," as they call it, far better than the Presidency : it is much more amusing. Of course everybody tried to make Madras as English as they could, though without much success, except doing away with everything curious; but this place is real India, and I am every day seeing something new and foreign. This is the country of the old Rajahs, and they are very sociable and fond of paying us visits. They think it a great incivility to appear without something in their hands as a present. It is contrary to regulation to accept anything of value, so they bring limes, oranges, yams, &c. The other day we received a basket of oranges, with a message that a Rajah whom we had not before seen would come next day and pay us a visit. Accordingly next day, at the appointed hour, we heard a queer kind of twanging and piping, like a whistle and a Jew's-harp. This was the Rajah's music, played before his palanquin: then came his guards, – men with halberds; then his chief officer, carrying a silver mace; then his principal courtiers, running by the side of his palanquin to keep him "pleasant company." When they all arrived, the halberdiers grounded their arms, and the whole cortège stopped at the military word of command, "*Halt! Present! Fire!*" but the firing consisted of the old gentleman's getting out of his palanquin, and quietly shuffling into the house, between two rows of his own servants and ours, salaming him at every step. He was dressed in a clear muslin pelisse, with his black skin showing through; the rims of his ears stuck full of jewels, gold bracelets on his arms, and a diamond locket hung round his neck. I call him "Penny Whistle Row": if that is not quite his real name, it is so like it, I am sure it must mean that. When he came into the drawing-room, he stopped at the entrance (N.B. we have no doors) to make us most profound salams, which we returned to the best of our ability: then he presented us with an orange each, and there were more salams on either side. At last, when we had all done all our "moppeing and moweing," he sat down and began his chirp. He paid a variety of set compliments, as they all do ; but, those over, he was more curious about European matters than the natives in general are. In particular he wished to know whether it was true that our King was dead, and that we had a woman to reign over us. This was quite beyond his comprehension – how she was to contrive to reign, and how men were to agree to obey her, he gave up in despair. He asked whether the King's death would make any difference to us: he was in hopes it might have given A—a step in the service. He invited us to come and spend a week with him, which we fully intend to do as soon as the weather allows. When he had sat about an hour, he took his leave with the same ceremonies as at his arrival: salams on all sides, pipe whistling, Jew's-harp twanging, guards recovering arms, courtiers putting on their shoes, and all marching off to the word of command as before, "*Halt ! Present ! Fire!*" At parting he shook hands to show how European his manners were, and he took leave of me in English: "My Lady, I now to your Excellency say farewell: I shall hope you to pay me one visit, and on one week go (meaning hence) I shall come again to see the face of your honour civilian."

Besides the Rajahs, there are a number of natives of lower rank who are very fond of calling to keep themselves in remembrance in case of an appointment falling vacant. Some only come as far as the gate, and stand there to make a salam when we go out. These never speak, but they put on some part of the dress belonging to the situation they want, in order that we may understand their meaning. A Court writer in expectance holds writing materials in his hand; a Peon sticks a dagger in his belt, &c. Others of rather higher pretensions come to the house and pay a visit. One of them calls regularly twice a-week, and the same dialogue takes place whenever he comes.

> Visitor. – Salam, great chief!
> A. – Salam to you.
> Visitor. – Your Excellency is my father and my mother!
> A. – I am much obliged to you.
> Visitor. – Sar, I am come to behold your honourable face.
> A – Thank you. Have you anything to say to me?
> Visitor – Nothing, great chief.
> A. – Neither have I anything to say, so good morning: enough for today.
> Visitor – Enough; good morning, sar; great chief, salam!

OCTOBER 1837

One has to dismiss one's own visitors, as they generally think it an impoliteness to go away of their own accord. We are obliged to appoint a particular hour at which they may come, else they would be hindering us the whole day.

Notes
In a letter dated 3 October Julia mentions the possibility of moving to a new posting to be nearer the Neilgherries (the Nilgiris, some of the most spectacular mountains in southern India and the hill-station of the Southern Presidency, the retreat from the heat of the Plains. It was in this period that the tea plant was being reported as flourishing in the hills. The experiment was begun by a Colonel Crewe, and followed up by the French botanist M. Perrottet). Julia herself says she is happy where she is. She has heard that Lord Elphinstone is to return to Europe and is to be replaced by Mr Stuart Mackenzie, currently in Ceylon. She asks her mother to acquire a letter of introduction from Miss Mackenzie. 'Lord Elphinstone', she elaborates, 'is a harmless young chap, does no mischief, but is not used to work for his bread and is heartily tired of the job. At last he fairly took himself off to Bangalore where he has been for the last two months randying, rather to the surprise and dismay of the old men of business at the Presidency' [13 September 1837].

altogether twenty-seven: Julia was relatively economical. Fanny Parkes had 'only fifty-four' servants, 'and I find it quite difficult enough to keep them in order' *(Wanderings of a Pilgrim in Search of the Picturesque)*.

rack and bang: arrack was the sap drawn from the date palm, but the term came to apply to any alcohol liquor distilled by natives. Bang, or bhang, is Indian hemp, a narcotic; its leaves, stalks and seeds are smoked, chewed or drunk.

the new registrar and his wife: Julia describes the post of registrar as 'Judge's muddle.' Mr and Mrs Jellicoe 'coolly established themselves with us till another [house] which they prefer shall be vacant, which it will not be for another fortnight. This I call an impudent thing.' Mrs Jellicoe she describes as 'very silly but worthy', and her husband as having 'a "turn" for languages but is "not deep"' (15 October 1837).

the English service: with the arrival of the Jellicoes there were enough people to make up a congregation. The service is attended by the Harrisons, Jellicoes, Sergeant Keeling with his son and 'a half-caste friend of his'. The doctor occasionally attended and they used 'commonplace but short' sermons, including those of Mr Maitland, her future father-in-law (15 October 1837).

LETTER TWELVE

I continue to like "up country": this October 27 entry is made up of extracts from three letters, to her mother, her grandmother, and her cousin Minette Kingston. Her belief that she is seeing the 'real India' is, however, not expressed in any of the three. Julia did not enjoy British society life in Madras, 'one never saw enough of anybody to really care for them, and yet there was always the fuss and bother of visitors' [to Minette Kingston, 1 October 1837]. The 'real India' to Julia seems to be a place remote from 'Englishness' and full of curiosity. It is not a place where she makes real relationships with local people, but she does appear to meet and converse with Indians more than anyone she knows around her. Accounts of 'Penny Whistle Row' were both colourful tales for her family and a demonstration to them that she was in touch with the 'real India.' Elizabeth Eastlake, writing in the *Quarterly Review*, certainly thought she was reading something authentic when she compares two other texts written by British women in India, 'neither of these gives the humours of this antipodes state of society like our nameless lady.' Julia's publication counters another 'nameless lady,' quoted in Letter Seven, 'I know nothing at all about them [the natives], nor I don't wish to: really I think the less one sees and knows of them the better!'

The two women whose work most closely resembles Julia's in type are Fanny Parkes and Emily Eden, and while both these women were in India at the same time as Julia neither of them published until later, 1850 and 1866 respectively. The two women who were in print, mentioned by Elizabeth Eastlake, were Emma Roberts and Anna Katharine Elwood. Emma Roberts, who in 1855 published *Scenes and Characteristics of Hindostan, with Sketches of Anglo-Indian Society*, seems to have hated her life in India but according to Jane Robinson 'produced the best vade-mecum available, and a ruthlessly objective and cautionary tale of Anglo-Indian society' (*Wayward Women*, 1990). Anna Katharine Elwood's *Narrative of a Journey Overland from England, by the Continent of Europe, Egypt, and the Red Sea, to India; including A Residence there, and Voyage Home, in the years 1825, 26, 27 and 28* (1830), describes only a few months in India.

contrary to regulations to accept anything of value: an obvious rule to curb corruption. Emily Eden and her brother, the Governor General, Lord Auckland, accepted sumptuous gifts while travelling on official business in North India in the late 1830s, knowing that these would go to the Company. This did not deter Emily from accepting a few trinkets for herself. Julia later has to turn down a delightful gift, which she describes in Letter Seventeen.

Penny Whistle Row: 'Row' or 'rao' was an honorific title given to a prince or otherwise distinguished man. In south India it could also be a family name.

Letter the Thirteenth

Rajahmundry, October 31st

We are very eager about our intended Native School – writing, and planning, and preparing. The difficulty, as usual, has been to find a proper master. In this part of India there are no native Christians, and of course we did not wish to have a Heathen master. On Sunday there came unexpectedly to the service a half-caste stranger. As we had never seen him there before, A— made some inquiries about him afterwards, and heard that he was here only for a couple of days on some business of a lawsuit; that he understands English well, writes a good hand, and spells correctly; and it looked respectable and well-disposed his taking the opportunity of coming to church. He is now gone back to his own home; but, as he seemed promising, and we knew of no one better, A— has written to offer him the schoolmaster's post, if he understands Gentoo; and we are now waiting for his answer. Meanwhile we are busy giving it out among the natives, and collecting promises of scholars. To-day one of the upper Court servants (post-office head writer), called for a chat, so we documentized him, and he offered to look for scholars. A— asked whether, if we set up a girls' school, any girls would come; but Seenevasarow said, "No: what for girls learn?" We had a great discussion on the subject, but he ended by saying that if a girl learned to read, some misfortune was sure to happen to her relations – most likely her father or mother would die. We told him that *I* had learned both to read and to write, and my father and mother were alive and well, and that all European ladies learnt reading and writing, and yet no misfortune happened to any of their relations in consequence; but he said, "Ah! Europe people never mind – never hurt; only native

LETTER THIRTEEN

people hurt." A— told him that it was a notion the Pishashi (devil) put into their heads in order to keep them from any good – and a great deal more besides; to which he answered, "Hum! sometime very true; but how can do? girl got no sense!" The consequence of this notion is, that the women, from being utterly neglected, are a hundred times worse than the men. As soon as European children are old enough to talk and understand, one is obliged to have bearers to attend upon them, because it is not safe to trust them with the women; they are so wicked, so lying, and so foolish.

The cool weather is coming on now: thermometer 86° and 84°. From having been completely *heated through* in the summer, I am now pretty well Indianized, and find the present temperature quite cool and pleasant. In the early mornings it is 74°, which feels so cold that I am glad of a cloak to go out with. The same degree of the thermometer certainly does not feel so hot here as it would at home.

There are so many changes in the service, that we shall probably not remain at this station very long, and we may be glad of a removal when the hot season returns; but, for the present, this place is so pleasant and so very pretty, that I should be quite sorry to leave it. Everybody says that the view from our windows is one of the most beautiful in all this part of India. We have just succeeded in putting the garden into nice order, and are feeling quite settled and comfortable. I have three little deer tethered on the lawn: they are very pretty creatures, and quite tame and friendly. Also I am taming some fine jungle peacocks.

To-night the hunter brought in a superb leopard (dead); they had shot him in looking for game: his beauty was still perfect, and in my own heart I was almost sorry such a handsome creature should have been killed; but they are very mischievous among the cattle, and a price is paid by Government for every one killed. The skins all belong to the Collector; but I mean to beg this one of him, as it was caught during our reign.

OCTOBER 1837

Now, in the cool nights, the hyænas and jackals come constantly into our garden, and howl under the windows: it is a most unpleasant noise, like a human being in agony. This morning I was told that "a cat had run away with a child." I was horror-struck, and thought it must have been a hyæna; but on inquiry I found the child was nothing but a young pigeon – "pigeon-child", as they explained it. The ducks laid a number of eggs, which were brought for us to see. "You must make little ducks", said the Master. "Sar, I shall do", said the butler. I laughed at the order; but a hen was caught, put into a basket with the eggs, and the lid shut down upon her; and in a little time I was told there were "four babies" in the poultry-yard.

I have just received a letter from the Madras Moonshee, who begs to express "the concern I have for your happiness as my matron, your state of health, and the state of my rising matron, your child." I suppose he thinks matron is the feminine of patron.

November 3rd – One evening, while the Hamiltons and several other visitors were still with us, I had gone to my room to rest a little before tea, when I suddenly heard a queer familiar twang in the drawing-room, which, though I could not distinguish a word, I was sure could only come through a French nose. Presently Maty brought a note from the Collector to beg us to help his friend M. d'Arzel on his journey; so I went into the drawing-room to receive him. There I found all my party of Englishmen working for their lives at French politesses, such as, "Permetty, Mushoo" – "Mushoo, je suis très aisy," &c. Monsieur himself was a true Frenchman, not at all distingué (an agent to one of the great French mercantile houses), but most completely at his ease, and ready for his company whatever it might be – keeping up conversation, and finding answers to English speeches in French, that I am sure it was impossible for him to understand. He addressed some remark to Mrs Hamilton, which only

LETTER THIRTEEN

meeting with a stare from her, Mr Hamilton answered for her, "*Elle ne parle pas, Moseer!*" – "A—h!" said the Frenchman, in a tone of most commiserating surprise. I believe he thought she was dumb.

He had contrived to travel from Madras, four hundred miles, without knowing one word of any of the native languages, or of English, making himself understood merely by signs. We gave him his supper, ordered his bearers, and sent him on. After he was gone, the Englishmen began talking over all the French adventures of their past lives, and I discovered that they were, as school-girls say, "very fond of French," not to say proud of it, and many Frenchmen had told them all – the innocent birds! – that they spoke it quite like natives. When Mr Hamilton and some friend of his were travelling in France together, they took it in turn to give the orders at the inns, because "one man could not speak French every day": but the friend often grew restive; he used to call to the waiter, "Gassor!" "Monsieur." "Now, Hamilton, I wish you would tell him." "No, indeed; it is not my turn; I spoke French yesterday." "Well then, I won't. It is impossible to talk their nonsense: Gassor, ally vous or."

One of our visitors at this time was a young ensign of seventeen, travelling in command of a company of Sepoys in charge of treasure, and it was quite a pleasure to see a creature so innocently important and happy. He travelled on horseback, and had a pony which he talked of just like a human being, and admired as much as any hero. He was attacked by some wild native horses at the entrance of the village – so, he said, "I took off my saddle and bridle, and set my pony at them; and if the people had not come and separated them, I know he would soon have licked them all. He is a capital fellow!" I saw his pony afterwards, the ugliest Pariah beast I ever set eyes on! You must know people here talk of high-caste and Pariah horses, Pariah dogs, &c. The native horses are Pariahs, the high-caste are Arabs. I have a high-caste horse,

'From our Verandah at Samuldavy. Finished June 7 1838.'

'Rajahmundry. View of a Moorman's Bungalow on the banks of the Godavery. September 1837.'

who is so excessively puffed up with pride that he will not bear the sight of a pony: I am obliged to make the horse-keeper run before me to clear the way of all ponies, or else this creature fights them, with me on his back.

November 23rd — Our school is now opened with about twenty-five boys, and more coming. All caste boys. A— thinks it better to teach them whenever one can, as it is far more difficult to get at them than at the Pariahs, and also the education of the upper ranks has much more influence than that of the Pariahs. We have a Bramin to teach Gentoo, and David Gonsalves, the half-caste, to teach English. I went to see them the other morning. (Tell your charity-school girls at home that they come at six o'clock, and are always in time!) The Bramins and merchant boys sat together; there was another row of the Moochy or workman caste; another of Mussulman boys; and, behind all, a row of grown-up men, who come to amuse themselves by watching and picking up a little by listening: but they talk, and are very troublesome, so they are in future only to be admitted on examination days. We have but few books, as they are very expensive, and the whole cost of the school must devolve upon the Hamiltons and ourselves; therefore we mean to spend our money in good books, which will be useful for them to read, and not in mere spelling-books. I make great pasteboard columns, with alphabets, spelling and first lessons, in large printing hand. One column does for the whole school to learn from at once, and we mean to keep to these till the boys can read a little, so as really to make use of a book. I have printed a number of texts to hang round the school-room, and the first text I chose for my poor little heathens was Psalm cxv. 4-8. I dare say by sending to Madras, by and by, we may be able to get printed sheets of lessons; but the wind has set in now the wrong way for ships coming from Madras, and parcels sent by land are a long while on the road, and, as our scholars are ready, we do not like to wait. You must understand that we have no immediate hope of making Christians of these boys by our teaching, but we wish to "do what we can": this kind of school is all we can do for them, and I fully believe that, if schools were set up all over the country, it would go far towards shaking their Heathenism, by putting truth into their heads, at any rate, instead of falsehood.

Notes
Seenevasarow: one of the upper Court servants.

We shall probably not remain at this station very long: Julia reveals to Minette in February the following year, 'I like the place and should not want to move but the gentleman does not think himself quite grand enough' (8 February 1838).

your charity-school girls at home: when telling Minette that all her plans seem to come to 'no more in India than they did at home,' she explains that she and James are always late for their planned breakfast at 9.00 am, so they set themselves a system of fines, 'to go towards a fund for feasts for Mama's Brighton Schools' (1 October 1837). In August Julia sent her mother £3 for her schools, 'I want you to be so kind as give a feast to Green girls or Sweeps, or whatever school you are fondest of at the present moment.'

Moochy: a worker in leather, and not one of the main sub-divisions of caste.

Mussulman: Muslim.

I make great pasteboard columns: she reassures her mother in the same letter: 'I keep my promise to the archdeacon faithfully, and do no schooling to tire myself, but sitting writing those Columns is no more work than writing a letter' (27 November 1837).

Psalm cxv. 4-8: Their idols are silver and gold, the work of men's hands. / They have mouths, but they speak not: eyes have they, but they see not: / They have ears, but they hear not: noses have they, but they smell not: / They have hands, but they handle not: feet have they, but they walk not: neither speak they through their throat. / They that make them are like unto them; so is everyone that trusteth in them.

A letter of 27 November includes a long shopping list for her mother. She sends £105:
 'fifty for the children's clothes [John Thomas's children], thirty for their picture, fifteen for me in commissions, five for James the same, five to go to Minette for the music she sent some time ago.'

NOVEMBER 1837

For her fifteen she wants what it will buy of: '2 silk (<u>good</u> silk) bonnets (v. light pink, v. light lemon, v. light French grey); 2 pair of strings to each bonnet (no flowers and no illusion); 3 pairs black silk shoes; 1 gown (for dinner); a belt to match the gown; cambric muslin to make frocks for baby (c.4); fine muslin for frocks; cambric muslin for baby shimmys; gauze flannel; Annual for Armagum, English views would give most satisfaction to a Hindoo; edging to trim the baby's frocks; 2 pr. white silk short gloves; pins, needles, cotton bobbin tape, hooks and eyes; 2 or 3 sheets of cardboard for drawing; 2 or 3 good camels hair brushes; 1 cake of yellow ochre; one of those patent drawing books the leaves fixed in on all sides; silk net to make bonnet; one of those barking dogs covered with wool which we used to have when we were children – and a soft ball.'

For James's money: '2 pr. linen sheets; 12 yds gauze flannel; half a ream of large sized square writing paper – the blue sort – not greasy and not too thick; a magic lantern to show the natives; a cylinder or plate for an electrical machine; 5 or 6 dozen thread shirt buttons; a piece of black shoe ribbon; 4 tooth brushes (also I want 6 toothbrushes and a box of charcoal toothpowder out of my money); 2 lbs brown windsor soap; a bottle of lavender water.'

Letter the Fourteenth

December 15th

We are just returned from our long-promised visit to Penny-Whistle, after a very amusing excursion, though, if I had known what an undertaking the journey would be, I should never have attempted it, or rather A— never would have consented to it, however urgent my curiosity might have made me. However, we are safe at home again, and the journey has done us nothing but good. When the time came for us to start, according to appointment, A— said he thought it would be scarcely worth the trouble, and that we should be "more quiet and comfortable at home" – such a thorough John Bull! – but I made him go, as I wished to "see a little of life." The people had told us that the distance was fifteen miles; so we expected that, starting at half-past five in the afternoon, we should arrive about ten o'clock, in time for a good night's rest. But it turned out to be thirty miles, and no road; we had to grope our way over cotton-fields, a pouring rain during almost all the night coming down in such torrents that I could not hear the bearers' song, pitch-dark, and the ground almost all the way knee-deep in water. We were twelve hours splashing and wading through the mud, and "plenty tired" when we arrived. But a palanquin is much less fatiguing than a carriage, and an hour's sleep and a good breakfast soon set us to rights.

When we arrived at Dratcharrum, the Rajah's town, we were taken to a choultry,* which he had prepared and ornamented with bits of old carpet for our first reception. I could

---

* Building for the reception of native travellers. It is generally open to the air, and much less convenient than a 'Traveller's Bungalow'.

not imagine why we did not go to his house at once, according to his invitation; but I found afterwards that he had arranged our going first to the choultry, in order that he might send for us in state to his mud palace. All his principal people came to pay their compliments, and he sent us a very good breakfast; and when we had eaten it, his Gomashta (a sort of secretary, at least more like that than anything else) came to say that all things were ready for our removal. I expected something of a row at starting, but I was quite unprepared for the uproar he had provided for us. As soon as our palanquins were taken into the street, a gang of musicians started up to play before us with all their might; a sort of performance much like an imitation of one of Rossini's most noisy overtures played by bagpipes, hurdy-gurdies, penny trumpets and kettle-drums, all out of tune. Then came banners, swords, flags, and silver sticks; then heralds to proclaim our titles, but we could not make out what they were; and then dancing-girls. A— looked rather coy at being, as he said, "made such a fool of"; but when the dancing-girls began their antics, ankle-deep in the mud, the whole turn-out was so excessively absurd, that mortal gravity could stand it no longer, and he was obliged to resign himself to his fate, and laugh and be happy like me.

When we arrived at the palace, on entering the gateway, the first thing I saw was a very fine elephant making his salam; side by side with him a little wooden rocking-horse; the court filled with crowds of ragged retainers, and about fifty or more dancing-girls, all bobbing and bowing, salaming and anticking "nineteen to the dozen." At last we came to the Rajah's own hall, where we found him, the pink of Hindoo politeness, bestowing more flowers of speech upon us in a quarter of an hour than one could gather in all England in a twelvemonth. He ushered us to the rooms prepared for us, and stayed with us for some time to have a talk, surrounded by all his retinue. His palace consisted af a number of courts,

LETTER FOURTEEN

walled in, unpaved, and literally ankle-deep in mud. We could not cross them, but all round there was a raised narrow pathway of hard earth, which we crept round, holding on by the wall for fear of slipping into the mud beneath. Our apartments consisted of one of these courts and the rooms belonging to it. At one end was a room, or rather gallery, which they call a hall, open to the court on one side, without any doors or windows; a small room at each end of the large one, and a sort of outer yard for the servants. The three other sides of the square communicated with other courts of the same kind, one opening into the Rajah's own hall. In the middle of our gallery there was a wooden alcove overhanging the street, in which Penny-Whistle sits and smokes when he is alone. The furniture was a table, a carpet, four chairs, two cane sofas, and a footstool. The room was hung with pictures of Swamies by native artists, two French looking-glasses in fine frames, fastened to the wall in their packing-cases, the lids being removed for the occasion, and two little shaving-glasses with the quicksilver rubbed off the back. Penny-Whistle was very fond of his pictures, and sent for some other great coloured prints of hares and foxes to show us. They had been given him by an Englishman long ago, and the colour was rubbed off in many places, so I offered to mend them for him, which greatly pleased him. While I was filling up the holes in his foxes' coats with a little Vandyke brown, he stood by crossing his hands and exclaiming, "Ah! all same as new! wonderful skill!" and A— took the opportunity to put in his usual lecture concerning the advisableness of girls' education. Penny-Whistle said he thought it was a very fine thing to teach girls, but that his people were "too much stupid," and did not like it, and he would not go contrary to their prejudices, &c. When we were tired of him we dismissed him, as the natives think it a great impoliteness to go away till they are desired; so, when we had talked as long as we could, A— said that I was going to sleep, for that he (Penny-Whistle) "must be aware that sleep was a very good thing." That is the proper formula. When the peons come to report their going away to eat their rice, they always inform me that I "must be aware that eating is a very good thing, and necessary to a man's life."

After we were rested and brisk again, Penny sent us our dinner. We had brought with us, at his desire, plates, knives and forks, bread and beer, and he sent us, besides, all his own messes, native-fashion, brass trays lined with leaves, and a different little conundrum on each leaf; pillaws, quantities of pickles, ten or a dozen varieties of chutnies, different vegetables, and cakes made of grease, pepper, and sugar. The Bramins of Penny-Whistle's class always have their food served on the leaves of the banyan-tree.

After dinner he took us out to see the town: we in our palanquins, and he in his tonjon*, and all his ragged robins piping and drumming before us. The whole town of course turned out to see the show : one of A—'s palanquin doors was shut, so Penny stopped his procession and came to beg that A— would do him the favour to keep it all open, and "show himself to the multitude." The town was all built of mud: the bettermost houses whitewashed, but the others not even that, and the streets ankle-deep in the mud washed off from the houses; but in the midst of all this dirt and discomfort, some little bit of tinsel would peep out at every opportunity: women covered with ornaments from head to foot, peeping out of the mud-hovels; men with superb Cashmere shawls looking quite beggarly from rags and dirt. This is "Eastern splendour", – a compound of mud and magnificence, filth and finery. Penny-Whistle is a great Prince in his little way, one of the old hereditary Rajahs of the highest caste. In the course of our expedition he took us to see the pagoda. I had never before been inside one, and was very curious to know what it really was. First, there was a high wall round a large

---

* A kind of open sedan-chair.

LETTER FOURTEEN

square compound; in the middle of each wall an immensely high gateway. This gateway is the pyramid-like building that one sees outside, and that I always supposed to be the pagoda, but I find it is only the portico. On entering the principal gateway, it was such a large place, that I thought we were inside the pagoda itself, but we went through to the compound, and inside that there was another very high wall round a square court, with one porch opposite the principal entrance: on going into this we found ourselves in the pagoda. It was a wonderful, dreamy, light-headed sort of a place, a low roof, and an interminable perspective of rows of massive, grotesque pillars, vanishing in darkness – I could not see the end of them – with many dark recesses in the walls, and here and there a strange, white-turbaned figure, just glancing out for a moment, and disappearing again in the darkness: altogether I never was in a place that gave me so much the feeling of a light-headed dream. In the middle of the court, round which these galleries of pillars ran, was the Swamy-house, or place in which the idol is enshrined. They brought us opposite to it, and by stooping a little I could have seen all the inside, but I thought that perhaps some of the lookers-on might fancy I was bowing down to the god, so I would not run the risk.

When we came back to Penny's house, we found it all lighted up with stinking torches, and the constant native amusement of nautch[*] and fireworks, and crowds of spectators. We stayed with him as long as we could endure the heat, din, and glare, and then went to our own rooms. There we found everything such a complete contrast to the native taste, that we could scarcely fancy ourselves only a hundred yards from all the Rajah's row. Our matee had lighted the candles, and placed our tea-things, books, and drawing materials on the table, all looking as quiet and comfortable as

---

[*] Dancing-girls.

at home. I never saw anything so curiously different from the scene of the minute before: every feeling and idea was changed in an instant. But the next day we were to see, as the Hindoos say, "all things native" again; so I asked Puntooloo (that is his real name) to let me have a ride on his elephant. He had it brought out directly, but it was such an awful affair, such an awkward ladder to mount by, so many people in the way, such a bad howdah, a present from some English gentleman of his own carpentering, and altogether so very inconvenient, that I was frightened and would not go; so I went out in my palanquin, and the elephant walked before me, to see Penny's garden, as he called it, a muddy swamp full of betel-nut and cocoa-nut trees.

When we returned to the house, he introduced me to his wife: I had been longing to see her, but did not dare ask it for fear of distressing his feelings; however, he proposed it himself. They brought her when A— was out of the room. She was an immense creature, but young, with rather a good sphinx-like face, – altogether much like a handsome young feather bed, – dressed in green muslin embroidered with gold, and covered with jewels from top to toe, besides a belt of gold coins round her waist. All her attendant women came with her and stood at the door. The Rajah's Gomashta stood by, to order her about and teach her manners, and one of my peons acted as interpreter. When she first came in, she twirled, or rather rolled, round and round, and did not know what to do, so the Gomashta bid her make salaam, and sit down on a chair: and then I did the same. We did not know much of each other's languages – she nothing of mine, and I only enough of Gentoo to be aware that the peon mistranslated every speech we made, and invented the conversation according to his own taste, making it consist entirely of most furious compliments on either side. She was very curious about my clothes, especially my bonnet, which she poised upon her forefinger, and spun round like a top. I showed her some pictures; she

LETTER FOURTEEN

held them upside down, and admired them very much. She seemed well amused and comfortable till A— came accidentally into the room, when she jumped up, wheeled round so as to turn her broad back to him, and waddled off as fast as her fat sides would let her. Of course, he went away directly, not wishing to hurt her modesty; and as soon as he was gone she came mincing back again, reseated herself with all sorts of affected airs and graces, and sent him a condescending message to "beg he would not distress himself, for that he was her father and mother." She did not mind the peons and servants standing by.

While she remained with me, A— went and sat with Penny-Whistle, and took the opportunity of being alone with him to try to do him a little good. He was very ready to listen, unusually so for a Bramin, and did not refuse to take some books; so next day we sent him plenty, and I have written to Madras for a Gentoo Bible for him, well bound, that he may like it. I wish, when you have an opportunity, you would send me some of those twopenny "moral pocket-handkerchiefs" with alphabets and pictures on them; also some children's penny pictures, especially anything of the Queen. They would be most acceptable presents to the natives. I took Penny some drawings I had made for him of subjects likely to suit his taste, particularly an eruption of Mount Vesuvius, on account of the red flames. I put the drawings in a blue satin portfolio, embroidered with scarlet and gold, and poor Penny was enchanted with the whole concern.

We came home on a dry night, quite safely, and found all well; but another unexpected stranger visitor had arrived the night we were away, and was established in our house ready to receive us: however, he was an agreeable person, and we liked his company.

In your last letter you ask if we have been alarmed by an insurrection of which the newspapers have spoken. I never heard of any one being frightened at it, and it is all quiet now.

DECEMBER 1837

It was six hundred miles from Madras, and I never even heard any particulars of it till this gentleman passed through. He had been engaged in helping to quell it. He told me that a new tribe, hitherto unknown, had been discovered among the rebels: a fine, manly, but fierce race, showing many traces of Jewish origin, both in countenance and habits. They worshipped an invisible God, but had also one wretched image perched on a tree, which they seemed to look upon as a sort of devil to be propitiated. Unlike the other natives of India, they all lived in houses, boarded, floored, and ceiled with cedar-wood.

Notes

Dratcharrum: Dracharam or Draksharamam is a Shaivite shrine. It was listed in the Rajahmundry Survey of 1821-24 as 'a large and populous village, containing 2118 inhabitants; there are several Pagodas of antiquity here, and consequently a great proportion are Bramins. There is also a weekly market established at this place, distance from Rajahmundry 27 (and a half) miles, but the roads except in dry weather almost impassable.' The Rajahmundry Survey shows that Dratcharrum was the only village in the area with a significant Muslim presence. In the *Madras Gazetteer* for 1915 the village was noted for 'its fine temple and for its sanctity.' The temple of Bhīmesvara-svami contains a fourteen or fifteen feet high lingam which is supposed to be part of a lingam 'which broke into five pieces and fell at five holy places.' The village is also a sacred place for Muslims as it has the tomb of the saint Saiyid Shah Bhaji Aulia.

pyramid-like building: Julia is describing the gopuram, the heavily ornamented pyramid-shaped tower over the entrance gates of south Indian temples.

A *matee* was an assistant servant.

A *howdah* is the litter carried by an elephant.

Puntooloo: in her original letter, Julia spells out the Rajah's name as Pentolo. It hasn't been possible to track down Puntooloo in the records of the Company. Julia later sent home a camphor necklace she receives from 'Mrs Pennywhistle'. 'James says it is more of a curiosity than I thought. He never saw one before, and thinks it was a particular compliment from Mrs Pennywhistle' (21 December). Julia provided a list of the items she was sending:

LETTER FOURTEEN

'A catalogue of articles accompanying:
- 1 box insects (<u>not</u> a Pisana)
- 1 model of our house for Mrs Thomas
- 5 cheetah (leopard) skins: yourself, Dick, Mrs Maitland, Maria to give to her uncle, and the other keep for the present
- 1 bottle of scorpions and centipedes
- 30 Rajahmundry pebbles for the children
- 1 swordfish's sword for you
- 1 pr Mussulman ladies' slippers "last new fashion – tip of the mode" for you
- 6 drawings for you: there are two of the jungle, No1 – horribly bad Pencil view in the Jungle, No2 – perhaps we might say it was rather good, you know, but that is quite confidential
- 1 camphor necklace
- 1 jar mango pickles
- 1 jar citron marmalade
- 1 jar citron preserve
- 1 jar chutnie sauce for curries
- 1 jar Guava jelly
- 3 bottles of snakes, all poisonous, the last one is a Cobra Capel – bite fatal
- 1 bottle of cashew nuts – half roasted
- 1 roll of papers containing the pleadings in a case in Court
- 1 number of the *South Indian Christian Repository*, ed. Mr Cotterill, to tell the truth I do not think very much of it.'

In August she had sent back 4 bottles of curry powder. 'It was made on purpose by a particularly capital curry maker. 1 for Minette, who is a great cook, 2 for Governor, 1 for you to give away' (11 August). She also reported: 'You ask if I have eaten banana and what it is like – it is rather nasty – something like bad medlars but more solid. Banana is the West Indian name – it is here called Plantain'; and she asked for small gifts she could give out at the school: 'Send a few little elegancies <u>cheap</u> for rewards for our school – penknives, pencils such as Dick can buy off the Jews at the coach doors – memorandum books – multiplying glasses – Kaleidoscopes – Humming Tops – inkstands – slates and slate pencils – strong large scissors – and anything else you think might be pleasing' (15 Jan 1838).

insurrection ... six hundred miles from Madras: Julia probably refers to the insurrection at Canara. The *Madras Almanac* for 1838 wrote in its summary of events for 1837: 'An alarming, formidable, and serious insurrection broke out in Canara – the Insurgents with an irregular force of 5000 armed men, principally Moplas [Moslem inhabitants of Malabar] of that country, and of Persian origin, attacked the town of Mangalore, murdered the Dawk runners [messengers] and cut off all communication by land, – the Collector was driven out, the town set fire to from one end to the other and a Powder Magazine blown up.'

Letter the Fifteenth

December 21st

I have just despatched a letter to you, and I owe eight to other people, therefore I begin another to you; that, I perceive, is your method with regard to me, which I highly approve.

To-day arrived the little parcel which you sent from England by the Hindoo servants. Poor things! the ship in which they sailed was wrecked off the Cape: no lives were lost, but the whole of the cargo was destroyed – all the little property of these two poor boys, the presents they had received in England, &c.; but in the midst of all their distress and alarm, they contrived to save my little package, and, to my very great surprise, brought it to me quite uninjured. Was it not a pretty instance of care and faithfulness?

Many thanks for the insect-box and pins, which are great treasures. I had been trying in vain to procure some, and had even sent to Calcutta, but they were unknown there. I wish we could have seen the friend you introduced to us, but he is at Madras, and we are four hundred miles off. It is very seldom that people introduced to each other from England really meet in this wide India. However, those young cadets are generally sent up the country soon after their arrival, and I hope Mr M— may come our way.

Our school is very pretty and satisfactory, the numbers daily increasing, and no objection made to the use of our books, which is in itself a great thing. Our boys learn such parts of the Bible as have been translated, and sensible lesson-books, instead of the rubbish they are taught in their own schools. The Hamiltons and ourselves take it in turn to examine the school every Saturday evening, when all the natives who choose to come are admitted to hear what goes

LETTER FIFTEEN

on. Besides this, we pay private visits in the week; and as long as the "Doories" keep up this constant superintendence, I hope all will go on well. We have not many rules – the boys receive tickets for regular attendance, and forfeit them for non-attendance, and their rewards depend upon those tickets. When we examine them, I hear the English, and A— the Gentoo scholars. Their English learning at present only extends to B, A, Ba; but they read the Bible in Gentoo, and A— tries to make them understand it a little. We have a Gentoo master, a Bramin, at about 6l. per annum; an English master, at 30l.; house-rent, peon, and sweepers, about 6l. more; and the only other expenses will be books and rewards. The little half-caste English master is clever and willing, and does his work well. The Bramin is a solemn, stately creature, clever at teaching, but a mean old thing. He made all the boys give him a pice (half a farthing) apiece whenever he obtained them a holiday, and he was always inventing excuses and pretences for holidays, till we found out the trick.

A— and Mr Hamilton, who is a most kind and active coadjutor, are also establishing a Pariah school. This will be only for Gentoo. At first we had a great deal of consultation as to whether it would be best to make our scholars pay anything for admission; but, on talking it over with the natives themselves, we found it would not answer our purposes, as there were very few, even among the richest, who would be willing to pay, and we must have made the same rule for all, and our object was to teach as many as we could.

There is one little boy who comes dressed in the finest muslin, with a gold cap, and silver bangles, and emerald earrings, looking quite a little prince; but they all prefer a charity-school. They learn very quickly, and are in nice order; Mr Hamilton says it is already superior to the N— school, though that has been established nearly a year; but into that school they admit Pariahs, which always ruins a caste school. Even in England you could not expect a gentleman to send his son to the same school with the children of his footman, and here caste is a religious distinction, as well as a difference of rank. After any natives become Christians, it is doubtless highly desirable for the missionaries to do their utmost to induce them to give up caste, as far as it is a religious distinction; but while they are Heathens, it seems merely waste of time and trouble to attempt it, and only prevents any but Pariahs from coming under their influence. In Bengal I hear that it is easier, as the natives there have associated more with Europeans, and their prejudices are less strong. This is strange, as their Heathenism is still worse: the suttees, Juggernaut's sacrifices, &c., were all peculiar to Bengal.

The castes are not now so unmixed as when first invented. Indeed I believe that some of the original divisions no longer exist; but they make up for it by subdividing the Sudra or merchant caste, and the common people call every different trade a caste. Ayah continually tells me "that man moochy (carpenter) caste" or "bearer caste," &c. The shoemakers, I believe, are the lowest of any. The Pariahs are of no caste at all. Learned men think that the Sudras were the original inhabitants of the country, and the three higher castes the conquerors. Nobody seems to know much about the Pariahs; I suppose they were the refuse of all. The trades are as hereditary as the castes; every man follows his father's business, and seems to have no idea of raising himself in life, beyond making a little more money.

I wish I could, as you ask, tell you any pretty stories for your schools; but I am sorry to say they are not at all plentiful: there are very few natives who are even nominal Christians, and still fewer whom we can reasonably believe to be anything but what is here called "curry-and-rice Christians." In England, I think people have a very false impression of what is done in India. That is not the fault of the Missionaries, who write the real truth home; but the Committees seem to publish all the good and none of the bad, for fear of discouraging

LETTER FIFTEEN

people. In fact, it is unreasonable to expect more to be done without more efficient means. Suppose thirty clergymen to the whole of England, – what could they do? And that is about the proportion of the Missionaries in Madras, and they have to work amongst Heathens. Perhaps about half of them know the language well, and the rest speak it like school-French. The chaplains are not Missionaries: their duties lie almost as completely amongst Europeans as if they had remained at home. Mr C., for instance, is a very excellent, useful clergyman, with a large English and half-caste congregation, but no more a Missionary to the Heathen than your vicar. There are thousands needed where one or two come; and schoolmasters are wanted as much as preachers.

There is great difference of opinion as to the class of men most wanted, and most likely to be useful as Missionaries. Some people have an idea that it is scarcely necessary to have persons of the birth and education of our English clergymen, but that a larger number of rather inferior men might be employed at a smaller salary, and be quite as efficient. Of course any Christian really working among the Heathen is likely to do some good; but I believe that the more educated and the more of a gentleman he is, the more influence he will have among the Hindoos. They are themselves most excellent judges of manners and standing in society, and invariably know a gentleman, and respect him accordingly. Their own priests are of the highest caste, and it lowers our religion in their eyes if they see that our *Padres*, as they call the Missionaries, are of what they consider low caste. Perhaps you will think this idea worldly, and too much like the proceedings of the Jesuits when they pretended to be a new class of Bramins; but our home clergy are gentlemen and educated men, and I cannot see why we should send out Missionaries less qualified for a much more difficult work. An English University education, and the habit of really hard study, prove immense advantages in mastering these native languages.

JANUARY 1838

I am, as usual, expecting several visitors to-morrow, to stay till the end of next week. "Missis don't want, but no can help!" After all, perhaps, it is as well that we are obliged to have people come in this way, or we should grow quite *farouche*, for we are both always so busy, and so fond of our own habits and occupations, that I am sure we should never invite interruptions. You ask what our visitors say, "if ever they say anything?" That, you know, depends upon taste; there is anything, and anything – "fagots et fagots." However, some of them are very sensible and agreeable; and when I have them alone, they talk very well, and I like their company; but as soon as three or four of them get together they speak about nothing but "employment" and "promotion." Whatever subject may be started, they contrive to twist it, drag it, clip it, and pinch it, till they bring it round to that; and if left to themselves, they sit and conjugate the verb "to collect": "I am a collector – He was a collector – We shall be collectors – You ought to be a collector – They might, could, should, or would have been collectors"; so, when it comes to that, while they *conjugate* "to collect", I *decline* listening.

January 18*th* – A— and I have been out in the district, travelling about to see the world a little. He had a few days' holiday in his Court, and we took advantage of it to go and visit some of the places on the coast, in order to see which would be the best refuge in the hot season. Also A— wished to inspect the proceedings of some of the District Moonsiffs, or native judges, under his orders. We left the baby at home, as she was quite safe with the old ayah, who really deserves the character she gives herself, "I too much careful woman"; and baby would have been tired, and perhaps have caught cold, with a hurried journey at this time of the year. The nights are now really cold, and the days pleasant. First we went to Narsapoor, a large native village about six miles from the sea. We did not expect to find that a good place for ourselves; but we had heard that two Missionaries were established there, and we wanted to see them, and learn how they went on, and whether there was anything we could do to make them more comfortable. They were English shoemakers, Mr Bowden and Mr Beer, dissenters of Mr Grove's class, but good, zealous creatures, and in the way to be very useful. They have two pretty, young English wives, as simple as themselves. They are living completely among the natives, teaching and talking to them, and distributing books. One of them is a man of great natural talent, strong-headed, and clear and sensible in his arguments; if he had been educated, he would probably have turned out a very superior person. They compained much of the difficulties of the language; but A— says that the two men spoke it really much better than the general run of missionaries. One of the wives said to me very innocently, "It is pertickly difficult to us, ma'am, on account of our never having learnt any language at all. I don't know what to make of the grammar." I advised her not to trouble herself with the grammar, but only to try and learn to speak the language so as to converse with the natives – to learn it, in short, as a child learns to talk. At her age, and without any education, it was next to impossible for her to learn the grammar of an Oriental language; but I do not suppose she will follow my advice, as she had a great notion of studying, reading with Moonshees, and so on. They live almost like the natives, without either bread or meat, which in the long run is a great privation to Europeans; but they have rice, fish, fowls, and vegetables, and they say, "The Lord has brought down our appetites to what he gives us to feed them on." Though *they* could get no meat, we had our choice of all the sheep in the village, as I suppose the natives would kill themselves for the Judge if he would but eat them. We did not want mutton for ourselves, but we had a sheep killed in order to send it to the Missionaries, together with some bread, and a little supply of wine, to have by them in case of illness. They had not much of a school, only five or six boys; I do not think that schooling

JANUARY 1838

will ever be their vocation. They seem most likely to do good by conversing and associating familiarly with the natives. They said that the people in general were not only willing, but anxious, to talk with them and take their books, and to come and ask them questions; but one day Mr Bowden went out with his tracts, and took his stand as usual in the bazaar, when a number of people, headed by some Bramins, came round him "a jeering and a hooting." The Bramins had nothing to say for themselves, but stood interrupting, mocking, and sneering, till they were tired, and then they said, "Now we have done laughing at you, you may go away – Go!'" "No," said Bowden; "now you have done laughing at me, I shall stay here, and give away all my books"; and so he did, and the Bramins walked off, and left him the coast clear. One man said that it was of no use preaching to *him*, for that he was quite perfect and free from sin – he was sure he had no sin at all. Bowden gave him a sheet of paper, and told him to write down in black ink all the good things he did, and in red ink all the bad things he did, and to bring the paper to him at the end of a week. At the end of the week the man came, and said he still considered himself free from sin, but did not wish to show the paper! However, he seemed a little disconcerted, and will probably return before long with more inquiries.

After we left Narsapoor, we went round to several different villages on the coast, and have decided on establishing ourselves during the hot weather at Samuldavee. There is only one small bungalow, and no village near it; but it is close to the sea, and I hope will be cool. We returned home in one night's run of fifteen hours, which was "plenty long"; but a palanquin is much less fatiguing than a carriage. I find it the best way, instead of undressing and settling for the night at first starting, to begin the journey, all as usual, and to send on a Peon about twelve miles before us, to get ready fire and milk; and when we come up with him we have our palanquins put under trees, and remain there about half an

LETTER FIFTEEN

hour, undress and take some coffee, and so settle for the night much more comfortably. Palanquin travelling pleases me very much: I can sleep a good part of the night, and, being able to sit up or lie down at pleasure, with plenty of room, I find it far less fatiguing than being cramped up all day in a carriage.

In passing through the villages, the head men, Moonsiffs,* Cutwalls,† &c., always turn out to come and make salaam while we are changing bearers, and we sit up and do our congées in our dressing-gowns and nightcaps, quite agreeable. However, as we had seen them all in coming, and as it was a very long run, we did not want to be disturbed again in the middle of the night; so we sent a Peon on before to announce that the Judge certainly was to pass through, but that he would be fast asleep and could speak to nobody, and that he must be transferred from the shoulders of one set of bearers to the other without touching the ground, all of which was performed according to order. About three in the morning we were awakened by the silence and stillness: the bearers' song had stopped, and our palanquins were quietly set down on the ground, and no one near us. A— got out to see what was the matter, and he found that we were in a cocoa-nut tope, the bearers all employed in stealing toddy,** and our palanquins completely laden with paddy,†† which they had stolen from the fields in coming along! It would have been a pretty story, if we had not found it out in time, the Judge returning to his Zillah, with his palanquins laden with stolen paddy, and his bearers tipsy with stolen toddy!

We found all well at home, and a large packet of European letters waiting to greet us, which would in itself be enough to make all well.

---

* Native judges.
† Head men of a village.
** Juice of the cocoa-nut leaves. It is collected in earthen vessels, and left to ferment, when it becomes very intoxicating.
†† Rice in the ear.

JANUARY 1838

Notes
Mr. M.: Mr Montague Cholmeley.

N— School: Nellore, a town approximately ninety miles north of Madras.

Suttees: in the original letter Julia refers to 'the burning of widows.' This practice, the burning of widows on the funeral pyres of their husbands, was outlawed by Lord William Bentinck in 1829. Wendy Doniger, in a review in the *TLS* (14 September 2000) of three recent books on the subject provides a comprehensive discussion of *sati* in colonial discourse. According to the various points of view, *sati* can be any one or more of the following: a voluntary and heroic act, a religious act, a sacrifice, a murder, a barbaric violation of human rights. When reporting on the death of Ranjit Singh in Letter Twenty-five, Julia's outrage is reserved for the British Government and its failure to stop 'the horrors.' His four wives 'burnt themselves at their own desire, from pride of family or caste,' but the 'poor slave-girls could have had no such motives, and must have been burnt by the wretches around them.'

Juggernaut's sacrifices: once a year, in the town of Puri in Orissa, images of Jagannatha, a form of Krishna, his brother, Balavama, and sister, Subhadra, are dragged through the streets on massive temple chariots. It is said that devotees threw themselves beneath the wheels of the chariots so as to die in the god's sight. Thomas Bacon visited Puri in 1831 and wrote, 'Since the year 1821, not a single instance of self-immolation has taken place at Juggernaut, and for two or three years previous to that date only three examples had occurred, one of which was accidental, and the other two victims gladly embraced death as a happy escape from loathsome and intolerable disease. It is scarcely possible to account for the gross misrepresentations which are daily imported into England.'

the castes are not new: this is not in the original letter and was perhaps added for the sake of explanation. The origins of the caste system are obscure, but it was eventually formalised into four distinct classes. The system was outlawed in 1949, but remains a deeply ingrained social structure, particularly in rural areas. At the top of the system came the *Brahmins*, or priestly caste, followed by the *Kshatriya*, the warrior caste, the *Vaisya*, the merchant caste, and the *Sudra*, the farmers and craftsmen. Beneath all these were the Untouchables, now called *Dalits*, Julia's Pariahs, who performed the most menial jobs. As Julia writes, you were born into your caste, a fact exploited by Christian missionaries.

Mr. C—: Mr Cotterill.

your vicar: he is named as Langdon. He was one of Julia's possible suitors; Charlotte Barrett wrote to her mother in June 1836, 'Poor Langdon, if he

109

LETTER FIFTEEN

had betrayed it six months ago Thomas wd never have secured her, for she liked Langdon best' (Barrett Eg3702A 137-8).

The moonsiffs Julia describes as 'native judges' were considered the lowest grade of native civil judge.

Mr. Grove's class: Henry Grove (1684-1738) was a dissenting tutor from Somersetshire, and from 1706 a tutor at the Taunton Academy. For Grove, the function of morality was to meet the universal demand for happiness, and human happiness was to be found in relationship with God.

stealing toddy: Julia's note is mistaken. Toddy is the fermented sap of the coconut palm.

Letter the Sixteenth

We have had a good deal of trouble with the school lately, which is very vexatious, because it really was going on beautifully; forty-five boys in constant attendance, reading and translating the Bible, using our books in school without the slightest objection, and asking for tracts to take home. But a little while ago there came a Mr G., a Dissenting Missionary, to visit the Hamiltons: he was a conceited, show-off sort of person, and curiously ignorant. He dined with us one day, and also the Prices, who were staying with us, Mr Lloyd, Commander of the detachment, and our Scotch Doctor. The Hamiltons had headaches, and did not come, and I am sure I do not wonder, after their having had to attend to Mr G.'s clatter for two days. At our house he chose, *à propos* of nothing, to begin a discussion concerning the evil of the Bishops being in the House of Lords, and various other delinquencies and enormities of the Church, including the bigotry of supposing that ordination would make any one a minister, unless he was a godly man. Lloyd said nothing – he never does; the Scotch Doctor sided with Mr G.; Captain Price thought the Church of England must be right, though he could not say why; A— quoted all the old divines, and I slipped in texts; Mr G. quoted Mosheim (that is to say, he did not quote him, but he mentioned him) as an authority, not in matters of history, but on points of divinity ; and he declared that he did not know of any such text as "Not forsaking the assembling of yourselves together"; and when it was proved by chapter and verse, he said one must consider such a text as that well before one could arrive at the real meaning, for that it never could mean us to meet for public worship with an indifferent minister, and that it would be much better to stay

LETTER SIXTEEN

and read one's Bible at home. The Doctor said, "According to quhat ye're a saying then, ye must have got yer Church of England airdination from some o' the Pops." A—: "Very likely." Doctor S.: "Wall, and d'ye think it can be good for anything whan it's passed through all those rogs?" I suppose the end of the discussion might be, that Mr G. thought us very bigoted, and we thought him very superficial and ignorant. After this, Mr Hamilton look him to preach at the school, and ordered all the boys to attend. They did not tell A— what they were going to do, or he would not have allowed it; for although he is only too thankful to be able to help the Missionaries to preach on their own responsibility, when, where, and however they can, he thinks it both wrong and inexpedient for people in authority to accompany them, as it sets the natives on their guard directly, and persuades them that the Government are going to make them Christians by force, as the Moormans made them Mohammedans. In the present instance it raised a great disturbance. In addition to the preaching, Mr G. got hold of a man's Lingum, or badge of caste, and took it away; and though he was forced to return it, the whole town has been in a ferment at the insult, and our school is almost broken up in consequence. The boys brought back in a rage all the bags I had given them to put their tickets in, and said they never would come to school again. We have now only twenty boys instead of forty-five, and they are all petitioning to use their own Heathen books, instead of ours, and we have no more requests for admittance. A little while ago, when we came in from our morning's ride, we used almost every day to find a pretty boy waiting at the gate, salaaming, and presenting his petition to be sent to school. I hope we shall be able to bring it round again in time, but it is very vexatious.

We are reading Shore's 'Notes on Indian Affairs', – very clever, true, and amusing. He complains much of the English incivility to the natives; and I quite agree with him: it is a

JANUARY 1838

great shame. A— says he exaggerates, but I really do not think so. A—, being an old Indian, is grown used to things that strike us griffins. The civilians behave better than the military, though all are bad enough. The other day an old Bramin of high caste called on us while the Prices were in the house; Captain Price, hearing his voice, sauntered out of the next room with his hands in his waistcoat-pockets, and planted himself directly before the poor old creature, without taking any other notice of all his salaams and compliments than "Well, old fellow, where are you going?" in a loud, rude voice. The Bramin answered with the utmost apparent respect, but I saw such an angry scowl pass over his face. A little politeness pleases them very much, and they have a good right to it. The upper classes are exceedingly well bred, and many of them are the descendants of native princes, and ought not to be treated like dirt.

A new magazine is just advertised as coming out at Madras. It is to be conducted by some of the clergymen, in opposition to another periodical, conducted by some others of the clergymen. The first number is to contain strictures on a review which appeared last month in the other magazine. I grudge the waste of time and thought upon such useless work. The writers come out here, they themselves, and everybody else, believing they will work among the Heathen; and while the Idol services are going on all round them, they sit writing their reviews and anti-reviews to the sound of the Pagoda bell!

The other night I was sitting in my Tonjon sketching a pagoda, when I saw a long procession of Bramins go in, and suddenly the service began. I could hear it all, through the walls. The first part sounded exactly like a Roman Catholic mass. There was music, and the mumbling chant of the old priests who could not sing, and the shrill voices of the choir-boys, and at intervals a little bell tinkling; till it was all interrupted by violent screams from girls' voices – perhaps they were meant for singing, but they sounded very horrible: then came loud beating of drums and ringing of bells, and it was all finished.

February 3rd – We are just come in from the school, the first time I have been there since Mr G.'s unlucky visit. Some of the deserters have returned, but about fifteen are still obstinate. They all crowded round me, saying, "Good ivning, Sar!" I tried to teach them to say "Ma'am", and explained that "Sir" belonged to the "Doory"; but a Peon who understands a little English, and is extremely proud of his knowledge, would help, and teach them to say "Mammon": so they got it perfect, "Good ivning, Mammon!" They are very boasting and confidential, and I am very sympathetic. "Sar! I larn very good; I am second man." "I am very glad to hear it – very good man." "And *I* larn too much good too! I am tree man." "That is right; you are a very good man too." Then they salaam and grin, and are very happy. I show them pictures, which makes me popular. The head boys are learning to write English: and today they made a petition to be allowed "Europe ink," as they could not write English words with Gentoo ink.

I have been trying to procure some of the cobra capello's poison for Frank to analyse; and also the native antidotes, the principal of which is a small, smooth, very light black stone which they apply to the bite, and they say that it adheres till it has drawn out all the poison, and then falls off. To-day the snake-charmer brought three fresh caught cobras to give me their poison. He set them up, and made them dance as usual, but did not allow them to strike, as that exhausts the venom. When he had played with them as long as he liked, he shut up two of them in their baskets, and proceeded to catch the third by putting one hand on its tail, and slipping the other very quickly up to the nape of its neck, when he held it so tight as to force it to open its jaws, and then squeezed the poison into a teaspoon. It is yellow at first, and turns red in about ten days. Each snake yielded only three drops; so think how powerful it must be! The cobra did not struggle or writhe at all while the man held it, but afterwards it seemed quite changed and subdued: it lost its spiteful look, and could not be made to stand up and strike, even when the man did his utmost to provoke it, but tried to slink quietly away, looking as if it knew it had lost its power, and was ashamed of not being able to do any mischief. I have put the poison into a little bottle, and keep it carefully covered up from the light. I shall send it home by the first opportunity. It will dry up, of course; but Dr Stewart says it will not lose its virtue, or rather its vice, and that Frank must be careful what tricks he plays with it. The natives make pills of it, and take them for fever: I believe it is a strong narcotic. I know the bite of a cobra throws people into a stupor. General W. told me that one of his servants was bitten, and wanted to lie down and go to sleep, but the General made him run before his horse for several miles till he was quite exhausted. No harm came of the bite; but, as the snake was not caught, it was impossible to be certain whether it actually was a cobra. The natives think their own remedies are much assisted by conjuring. Once, when we were travelling, my bearers stopped, and one of them began to cry and howl and writhe about, saying he was stung by a scorpion in the road, and could not go on. We gave him eau de luce to rub the place with, but it did no good. One of the Peons then said he could conjure him: so he sat down before him, and began muttering, and sawing the air with his hand, making antics like animal magnetism; and in a few minutes the wounded man said he was quite well, put his shoulder under the palanquin-pole, and set off with his song again. In your last letter you ask me if the snake-charmers have any herb with them. I do not think they have anything but dexterity and presence of mind. They pretend to be conjurers, and play a number of antics, all quite absurd, but which impose upon the people. Their music seems to irritate the snakes and incite them to strike: but the snake-charmers know their distance exactly, and jump

LETTER SIXTEEN

on one side. They take the snakes with perfect safety, as they know exactly where to seize them in the neck. The snakes grow very tame after a time, and the men extract the poison as fast as it collects. They begin their trade as children, so they grow up expert and fearless. The man who brought me the poison told me all his proceedings "for a consideration." He said his father was a snake-charmer before him, and used to take him out when he was quite a child, and teach him the manner of laying hold of the creatures, making him first practise upon harmless snakes; that there was no secret in it beyond dexterity: but that the people were so afraid of such "bad animals," that they "always tell conjure" when anybody was able to touch them.

Notes

Dissenting Missionary: a Mr Gordon. He is not to be found in the *Madras Almanac* which included only the names of Church of England missionaries under the entry 'Religious Establishment.'

Mosheim: Johann Lorenz Von Mosheim (1694-1755), ecclesiastical historian and divine, professor of Theology at Göttingen.

a man's Lingum or badge of caste: the literal meaning of the sanskrit word 'lingam' is 'mark.' The Lingam is a phallus worshipped as a symbol of the god Shiva. Marks made with a seal and paste probably designated sectarian allegiance rather than caste, as they can do today. It is difficult to know to what Julia is referring to in a removeable 'badge.' But it is clear Mr Gordon was carrying out a highly offensive act.

Shore's 'Notes on Indian Affairs': F.J. Shore, the son of the Indian administrator Sir John Shore, had twenty years' experience in India before publishing his *Notes*. His 63 articles were published in book form in 1837 and address such subjects as, 'On the Government of British India,' 'On the Intercourse between the English and the Natives,' 'On the Improvement of the Country,' 'On the Formation of a Code of Laws,' 'Propriety of Interfering with some of the Native Customs,' 'On the State of Feeling among the Natives towards the British Government' and 'Behaviour of the English towards the Natives.' Shore's articles are highly critical of British attitudes and behaviour and aspects of British rule in India.

'new magazine': the new magazine was *Christian Knowledge*, begun in opposition to Cotterill's existing *Christian Repository*.

FEBRUARY 1838

A month later Julia mentions to her mother having received a letter from Dick with plans to start a magazine. She suggests this should be printed in India where there are no copyright laws. She sends a sample of a magazine by Rushton of Calcutta which she doesn't think good, 'very meagre politics and miserable rubbishing sentimental stories from the magazines by way of literature' (24 April 1838).

By August she suggests working with the publisher and bookseller Pharoah. Pharoah is listed in the *Madras Almanac* of 1839 as the publisher of the bi-monthly *Madras Observer*, the monthly *Illustrations of Indian Botany*, the quarterly *Army List*, *Journal of Literature and Science* and *Missionary Register*, and the annual *Madras New Almanac*, *Pocket Calendar* and *Sheet Calendar*.

eau de luce: a mixture of alcohol, ammonia and oil of amber, used as an antidote to snake-bite in India, and in England as smelling salts.

Letter the Seventeenth

Today the Narsapoor head of police sent me a present of a toy of his own invention. It was a representation of a justice-room. There sat the English Judge in his jacket, writing at a desk; round him all the native Gomashtas, squatted on the floor, writing at their desks; at the end of the room a wretched prisoner in the stocks; and, in front of the Judge, another prisoner being tried, with a great Peon by his side, holding a drawn sword in his hand to take care of him. The Englishmen and Court servants were made enormously fat, and when I asked the reason I was told it was to show how rich they were! It was a very droll performance; but I was obliged, much against my will, to refuse it. A— said it was too good to accept, for fear of that tiresome plague John Company's finding fault. However, I confess it is a good rule. If I had accepted that, some one else would soon have brought something of more value, and in a little while they would arrive at shawls and pearls, and expect injustice in Court in consequence. When A— is out, visitors often come to me privately, begging that I will persuade him to give them offices, or to excuse them fines and punishments, &c. Sometimes they go and make their petition to the baby if she is in another room, but she only sucks her thumb at them. When we are out in our tonjons without the "Master", the wives of the petitioners assail me, and their children the baby, screaming and throwing themselves on the ground before us. Baby likes the uproar extremely, and crows and dances in great glee. Then the petitioner comes to A— next day, and gravely tells him that "Missy" has promised him the post in question. This Court has been for some years past very badly managed – idle men sent as Judges, nothing inquired into, cases neglected, and so on; and the consequence is, that some of the rich natives have quite got the upper hand of honesty. One very rich Zemindar's widow owed, and still owes, five thousand rupees to a man in this village. Instead of paying her debt, she took refuge with her son, the present Zemindar, and shut herself up in his house. One Judge after another has sent Peons with summonses to the old lady to make her pay the poor man his just due; but she cares for none of them, and the Zemindar's servants always beat the Peons, and send them away. One Judge summoned the Zemindar to account for the assault on the Peons, but he said it was no fault of his — it was the servants' pleasure: then the servants were summoned, but they ran away and hid themselves, and were not to be found all over the district. The same thing has just now happened again; but A— will not take the excuse, and has summoned the Zemindar to account for his servants' misdemeanors, as they are in the habit of taking their pleasure in that way. He has fined him two hundred rupees, and sent word that, unless his mother's debt is paid, he shall send a battalion to seize her jewels. It remains to be proved which will gain the day: I am curious to see how it ends. Another Zemindar, choosing to protect a man who had a notification sent to him, fought the peons who delivered it, and sent it and them back again: so A— then sent the notification to the Zemindar himself, with a polite request, or rather command, that he would himself see it served without delay. The Zemindar was frightened at this, and obeyed directly, as humbly as possible. All the Court histories and adventures amuse me very much.

The business is all taken down in writing, and translated into English. The trials, examination of the witnesses, sentences of the Judge, &c., all go under the general name of "Decrees", and every day a certain number of copies of these Decrees are brought in for the Judge to examine and verify. I often get hold of them to read, and very curious they are; but the lying and false witnessing are quite horrible. Sometimes the whole case is

LETTER SEVENTEEN

one great lie supported by innumerable forgeries. The other day a man laid claim to the house and land of another: the claim was well established; there were all the proper documents to show that the estate had been in his possession, witnesses in plenty to swear to the same, and a plausible story as to the manner in which the defendant had cheated him out of it; and, in short, everything to prove him a most ill-used man. But the defendant had just as good a story, as carefully arranged papers, and as many respectable witnesses on his side: but here and there different little things were allowed to transpire which weakened his cause, and gave the plaintiff rather the best of the story. A— made me guess how the matter had been decided; and, of course, I supposed that the land had been restored to the poor injured innocence who claimed it. No such thing: A— says, in the midst of such constant cheating, he is obliged often to judge by the manner and countenance of a witness rather than by his evidence, and in this case it struck him that there was a cunning under look that did not belong to a true man; he therefore set on foot a strict inquiry into the affair, and discovered that the whole was a concerted scheme between the two men; that neither the one nor the other had the property in his possession, nor the slightest claim upon it; and that it belonged altogether to another person, who knew nothing whatever about this lawsuit. The object of the two false claimants was to get a Decree passed in favour of one of them, it did not much signify which: the Court Peons must have seen it executed, and the real owner would have been turned out of his property, while the two cheats divided the spoil.

There seem to be very few cases that are not supported by some forgery or false evidence in the course of the trial. Even when the truth is on their side, and would be quite sufficient, they prefer trying to establish their cause by falsehood, though it discredits rather than helps them.

February 16th – For the last few days we have been occupied with company again. A regiment passed through, and we had to dine all the officers, including a lady; now they are gone. I perceive the officers' ladies are curiously different from the civilians. The civil ladies are generally very quiet, rather languid, speaking in almost a whisper, simply dressed, almost always ladylike and *comme il faut*, not pretty, but pleasant and nice-looking, rather dull, and give one very hard work in pumping for conversation. They talk of "the Governor","the Presidency", the "Overland", and "girls' schools at home", and have daughters of about thirteen in England for education. The military ladies, on the contrary, are almost always quite young, pretty, noisy, affected, showily dressed, with a great many ornaments, and chatter incessantly from the moment they enter the house. While they are alone with me after dinner, they talk about suckling their babies, the disadvantages of scandal, "the Officers", and "the Regiment"; and when the gentlemen come into the drawing-room, they invariably flirt with them most furiously.

The military and civilians do not generally get on very well together. There is a great deal of very foolish envy and jealausy between them, and they are often downright ill-bred to each other, though in general the civilians behave much the best of the two. One day an officer who was dining here said to me, "Now I know very well, Mrs —, you despise us all from the bottom of your heart; you think no one worth speaking to in reality but the Civil Service. Whatever people may really be, you just class them all as civil and military – civil and military; and you know no other distinction. Is it not so?" I could not resist saying, "No; I sometimes class them as civil and uncivil." He has made no more rude speeches to me since.

February 17th – Yesterday the old Braminee post-office writer came to pay a visit and chat. He had been to a great Heathen feast at some distance – thirty thousand people present. He told us that the Narsapoor Missionaries and Mr G. were there, preaching and giving away books, and that they said, "What use your feast? *arl* (all) too much nonsense!

LETTER SEVENTEEN

What for make noise, – tumtums, – washing? – arl that, what for do? pray to God, that *prarper* (proper)!" We asked if the people understood and listened, and if any of them believed the "padre's" words. He said, "Understand, very well; – listen, plenty; – believe, no, sar!" Then he went on to tell us that they could not believe now, no more could he, but that their children's children would all believe; that we were now in the ninth Avatar, which would last sixty years longer; that then there would be "plenty too much great trouble", and everything "more worser" than it had ever been before; that all religion would be destroyed, and this state of confusion would last for some time, but that, within two hundred years from the present time, the tenth Avatar would take place, and Vishnoo would appear to put all in order; that he would not restore the Hindoo religion, but that caste would be done away with for ever, and all people be alike upon the earth, "just same Europe people tell." Then he went on with their usual story that all religions were alike in their beginning and would be alike in their end, and that all enlightened people believed the same thing, &c., &c. – just the nonsense they always talk; but I thought his tradition very curious.

I have taken a Moonshee to translate for me, and to teach me Gentoo. He is a tolerable translator, but a great booby. He was showing me some different forms of the same letter: I asked on what occasions each was to be employed. He said, "This one, carmon (common) letter, I teach boy; – arther (other) one, sublime letter, I teach hanner (honour) ma'am." Another time I was playing with the baby, and saying, "Talk, baby, talk!" when Moonshee rose from his chair and came to me very slowly and formally, holding his petticoats over his arm. After a solemn salaam, he told me, "I have one subject to inform your honour." – "Well?" – "I shall inform your honour that this baby cannot talk: it is not capable for her to talk until she shall have arrived at two years." – Did you ever know such an owl? They have no notion of anything in the shape of a joke, unless it is against the Collectors and the Board of Revenue. That touches their hearts and tickles their fancies directly.

So many people apply to us for books, that we are going to set up a lending library, to be kept in the school-room, for natives, half-castes, and travelling soldiers who may halt here. We cannot muster many volumes yet, and some of those are contrived by sewing tracts together. Tailor and I have been very busy making elegant covers out of bits of coloured paper. We greatly want some baby lectures on astronomy for our school. I am trying at them, but it is a tough job, because, first of all, I am a dunce myself, and next I have very few astronomical books, and those – such as Mrs Somerville, Herschel, &c – not suitable. All the elementary books are translated from English lesson-books, and are altogether out of the comprehension of the natives – not so much *above* them as *different* from them – expressed in terms which they cannot understand, from being completely unlike their own manner of thinking and explaining.

February 22nd – This is now the Indian spring. The garden is in full flower, and the scent of the orange-blossoms and tube roses quite fills the room as I sit with the windows open; but it is beginning to grow very hot: the thermometer is at 9C° in the middle of the day, but I do not find it so oppressive as at Madras; the air is much fresher and clearer. Dr Stewart advises me not to remain here after the middle of the month, so on the 16th we are all to go to Samuldavee. A— will settle baby and me there, and then he must return by himself, I am sorry to say, to his hot Court. We shall probably be obliged to remain on the coast about four months, but he will be able to shut up the Court and come to us for one month, and occasionally at other times from Saturday till Monday.

LETTER SEVENTEEN

Notes

Avatar: the incarnation of a god on earth.

Vishnoo: or Vishnu, the preserver of the world and one of the Hindu Triad, the others being Brahma, the supreme god of the trinity, and Shiva, the creator and destroyer.

Mrs. Somerville: Mary Somerville (1780-1872), mathematician. *The Mechanism of the Heavens* was published in 1831, and *On the Connexion of the Physical Sciences* in 1834. Julia probably refers to the former.

Herschel: Sir William Herschel (1738-1822), his son Sir John Herschel (1792-1871), and William's sister Caroline Herschel (1750-1848) were all astronomers. It is most likely that Julia is referring to Sir John Herschel's *A Treatise on Astronomy*, first published in 1833 and a general exposition of the science. Incidentally, Sir William and Caroline were both known to Fanny Burney D'Arblay and they appear in her *Journals*.

the garden is in full flower: Julia also lets her mother know what is growing in the vegetable garden: 'beans, carrots, lettuce, turnips and tomatoes ... all of our own planting.'

The new doctor's wife arrived in February, Mrs Wight. 'She is a poor dowdy as ever I saw and didn't know how to spell – I hope she will not call often – she looks rather a neighbourly sort of person I am afraid' (21 February 1838).

While happy to be out of Madras, Julia continues to absorb news from her sister-in-law Diana and passes this on to her mother. Intrigue surrounds the post of Accountant General, Thomas's hoped for position. 'False charges' have been laid against Turnbull, and a clique near to Elphinstone (a 'mere cypher' according to Julia) 'who are anything but upright and honourable' want to get the Accountant Generalship in their power. One of these dishonest managers is a Mr Sullivan, 'the same who was James's enemy in an equally unjust cause, and I believe even now uses all his influence against him' (13 February). Colonel Dyce's wife has died, 'the 4th of our fellow passengers (sic) who has been carried off.' By October Colonel Dyce is still inconsolable, 'and keeps the body of his poor wife always by him in a leaden coffin.' Miss Craven was to stay on having survived a liver complaint, 'to superintend a Boarding school for Half-Castes and rich Native girls, which Miss Tucker is going to set up' (22 February 1838).

Letter the Eighteenth

March 8th

I am very busy now, translating a story with my little squinny Moonshee. Moonshee chuckles over it, and enters into much conversation about it.

M. – Your honour has in this your handiwork taken much trouble to bring together *arl* things *prarper!*

I. – Because everybody ought to know those things, Moonshee.

M. – Those are from your honour's Shasters.[*] My people also have Shasters and Vedas; are not those the true words of God?

I. – They are *not* true; they tell to worship idols. Now you know very well, Moonshee, that those idols are only wood and stone; you do not believe them to be really gods.

M. – I know very well – piece of stone – nothing at arl. What enlightened person thinks them to be God? – No Bramin, no Moonshee will think – but idols are of necessity for arl carmon people.

I. – Now you see we can know those Vedas to be lie, because, if they were words of truth, they would not tell you to make lie to anybody, common people or Bramins.

M. – Ah, ha! But if not the words of God, who did make write the Vedas? No man could write, therefore God write.

I. – Some Bramins, a great many years ago, wrote.

M. – No any Bramins; Vedas are written in the Devinagree – the most holy Sanscrit – the language spoken by the planets. What man could write?

I. – *Now* could not write; but formerly the Devinagree was common language; Bramins could write very well.

M. – Will your honour tell me, is not Devinagree the language of the planets?

Upon this I gave him a touch of astronomy, and told him what astronomers could see with their telescopes, so as to

---
[*] Holy books.

know for certain that the astronomical legends in the Vedas are not true. Then he went off into a metaphysical disquisition on the nature of God, which I would not answer further than that man could know nothing of God but what he is pleased to reveal. Then he wanted to know why God had not taught all men to speak the same language, so that all might profit by each other's knowledge. I told him the history of the Tower of Babel, which he liked very much, except that he was disappointed at my not knowing how many cubits high they had raised it. He had been educated at a Dissenting Mission school, but left it almost as ignorant as he entered it. He thought that the Bible had been written in English, and that that was an argument against it, English being a modern language. He was charmed at the sight of some Hebrew and Greek, which he had never heard of. He supposed that our Saviour had come to England about a hundred years ago, just when the English first came to India; and, when set right upon that, he argued that, if God had meant the Hindoos to receive the Bible, he would have sent some teachers to India when Jesus Christ came into the world. So then I told him about the first preachers, the Black Jews, the Syrian Christians, &c. He said, "Will your honour not be angry if I ask one question, and will honour ma'am tell me that question?" "If I know I will tell, and I will not be angry." "Certainly no any anger upon me?" "Certainly not." "Then I would ask your honour, suppose any Europe lady or gentleman make much wickedness – never repent – never ask pardon of God – never think of Jesus Christ, but die in committing sin; what will become of them?" "They will go to hell." "What! Europe lady or gentleman? " "Certainly." Then he went on to tell me all about the transmigration of souls, which he said was a great advantage in his religion, for that going to hell was "very offensive". Then he told me a long story. "If your honour will listen to me, I shall make you sensible how it consists. One man had ten sons, and to his sons he gave rules. But those sons arl *ispeak* different languages; therefore he allow them take the rules every one in his own language, which may suit him best; is it not so?"

I. – Now, Moonshee, I will tell *you* how it consists. One man had ten sons, and to all he gave rules – *same* rules, understand. Those sons speak different languages, therefore he allowed them to translate the rules each into his own language, but always *same rules*. One son tell, "My father give too many rules; I don't want": so that son throw away half his father's rules. Another son tell, "Don't like some of these rules; myself I shall make": so that son change half his father's rules. Another son tell, "I will keep my father's rules; neither add nor take away." Which son best, Moonshee? He answered with his usual "Ah, ah!" and looked very cunning. I tried to persuade him to read the Bible, but he said it was too much trouble. I do not think these natives have the slightest notion of there being any beauty or advantage in *truth*. They think one way is good for them, and one way good for us. They are very fond of metaphysical subtleties, which at first makes one fancy them very acute, but one soon sees that they have no power of perceiving the real state of an argument. They are always caught and pleased with a cavil, when a reason has no effect upon them; but what they like best of all is any illustration or parable. That seems to be their own manner of reasoning. I do not suppose they ever have much real conversation with each other – mere chatter and gossip. They seem to have no pleasure in associating with each other on terms of equality. Everybody has a *tail*, consisting of poor followers, flappers, and flatterers. The head feeds the tail, and the tail flatters the head; and plenty of "soft sawder" seems to be in use. When head walks abroad, tail walks after him at a respectful distance. If head stands still to smoke his cheroot, tail, who has no cheroot, stands still and looks admiringly at him. If head condescends to make an observation, tail crosses his hands, bows, assents, and remarks what a wonderfully wise man head is!

LETTER EIGHTEEN

The other day we happened to tell the post-office writer that the officers were coming to dine with us, and that we did not want him to go and peer out all the gossip concerning them, which he had offered to do, like an obliging jackal. "Sar," said he, "very great charity, indeed, sar!" "Charity!" exclaimed I, rather astonished. "Ma'am ! too much great charity, indeed, ma'am! – but Master very charitable gentleman; always give bread to gentlemen passing through. Last Judge, when anybody pass by, Judge too much sick – gentlemen go 'way, Judge too much well again!"

A Government circular is just come to all the Zillah Judges, to inform them that "the Right Honourable the Governor in Council" has been considering the best means of facilitating the re-apprehension of prisoners who have escaped from confinement; and it has occurred to him that it would answer the purpose to make them always wear a dress of some particular colour or material, by which they might be easily identified. – The innocent bird! He must have kept his eyes in his pocket ever since he landed, not to know by this time that the natives strip off their clothes as soon as they are alone, or at work, or running; and, most certainly, runaway prisoners would not remain in full dress merely for the purpose of being identified.

To-day's *Gazette* brings word that Government have just issued their orders that "*no salutes to idols be discontinued*, but that all respect be paid to the native religions as heretofore." Is not this disgraceful? A fortnight ago, at a Mohammedan festival at Trichinopoly, the European troops – Artillery-men – were kept exposed to the sun for nine hours, firing salutes, and "showing respect" to Mohammed.

The Government lately presented a shawl to a Hindoo idol, and the Government officer, Mr D., with whom we are acquainted, was ordered to superintend the delivery of it. He does not pretend to be a religious man – a mere commonplace, hunting, card-playing dandy: but even *he* was disgusted at having such an office to perform; so he went with the shawl in his tonjon, and told the Bramins they might come and take it, for that he would not touch it with his own fingers, to present it to a Swamy. At the same place the Swamy was making a progress in its car, and the officiating Bramin came and told Mr D. that it had stopped at a certain point for want of sufficient offerings; so Mr D. went to see about it, and found that they had stuck a wedge under the wheel, which prevented its going on. He had the wedge knocked out, and gave orders that Swamy must arrive at his destination without delay, before all the poor offerers were ruined, or the cholera broke out, as generally happens at these horrid feasts, from the concourse of people, dirt, &c. In consequence of all this, Mr D. was much blamed and reprehended at Madras, for having caused the feast to be hurried over more quickly than the Bramins liked. The cars are drawn by men and very often these men are unwilling to leave their work for the service, and the Bramins cannot catch as many as they want; so the Government order the Collector to take unwilling men by force, and *make* them drag the car.

I believe that, if idolatry were merely tolerated and protected, the idol services would fall almost to nothing, from the indifference of the mass of the people; but our Christian Government not only support and encourage it, but force it down the people's throats. They have made a law that a Heathen Sepoy may not be flogged, but a Christian Sepoy may. If a Sepoy turns Christian, he is subject to a punishment which they are pleased to say would degrade a Heathen or a Mohammedan.

March 20th — We are going to Samuldavee on Friday, and we had a grand giving away of prizes at the school, by way of taking leave. Every boy with a certain number of tickets had a prize, and they took their choice of the articles, according to their proficiency. First boy took first choice, and so on. The favourite goods were English books, particularly Grammars.

LETTER EIGHTEEN

Next, the tracts with woodcuts, which you sent me. I had had them bound, so that they looked very respectable, and those wretched woodcuts were wonderfully admired. I gave one tract to the butler's "volunteer", a Gomashta, who writes his accounts for him, in hopes "Master" will admire his talents and give him the next vacant post. The Peons admired the tract so much, that they intercepted it by the way, and they sit in a circle by the hour together, pawing and stroking the frontispiece, and Volunteer explaining the meaning to them.

There have been many more applications for admission to the school again, and one learned old Moonshee has sent two sons, which is a great compliment. The boys, in fact, only wish to learn English in hopes of making money by it, obtaining places in Court, &c.; but they have no love of knowledge for its own sake. A— gave them a 'History of the World' in Gentoo, and desired them to read it, and answer questions from it; but they brought it back, saying they did not want to know anything that was in it, they only wanted to learn "vords". So then they were reproached with the attainments of parrots, minas, and such-like, till they looked very sheepish, and promised they would "get plenty sense".

We have a young officer staying with us now, who is to keep A— company while I am on the coast. He is a nice, innocent, good-natured boy, and as tame as can be. He has brought a cat and two kittens with him all the way from Bangalore, upwards of four hundred miles, and in the evenings he brings them into the drawing-room to pay me a visit and drink some milk, and he sits quite contentedly with them crawling up his great knees, and sticking their claws into him, just like Frank and our old cat at home. He has had six jews'-harps sent him by a brother in England, and he performs Scotch jigs upon them by way of "a little music"; and in the morning, when I go to lie down before dinner, he sits with Moonshee, keeping him to his work, and explaining matters to him. I hope he will be a pleasant companion for the ' Master", while I am obliged to be away.

A— has invited one or two other very young officers, but I do not know yet whether they will come or not. Those "boys" are very remiss about answering invitations; sometimes I do not know whether one of them means to accept an invitation or not, till he makes his appearance at the time appointed, bowing and smiling, with a ring and a gold chain, quite unconscious that he has not been the very pink of politeness.

Notes
Shasters, as Julia notes, meant any of the sacred writings of the Hindus and comes from the Hindu term for a sacred code or rule. *Veda* referred to ancient sacred books. *Devinagree*, or Devanagari, is a formal alphabet of the Sanskrit and Hindu languages. And *Sanskrit* was the ancient, and holy, language of India.

the Governor: 'they make a complete catspaw of him' writes Julia. The cabal around Elphinstone allows him to govern only when they believe the issue is one that does not matter, as in this case of prisoners' clothing.

Government Circular: the means by which centrally made decisions were communicated. These were published in the *Gazette*.

Mr D: William Dowdeswell. See note to Letter Ten.

young officer: Milne

Letter the Nineteenth

Samuldavee, March 26th

Here we are, safely arrived and established for the summer. The baby and I were beginning to be so ill with the heat at Rajahmundry, that A— brought us away in a hurry, and settled us here with Peons and servants, and is gone back himself this evening. He means to come every Saturday and stay till Monday, unless any particular business should prevent him. This is a most charming place – the thermometer eight degrees lower than at Rajahmundry, and at present a fine sea breeze from eleven in the morning till eleven at night, and a thick cocoa-nut tope between our house and the land-wind, so that I hope we never shall feel it in all its fury. I do not suppose there is a healthier or pleasanter summer place in all this part of India. Its only fault is its extreme loneliness. This is a solitary house on the shore of an estuary; not even a native village or hut near; forty miles from the nearest European station – Masulipatam; and no English people at all within reach, except the two Missionaries at Narsapoor, ten miles off. I have no one ever to speak to, but my own Hindoo servants. I mean to amuse myself with learning Gentoo, and have brought a Moonshee with me. Gentoo is the language of this part of the country, and one of the prettiest of all the dialects, but there is nothing very fine or beautiful in any of them. The idioms are quite disagreeable; they have neither simplicity nor finesse. I believe the old Sanscrit is a very fine language, but it is excessively difficult, and would be of no use to me. The Moonshee I have brought with me is not the little talkative magpie who told me about the language of the planets, but a very slow, sober, solemn gentleman, with a great turn for reading and sententious observations. Whenever I keep him waiting, he reads my books. The other day he got hold of a Church Prayer Book, which he began to read straight through – Dedication, Calendar, and all. He told me that he perceived it was a very scarce and valuable work, but that he would take great care of it, if my honour would grant him permission to read it at his own house, which of course my honour was very willing to do. He admires it greatly, and says, "Ah! good words! very fine words!" – but he says he thinks a man must have "a very purified mind to be capable of using those prayers." He says he much wishes to read our Shasters, so I am going to give him a Gentoo Bible as soon as I can get one from Madras.

April 2nd – Today I have had a specimen of the kind of company I am likely to see at Samuldavee. Three wild monkeys came to take a walk round the house and peep in at the windows; they were the first I had seen, and very fine creatures – what the natives call "*first-caste* monkeys", not little wizen imps like live mummies, such as we see in England, but real handsome wild beasts. They were of a kind of greenish-grey colour, with black faces and long tails, and their coats as sleek as a race horse's. They were as large as calves, and as slim as greyhounds. They bounded about most beautifully, and at last darted with one spring to the top of a rock ten feet high, and sat there like gentlemen taking the breeze and talking politics.

In the jungle behind our cocoa-nut tope there are clumps of prickly-pear, sixteen or eighteen feet high, and tribes of jackals sitting playing with their young ones on the turf – very pretty graceful creatures, like large foxes. I have found many shells on the beach, but I am afraid they are not good for much. They were, however, all alive, taking their evening walk, when I met them, taking mine. I set some boys to dig in the sand, but they brought me nothing but broken mussels and cockles.

April 23rd – We are very comfortable here, and the Master pays us his visit once a-week. Moonshee comes every day, and I potter a little at my Gentoo; but I have not learnt much. I do not work very hard, and no Moonshee has any idea of teaching, but I just pick his brains a little by way of amusement. He is a Bramin, and, like all of them, very fond of questioning and discoursing. He has now read my Prayer Book straight through from beginning to end, and with great admiration; but he says the finest words in the book are "Maker of all things visible and invisible;" those, he says, are "very great words indeed." Now he is reading the Bible. He told me that a learned Bramin came to pay him a visit and to look over his new Bible. The Bramin said that all the words against graven images were " good and very true words", and that it was certainly a "senseless custom" for a man to bow down to a stone; but that still it was necessary to keep images for the Sudras (low-caste people), for fear they should not believe in any God at all. That is their constant argument. They never defend their idols, nor own that they worship them, any more than Roman Catholics will allow that *they* worship the saints. Moonshee says there is one particular tribe of Bramins who keep a sabbath, and it is on the same day as our Sunday; so it seems like a Christian tradition, as the Jews' sabbath was on a Saturday. He thinks it is kept in honour of Kistna, but he says it is only a custom, and not commanded in the Shasters.

April 24th – In one of my letters I told you about a bad Zemindar who would not pay his debts, and A— threatened to send a *battalion* against him. Upon this the Zemindar sent a very polite message with a tray-full of oranges, and a request that his honour the Judge would keep much favour upon him, and look upon him as his own son! But his Honour was extremely indignant, and returned the tray of oranges, with an answer, that he would hold no intercourse with him till the debt was paid. The returning a present which may be accepted is the greatest possible affront, and it hurt the Zemindar's feelings so much, that he immediately sent another message to say that, rather than in any way displease Master's honour, and have his oranges refused, he would pay his debt. Master's honour thought he had gained the day, but the cunning old fellow despatched a party of his ragamuffins to make an attack on the Government treasury in the next district, and seize money enough to pay his debts here. However, the thieves were detected and defeated, so there the matter rests for the present, and we do not yet know which will win.

In my tonjon yesterday I passed a large old tree, inhabited by a family of monkeys – father, mother, and children of all ages. Don, A—'s dog, who was with me, was in a perfect fury to get hold of them, sitting upon his hind legs, and whining with agony. The monkeys were in a rage too, but they were very clever. The old father hunted his wife and children up the tree, on to one of the high branches; and when he had seen them safe where they could only peep out and grin, he came down again himself, and stood at the edge of a dancing bough, chattering, grinning, and evidently trying to provoke Don – taking excellent care, however, to keep out of harm's way himself – and sneering, till poor Don was so wild with fury, that I was obliged to have him tied up and led away.

Notes

Samuldavee: Julia explains that this was not always such a lonely place: 'Five and twenty years ago, many people came here to be cool, and at the same time in reach of the Factory at Narsapoor. Since the Factory has been done away with Samuldavee "got forgot," but we heard of it through the old Post Office Bramin' (26 March 1838). A 'Factory' referred to the place where 'factors' – or representatives of a merchant company – lived and traded.

Don: James Thomas's dog died in Hurst, near Brighton, in 1843.

Julia speaks well of Dr Wight, the new doctor, although she does not maintain this view of him. He takes her off the medicine prescribed by Dr Lane – 'a very strong one and would certainly do me harm if I took it too long.' Instead he has her take 'Rhubarb and Quinine in a glass of wine and water, which has strengthened me and done me good' (26 April 1838).

Julia frequently describes herself as taking calomel and this may be Dr Lane's 'strong one', although letters show that Dr Wight did later prescribe calomel for her. Calomel, or subchloride of mercury, was a powerful purgative. Julia suffered frequently from headaches and a pain in her side that 'I have had for so long' which all the doctors she consulted described as 'an Affection of the Splene.'

Letter the Twentieth

June 22nd

I hear that the river is come down at Rajahmundry, and I wish that, like Johnny Gilpin, I had "been there to see," for the manner in which these Indian rivers come down is very grand. When I came away it was one bed of sand, except a narrow stream just in the middle.

A— had made the prisoners dig some channels for the convenience of the neighbourhood, but they had all gradually dried up, and the poor people had to go nearly a mile over the bed of the river to draw water from the middle stream, and the heat and glare from the sand were almost intolerable. But one morning last week he was looking out of the window, and he saw one of his little channels suddenly filled, and the water presently spread as if it was being poured into the channel. In the course of six hours the river was quite full from bank to bank, eighteen feet deep and two miles broad, and rushing along like the Rhone. There will now be no more of the very hot weather. Here, at Samuldavee there has been no really intolerable heat; but at Rajahmundry A— had the thermometer at 100° in our drawing-room, notwithstanding watered tatties and every precaution. With us it has not been above 92°, and that only for a few days; generally 86° and a sea-breeze. I find the wind makes much more difference in one's feelings than the heat itself: 90°, with a sea-breeze, is far less oppressive than a much lower temperature with a land-wind.

Mr and Mrs Beer (one of the Narsapoor Missionaries and his wife) spent a day with me last week. He said they had been "very dull of late", that the people seemed to have satisfied their curiosity, and now never came near them; and that they had not seen a single instance of a wish really to know or inquire into the truth – only mere curiosity. That is the great difficulty with these poor natives; they have not the slightest idea of the value and advantage of truth. No one in England knows the difficulty of making any impression upon them. The best means seems to be education, because false notions of science form one great part of their religion. Every belief of theirs is interwoven with some matter of religion; and if once their scientific absurdities are overthrown, a large portion of their religion goes with them, and there seems more likelihood of shaking their faith in the remainder.

Our school goes on nicely and keeps full. The children learn what we bid them, and read the Bible, and give an account of what they read, just as they might in England – but it makes no impression: they look upon it as a mere English lesson. They know that the Bible is our Shaster, and suppose it to be as good for *us,* as their own Shasters are for *them.* Moonshee reads and studies the Bible, and often brings it to have passages explained. He says he believes all the "good words" against idolatry, but that the worship of any of the superior invisible beings is not idolatry, only the worship of graven images and demons. He was reading the story of Cain, and he supposed that the reprimand to Cain, "If thou doest well, shall it not be accepted," &c., was on account of his following "such a mean trade" as tilling the ground.

I have just been arranging some questions and answers for the school, and setting Moonshee to translate them. They were, of course, the most thorough *a, b, c* affairs possible; but Moonshee said they were "deep words," and his misunderstood translations were considerably quaint. For instance:"Water is a *fluid,*" he translated so as to mean "Water is *a juice.*" "Is it a *simple substance*?" – "Is it a *soft concern*?" "The sun is much larger than the earth;" – "Sun is a far greater man than earth:" &c., &c.

LETTER TWENTY

July 9th – We have had some very bad weather for the last week; furious land-wind, very fatiguing and weakening. We were scarcely ever able to leave the house either morning or evening, as the wind lasted all the twenty-four hours. Everything was so dried up, that, when I attempted to walk a few yards towards the beach, the grass crunched under my feet like snow. I have taken a good many beautiful butterflies, and Moonshee often brings me insects. He will not kill them, being a man of too high caste to take away the life even of a flea; of which the fleas, *con rispetto,* take great advantage, and hop about on his shawls and embroidery in a way that is apt to make me very uneasy. I told him, for fear he should hurt his caste or his conscience, that, if he collected insects for me, I should kill them and send them to Europe, and therefore he had better not bring them if he wished them to be preserved alive; but after a good deal of hesitation he came to the conclusion that it would be no sin in him to connive at taking away life, provided he himself did not commit murder.

I have a good many native visitors here. They like coming to me when A— is out of the way, in hopes that, when they can discourse to me alone, they will make me believe they are very clever, and that my private influence may persuade "Master" to think the same, and then perhaps he will turn out some one else to give them places. They sit and boast about themselves till they are enough to make anybody sick; and after having given me a catalogue of all their talents and virtues – which are all lies, or ought to be, for very often their boasts are of their own cleverness in cheating and oppressing their countrymen in order to obtain money for Government, squinnying cunningly at me the whole time, to see if I look as if I believe them – they put up their hands like the old knights on the monuments, and whine out, "Missis Honour, please recommend Master keep plenty favour upon me: I too much *clover* man !"

JUNE 1838

Moonshee asked me today whether the Governor of Madras was really the wisest man in England. He supposed that the Governors were always picked out for being the wisest men that could be found in the country.

June 22nd. – The other day some of the villagers came to me to make a complaint that one of our Peons had taken up goods in our name, and never paid for them. Of course, I scolded the Peon. Yesterday he brought me a petition addressed to "Your worshipful Honour", setting forth that it was the poor petitioner's opinion that, "when any gentleman come to this place for cool breeze, it is the *duty* of the villagers to give the gentleman's servants everything they want, and he therefore hopes your charitable honour will look upon him for the future as a most innocent man." See what notions of honesty they have! This "injured innocence" had received the money from us to pay everybody. But with all their badness, and all their laziness, there is some good in them. If their master or mistress is in distress or difficulty, they do not grudge any trouble or fatigue to help them. Last Saturday I was in a great fright: A— did not come, as I expected, and I had not heard from him for two days. There is no regular post to this remote place, so we have messengers of our own to carry letters and parcels, and we send each other a note every day to say that all is well; for in a country like this, where all attacks of illness are so frightfully rapid, we could not be easy without hearing from day to day. But on Saturday evening, as he neither came nor sent, I was quite frightened, and thought he must certainly have the cholera and be too ill to write, and that I must go and see after him immediately. Accordingly I despatched messengers to post bearers for me all along the road, bade Moonshee write me a letter every day about the baby, and in the evening I set out in a great bustle for Rajahmundry, attended for some miles by all the inhabitants of the nearest villages, all shouting. I took the cheating Peon with me, and told him that he was to go half-way, and then stop,

LETTER TWENTY

and send a chance village Peon on with me the other half; thinking twenty-five miles quite enough for a man to run in one night; but he said he would rather go all the fifty miles himself; for that he did not mind being tired, and should not be happy in trusting the Mistress to the care of a strange Peon. However, after I had gone about nine miles, I met the messengers with A—'s letters, which had only been delayed by the very common occurrence of the postmen being lazy – they were fast asleep by the river-side when I met them: so, as A— was quite well, and only detained by some unfortunate visitor, I returned home again. The bearers, Peons, and people whom I had scuffled half out of their lives to get ready in time, all laughed very heartily; but I was glad enough that it was only a laughing matter, and laughed myself as they shouted with redoubled vigour all the way home.

Notes
Johnny Gilpin: the final lines of William Cowper's *John Gilpin*, 'And when he next doth ride abroad/May I be there to see!'

I have a good many native visitors here: this section of the published letters, to the end of the entry, comes from one of the four surviving letters Julia sent her grandmother from India. It is possible that Charlotte Broome never read this letter as it may not have arrived before her death in September 1838. Julia had carried with her to India the first letter her grandmother ever wrote to her, 'when I knew only the letter A, and your letter was to teach me B' (24 October 1837).

In this same period, Julia writes that both Miss Craven and Miss Spiers are to be married. 'What humbug it is,' says her husband, 'the Society for sending out marriageable girls.' Miss Spiers was to marry an American missionary, a Mr Winslow, and Miss Craven, 'a medical man, with a good fortune, a widower with several children.' Julia notes, a little to counter her husband's ironic observation, that the Missionary Society would be repaid the cost of sending the girls out (25 June 1838).

While in Samuldavee, Julia occupied some of her time in writing and provides an interesting summary of a book she was working on. 'You have no idea what a slow scribe I am – it is as much as I can do to get through my letters, and the lessons for the school, and now and then a little bit of a book I am about. The book I am doing now is the history of a girl who

JUNE 1838

comes to India. I mean to shew the good one English family might do among the natives – she will live up the country, her father is a Zillah judge, and she has two young brothers – they will have boys and girls schools, conversations with moonshees etc – intimate with a Rajah – Rajah's little son becomes a Christian in consequence of his friendship with the Judge's boys – dies – the poor old Rajah's penances and offerings to expiate his son's loss of Caste – I have not settled the end yet – very little is written – the girl (by name Ellen Leslie) is only at Madras now, just landed – I mean to put in all the different things I see and hear myself among the natives, with some interludes of English visitors and their faults' (13 July 1838).

Letter the Twenty-First

Samuldavee, July 10th, 1838

There are large snakes here, seven feet long, and as thick as my arm, not poisonous, but I always have them killed, nevertheless; for they are horrible creatures, and, even if they are not poisonous, no doubt they are something bad: I have no respect for any snakes. But, worse than snakes, scorpions, centipedes, and even land-wind, are the GREEN BUGS. Fancy large flying bugs! they do not bite, but they scent the air for yards around. When there is no wind at night, they fly round and get into one's clothes and hair – horrible! there is nothing I dislike so much in India as those green bugs. The first time I was aware of their disgusting existence, one flew down my shoulders, and I, feeling myself tickled, and not knowing the danger, unwittingly crushed it. I shall never forget the stench as long as I live. The ayah undressed me as quickly as she could, almost without my knowing what she was doing, for I was nearly in a fit. You have no notion of anything so horrible! I call the land-wind, and the green bugs, the "Oriental luxuries."

You ask about the THUGS. They are a class of natives who live entirely by murder; they bring up their children to it, and initiate them by degrees – they feel no shame nor compunction; they strangle their victims and take all their property. They pretend that they look upon their horrid profession as commanded by some particular goddess, as her service; but I do not believe it. I think they mystify people about their religious obligations in order to lessen the horror, and get off when examined. I believe their offerings and sacrifices are intended as expiations, not as propitiations: the worst of these heathens have sufficient light of natural conscience to understand and allow their duty to *man*.

AUGUST 1838

Cocanada, August 10th – Finding the weather cool again, we started from Samuldavee about a fortnight ago, and made a little tour of five days along the coast in our way hither. It was "plenty hot" though, in some of the places we passed through. We went to one place, Amlapoor, where A— had to settle a dispute between a Moonsiff, or native Judge, and some of his clerks. The clerks wanted to make out that the Moonsiff had taken bribes and committed other enormities. They came to our bungalow to tell their histories, and A— said that he must go to their Cutchery (or office) to examine all the papers, and that he should bring with him *two ears*, and give one ear to the Moonsiff and the other to the clerks. This obliging promise was quite satisfactory; but the result was that the clerks' ear heard nothing but falsehoods, and the poor Moonsiff was honourably acquitted, and the clerks pronounced to be rascals. I was glad of it, because I always thought the Moonsiff a very innocent painstaking creature, and he has been worried quite thin by his clerks, and would have been dismissed from his post if A— had not sifted the stories. He came to see me after his trial was over, looking so pleased and so happy that for a minute I did not know him again, he had appeared so careworn a few hours before. I dare say, next time I see him he will be as fat as a porpoise.

We spent one day at a former Dutch settlement, *Nellapilly* and *Yanam*. It was really quite a pleasure to see a place so neat: the poor Dutchmen had planted avenues, made tidy village greens, chopped the prickly-pears into shape, clipped the hedges, built white walls, and altogether changed the look of the country. They had raised their old-fashioned houses quite high above the ground, as if for fear of the Dutch fens, and made little brick walks and terraces in the gardens, with water-channels on each side to drain them! In short, they had contrived with great ingenuity every possible unappropriateness that could be devised.

LETTER TWENTY-ONE

We paid a pleasant visit of a few days to our friends the L—s, whom we found comfortably established in their Collectorate, and objecting to nothing but the *black bugs*. These are not so horrible as the green ones, but bad enough, and in immense swarms. One very calm night the house was so full of them, that the dinner-table was literally covered with them. We were obliged to have all the servants fanning us with separate fans besides the punkah, and one man to walk round the table with a dessert spoon and a napkin to take them off our shoulders. Except Mr S—, who contrived to be hungry, we gave up all idea of eating our dinner; we could not even stay in the house, but sat all the evening on the steps of the verandah, playing the guitar.

Rajahmundry, August 16th – Here we are at home again; but on our arrival, instead of resting quietly, we found an uninvited visitor established in the house to be entertained for several days – altogether one of the coolest and least ceremonious persons I ever saw. He was lame; so A— one evening lent him his horse out of good nature, and always afterwards Mr – took the horse without asking any leave, and A— was obliged to walk all the time he was pleased to stay. One day A— made, in his hearing, an appointment with another person to ride to a particular spot next day: "Oh, no," said our guest, "you can't go tomorrow, for I am going there myself, and I shall want the horse!" When at last, to my great joy, he took himself off, he left, without asking leave, all his luggage in our only spare room, to wait till he should like to come back again – without any invitation!

August 31st – The present commanding officer here, and his wife, Captain and Mrs C—, are pleasant people, young and Irish, and well-mannered. *She* is *very* Irish, however – lets her tame goats run in and out of the house as they please, and break all the crockery. I sent her some fruit twice in plates, and both times she sent back the plates broken, with notes to say how shocked and confounded she was, but that "the goats had set their feet in them."

AUGUST 1838

Our school is going on nicely; and while we were at Cocanada A— taught one of the Collector's assistants there how to set up a school, and supplied him with books; and I hope there will soon be a good one at that station also.

When we came home I found that all the time I was away the poor old sergeant was busy raising flowers for me. He sent me most beautiful balsams and roses. Also the Mooftee sent me a present of a talc fan, in return for which I have sent Mrs Mooftee some heart pincushions, which I hope she will admire.

We hear that the M—s are going home overland in January. Everybody is very sorry to lose Sir P—. Even those who do not care for religious matters have found the advantage of having an upright and just man over them.

Here is a story of the encouragement given to idolatry, which I know to be true; it took place about six weeks ago. A Collector happened to inquire the destination of a sum of money he was required to disburse. He found it was for a grand ceremony, performed by the order and at the expense of Government, in honour of a particular idol. On making further inquiries he found that the natives had requested to be allowed to take a part of the ceremony and the expense upon themselves, but Government said No, they would do it all. Besides this, he learned that some years ago this wicked feast was first established: it was afterwards discontinued for ten years without the slightest murmur or symptom of discontent from the natives; and within the last two or three years it has been revived by the Government, and entirely kept up by them.

The Collector represented all this at head-quarters (I saw a copy of his letter), petitioning that the natives might be allowed to conduct their feast without English interference, and showing how utterly gratuitous it was, from the proof that the Ceremonies had gone on for ten years without the English having anything to do with the matter; but he was

LETTER TWENTY-ONE

assured that Government thought it would be dangerous and inexpedient to make any alteration, and that the feast must be carried on in behalf of the English, as usual.

September 21st – Have you heard of the Cooly Trade? "Emigration of Hill Coolies to the Mauritius" it is called, and divers other innocent-sounding names. In case you should ever hear anything said in its favour, this is the real state of the case. It is neither more nor less than an East Indian Slave-Trade – just as wicked as its predecessor, the African Slave-Trade. It is encouraged by Lord G—, who ought to have inquired more before he gave his countenance to such horrors. These Coolies are shipped off by thousands from all parts of India to the colonies, instead of Negroes. Twenty-one thousand are said to have been sent from Pondicherry only; for though Pondicherry is a French settlement, the Coolies were shipped for our colonies. Numbers are kidnapped, and all are entrapped and persuaded under false pretences. They are "as ignorant as dirt", do not even know that they are quitting the Company's dominions, and meanwhile their families are left to starve. There is now danger of a famine, from the large number of cultivators who have been taken away. They are so ill-treated by their new masters that few even live to come back, and those who do bring with them the marks of the same cruelties and floggings that we used to hear of among the slaves. As the importation is legal, of course all the throwings overboard and atrocities of the Middle Passage cannot take place; but there are great horrors from stowing numbers in too small a space on board ship. Many die, and many more have their health ruined. There is a great deal of verbiage in the Government newspapers about the Coolies "carrying their labour to the best market", and so on: but the fact is, these poor creatures are far too ignorant and stupid to have any sense or choice in the matter. Some slave-agent tells them they are to go – and they go: they know nothing about it. A Hindoo does not know how to *make a choice*; it is an effort of mind quite beyond any but the very highest and most educated among them. Gentlemen's native servants are very superior in sense to those poor wild Coolies; but once or twice I have, quite innocently, puzzled and distressed some of our servants exceedingly, by giving them their choice about some affair that concerned only themselves: they have gone away and pined and cried for two or three hours, or sometimes days, and then come back and begged that "Missis Honour would please make order, for they did not know what to do."

I long to see my kaleidoscopes and all the school rewards you have sent me. A— has an idea that we might manage to set up a little *Europe shop* in the Rajahmundry bazaar, to be managed by a native who would be paid by us. He thinks they would be so pleased by books, pictures, and conundrums of various sorts, that one might thereby introduce useful things *"di nascosto"*; but I fear it is impracticable, because they are so silly and so suspicious, that they would fancy we were trading and making money by it. We have the two first classes of our school now every Saturday evening at our own house, as A— finds he can instruct them better by that means. Our schoolmaster has taught them to read and write, but he is not capable of anything more; so now we send a Moonshee three times a-week to teach them some "sense". They are now busy upon a 'History of the World,' which is very good *learning* for them.

September 26th – It is now a great native holiday for the Dussera, a Hindoo feast. Here is a proof of how much they care about their feasts. There is always a holiday in the Courts for a week during the Dussera, and the Pundit, who is the principal Hindoo in the Court, and a Bramin of very high caste, sent to ask whether he might be excused from taking the holiday, because his work was in arrears, and he did not care for the feast. Of course, it would not be fair to let his underlings lose their holiday because he had been lazy and not done his work; but it shows how little stress they really lay upon these feasts, about which the Government makes so much ado.

The old postmaster Bramin is now come to make salaam, and inform us of an eclipse that will take place next week – a very frightful circumstance; and the people are preparing their drums, &c., "to frighten the giant, for who knows whether he may not eat up the moon entirely?" A— is trying to explain the matter to him, with the help of oranges and limes for the moon and earth. How charmed he will be to see the astronomical magic lantern!

September 29th – A— thinks there is serious danger of a war. The Russians have sent ten thousand men to help the Affghans against us, and we are at war with the Persians already. Sir H. Fane, the Commander-in-Chief in Bengal, says that thirty thousand men are necessary to conquer these combined Russians, Persians, and Affghans, and only five thousand are granted. All the Indian politicians declare that nothing but our obtaining a really sensible, energetic man as Governor-General can possibly save India to us – such a one as the Marquis of Wellesley again. Since I have been in India, and have seen the traces of his wonderful wisdom, I have learnt to think him one of the first of human geniuses.

October 1st – We have had two visits lately from Mr S—, the clergyman of L. He is to come to Rajahmundry once a quarter. He is a good man, but has given offence by his punctiliousness about minor matters, such as *public* baptism, &c.

We have also been favoured with the company of a Mr and Mrs G—; she is a bride, and as pretty and silly as any one I ever saw. S— seems to be the principal topic of conversation in this division just now, so Mrs G—, like everybody else, began to discuss him, and give her *piccolissimo parere* about him. "I think Mr S— is very uncharitable – very much so. He thinks it wrong for Missionaries to preach to the natives." "Does he?" said I, somewhat astounded: "why, I understood that he particularly wished the Missionaries to confine their preaching to the natives, instead of employing themselves among the Europeans!" "Ah!" said Mrs G—, "very likely that's it: I know he thinks something wrong – he's very uncharitable." She discoursed also a good deal on literature and science, chemistry and poetry, in a very innocent way, and I found she was, by way of being "blue." But, you know, ladies who are very *blue* are apt to be rather *green*.

October 5th – Everybody had a holiday on the day of the eclipse; all the Bramins marched into the river to bathe and sing while it lasted; *such* a clatter they made! An eclipse is a signal for particular purification. There was an old Bramin here in prison for debt; he would not eat anything for fear of defilement, and was literally starving himself to death. A— found that he could allow him to live in a separate house guarded by Peons, and therefore removed him out of the jail, and now the poor old creature has taken again to his food. The post-office writer came to have a chat about the matter, as he generally does when there is any such trifle of news. I asked him whether he did not think the Dewan a very foolish man to have run the risk of killing himself rather than eat in a prison. "Yes," he said, "too much foolish; but that man all same one jungle beast – never been in one Government office, never read the regulations!" They look upon employment in a Government office as the height of human dignity, and strut to and from the Court-house like so many turkey-cocks.

I hope we shall soon have a respite from uninvited company, and be able to ask young Ch—, whom we are both longing to see; but our house is a complete hotel for people we do not care to see, and I know not a greater bore than "Indian hospitality", as it is called by travellers. Some time ago there was an order given to build a public bungalow at this place; but the Government changed their minds, and desired that none should be built at the *stations,* "as the residents can always receive travellers." This is mean enough,

LETTER TWENTY-ONE

but all of a piece with the rest of their proceedings. In order to save money, Lord W. Bentinck reduced the army and sold the stores; and now there is a war beginning, and not soldiers enough to carry it on. They are trying to raise regiments in a hurry, and find that all the able-bodied men, who ought to be soldiers, have been shipped off as slaves to the Mauritius. The Commanders-in-chief at the three Presidencies are all going home, and the Governors can do nothing without them: India is, in fact, governed by the private secretaries, who are not responsible for the mischief they do, and are often intent only on feathering their own nests and promoting their young relations. Half the experienced men in the service who really understand matters are kept in subordinate situations, and young raw slips placed over their heads, to ride races and try fancies, whilst the country is in the most dangerous condition.

October 10*th* – Moonshee has been telling me a long story about snakes and giants eating up the moon, to account for the eclipse: upon this he received a lecture about the shadow, and so forth; and he now informs me that he shall "futurely not believe that giant." When the schoolboys came for their examination last Saturday we found that three or four had learnt very well, and all the others nothing at all, for which Moonshee gave most excellent reasons: but upon a little cunning inquiry we discovered that all those who had learnt gave Moonshee a little extra private pay, and that those who paid him nothing were taught in proportion. The next process was, to reprimand Moonshee, which being done, he informed me that he should *"futurely* teach all the boys without *parturition,"* meaning – partiality.

Yesterday I had an old Bramin to play the tamboura and sing to me. I was in hopes, if I heard a solo performance, I might be able to make out some of their tunes undrowned by their horribly discordant accompaniments. He sang one tolerably pretty Hindostanee song, but was too stupid to sing

OCTOBER 1838

it over again, therefore I could not catch it. The national airs of this country are remarkably ugly – like Spanish boleros, with a profusion of caricature flourishes.

October 21st – Today I had the delight of receiving your most welcome packet of letters. You may imagine what raptures I am in at hearing that Frank has gained the T— scholarship! If I were but strong enough, I think I should dance, just by way of effervescence; as it is, I can only lie on the sofa and grin! I am exceedingly pleased. You are quite right, though, in thinking that you had betrayed his intention of trying for this scholarship. You tried to *un-betray* it afterwards, and make me think there was nothing in your hints – but in vain; I was too cunning for you! I always knew he was going up for it, and calculated that this very mail would bring me the result.

Notes

green bugs...black bugs: these plagues of stinking bugs rarely go unmentioned in European accounts of life in India.

Dutch settlement: The Dutch East India Company had been the major competitor to the East India Company in the seventeenth century. It also provided the English Company with a model: a charter giving it some independence from the home government, its own armed forces, its financial management and the 'Factories.'

the L—s : this couple and other Europeans mentioned on these pages cannot be identified as the original letter/s are missing.

The M—s....Sir P: Sir Peregrine Maitland resigned as Commander-in-Chief in protest at the official countenance given to Hindu and Moslem religious festivals. In a despatch of the Court of Directors of the Company, 20 February 1833, the point was made that Company servants no longer had to attend 'idolatrous rites.' But a despatch of 18 October 1837, in response to a Memorial of the Madras Christians, ordered 'that no customary salutes or marks of respect to native festivals be discontinued at any of the presidencies; that no protection hitherto given be withdrawn; and that no change whatever be made in any matter relating to the native religion, except under the authority of the supreme government.' The story Julia tells is an illustration of the confused state between the various levels of the establishment in relation to Indian religious practice.

LETTER TWENTY-ONE

Cooly Trade: the so-called indenture system used by the British and French in their former slave-owning colonies. Indian emigration to Mauritius began in 1830 and most recruits in the 1830s were from the Tamil areas of Madras, from the United Provinces and from Bihar. Pressure from Evangelicals, in particular, led to investigations in each presidency into malpractices in the system. Julia's comment that there was now a danger of famine due to the number of cultivators taken away is an incomplete analysis of problems on the land and of the Indian economy. The slump in the cotton industry, a result of the developing cotton industry in England during the Industrial Revolution, drove many to work on the land where frequent drought led to starvation.

serious danger of a war: James Thomas also tells Julia that he believes the English could lose India, 'owing to their own folly.' Julia's references are to classic Great Game territory. For much of the nineteenth century Afghanistan was its backdrop. The Russian Empire in Asia had grown as fast as Britain's. In north India Britain had a 2,000-mile land frontier to protect and beyond its north-west corner lay Afghanistan.

A mixture of fear, intrigue and rumour led to Lord Auckland's [Governor-General of the Bengal Presidency] decision to invade Afghanistan in 1839, to remove the popular ruler Dost Mohammed, rumoured to be plotting with the Russians, and to replace him with the exiled, pro-British, Shah Shuja. By the end of 1841 all Afghanistan was in arms against the British. The retreat of January 1842 is described as the most terrible in the history of British arms; Dr Brydon, a few sepoys and 120 prisoners were the only survivors.

Marquis of Wellesley: Governor-General of India, 1798-1805, and elder brother of Arthur Wellesley, Duke of Wellington. In his relatively brief time as Governor-General, Wellesley defeated Tipu Sultan, of Mysore, and the Marathas, and brought under control the native governments in Arcot, Awadh and Hyderabad. It was a scheme of Wellesley's for the training of civil servants, considered too expensive at the time, which led to the establishment of Haileybury College.

Mr S.: the Reverend Vincent Shortland of Vizagapatam. 'He is a really good man,' wrote Julia, 'though very pragmatical. He is one of the new High Churches – all for discipline and infallibility' (10 July 1838).

Mr and Mrs G....young Ch: the Butlers and young Cholmeley.

The title *Dewan* in this instance probably means a person in charge of dealings in a business, or in charge of a large domestic establishment.

Lord W. Bentinck: William Bentinck (1774-1839) had been Governor of Madras from 1803 to 1807, and was Governor-General of Bengal from

OCTOBER 1838

1828 to 1835. With finances depleted by the prolonged war in Burma, his first duty was to devise means of reducing expenses in every branch of the administration. He was in effect carrying out the orders of the Court of Directors, but his actions made him unpopular.

the Commanders-in-chief....are all going home: Maitland was leaving Madras, Fane was attempting to leave Bengal (his resignation was refused because of the invasion of Afghanistan), and Sir Colin Halkett was leaving Bombay. *the Governors can do nothing without them*: in her original letter she wrote, 'the Governors are such utter dawdlers that they can do nothing of any sort themselves.' She adds that Elphinstone 'is a nice fresh coloured young man and a good dancer . . . but Lord Auckland is not even that' (1 October 1838).

tamboura: a four-stringed instrument providing a drone, usually to accompany the main instrument. Tamboura and voice may not have been the best way to persuade Julia of the merits of south Indian music.

Frank ... the T— scholarship: in May Julia's brother Richard was named Tyrwhitt Hebrew Scholar at King's College, Cambridge. A family friend, George Leonard Jenyns (1763-1848) of Bottisham Hall was Regius Professor of Hebrew at Cambridge. Julia must have felt very proud of her brother. Problems with his eye-sight had meant that most of his studying had to be done with the help of others. Charlotte Barrett wrote to Fanny D'Arblay in June of 1834 or 1835: 'Julia is at present highly useful to her Brother, preparing his hebrew lessons which she embosses so that Dick can read them in the dark: and this aid, mechanical though it is, is quite indispensible to him till he returns to College in November' (Barrett Eg3702A 56-57).

In her letter of 18 September Julia informed her mother that she was again pregnant. She enjoys her little daughter who is now walking about, helping, bossing the Matey 'like a grown woman' when she sees a dirty spoon. She puts Julia's shoes on her feet when she finds them lying on the floor, 'as they are apt to be.' In a later letter, in January 1839, she describes her baby playing with a looking-glass: 'she evidently takes it for another child – calling it "Baba" (Gentoo for "baby"), trying to shake hands with it, making salaam to it, feeding it with cake, and kissing it most tenderly!' She even takes her castor oil happily when accompanied by the glass.

Letter the Twenty-Second

Rajahmundry, October 31st 1838

Everything goes wrong – the overland post has been due this fortnight – all our letters are detained at Alexandria – everybody in a fume – nobody more so than I. The steamers are sent to make war against the Persians instead of doing their proper work – all the ships going on to China or Calcutta instead of to London – and when I shall be able to send this letter, *chi lo sa?*

The Bishop is arrived at Bangalore, within two hundred miles of Madras, and is taken ill, so that he is detained there; but they say his illness is not dangerous. Every one who has seen him likes him very much. We are all well here, only in a fury for letters. There is a great deal of distress among the natives, owing to the failure of the Monsoon, and a prospect of great scarcity. Poor creatures! they are so screwed by taxes, higher than the land will fairly bear, that they never have a farthing in hand. The natives and some of the European officers want the magistrates to force the sale of grain, and the grain-merchants want to hoard it. Some of the magistrates give way, and sell off all the hoarded grain: the consequence is, that the merchants decamp, there is no seed left for sowing, and what was a scarcity becomes a famine. Other magistrates, A— for one, will not interfere with the sale of the grain, because they have found, by much experience, that that method answers best; and it stands to reason that the merchants will bring the largest supplies wherever they find the freest sale and the best protection. Captain Kelly, the commanding officer here, wants to have the sale forced; A— will not allow it, and talks himself hoarse, all to no purpose, in trying to convince him that it does not answer, and that the merchants have as good a right to have their property in grain protected as in anything else. Kelly always ends with "I cannot see *that*: *I* think they ought to sell it"; and Mrs Kelly puts in her little word in confirmation, "I think they certainly ought to be made to." She has a great idea of people being "made to". She is considerably affronted because A— will not fine or imprison the butcher and baker till they give their meat and their bread at the prices she thinks proper. He assures her in vain that he has no power over that class of crimes, and also that in such a small station it is not worth the people's while to serve us at the same prices as in a large town with a certain sale and plenty of competition. She still persists, "Hem! with all that, I am sure it *might* be done." There has been so much discussion about it all, that I quite dread to hear the subject mentioned, for fear of a quarrel, besides the wearisomeness: so now, when they dine here, I have invented having two large dishes of barley-sugar at dessert, which is the time when the arguing always takes place; and the barley-sugar being something new and very nice, it quite answers my purposes, and sweetens matters beautifully. They eat it all up, and are quite good-humoured.

November 6th – To my greatest joy, the September steamer arrived the day before yesterday, and brought us a packet of letters. I go quite mad when the letters appear, and turn Moonshee out of the house without giving him time to make his salaams. But all the natives seem to understand and sympathise with our love of letters. They have plenty of queer notions about Europe letters, and think they add greatly to our respectability. One day I thought a letter from you had been lost, as it did not appear when I expected it; so I sent for the old post-office writer to ask if he was quite sure there were no more letters, as "Ma'am" wanted another. "Oh!" he said, "too much care arlways I take Ma'am's letters. Five letters this time come Ma'am! – Very high-caste lady indeed! – No any lady in this district so many Europe letters same as Ma'am! – No any lady such high caste!"

LETTER TWENTY-TWO

I am very glad you know Colonel B—y: he was the cleverest man in India when he was here, and has left no one able to supply his place. You ask how I get the pebbles from our river polished. I keep an old Moorman, with a long white beard, cutting and polishing them all day. He is a most lazy old creature, and will do nothing unless he is teazed. Sometimes he does not bring me a stone for days together then I send a Peon to ask whether he is *dead:* Peon brings back word, "Not dead, ma'am – that man 'live." Then I send to know how many more days he means to *sleep;* then they come back grinning and looking very cunning, with a pebble in their hands.

Here is a story for you and the national-school girls, if you can make a moral to it. There was a Moorman Hakeem, or doctor, at Calcutta, very anxious to cure one of his patients. The Moormans ought to know very well that idolatry is forbidden by their Koran, but they are often very ignorant and heathenish. This Hakeem thought it would make matters surer with respect to his patient if he secured the aid of some of the Heathen gods as well as that of Mohammed; so he went to the temple of the idol Punchanund, and promised him a large reward if he would help to cure the man, who was very rich, and had engaged to pay the Hakeem a considerable sum on his recovery. The patient died. The Hakeem went again to the temple and told Punchanund that he did not believe he had any power at all, and that, if he was a god, he must get up directly and eat the fruit and smell the flowers which the Hakeem had brought him out of goodnature, notwithstanding his disappointment. Punchanund, of course, sat still: the Hakeem, in a rage, broke off its head, and was found by the police walking about with the idol's head in his hand. On being asked why he had done it, he said, "What was the use of leaving a head on such a stupid fellow as that, who could not help either himself or me?"

November 26th – The Bishop is well again, and arrived at Madras. The religious people at Madras are going to present

NOVEMBER 1838

an address to Sir P— M— before his departure, to express their respect for his conduct, and regret at losing him, &c., &c.

The country and the Government are in a shocking condition: it seems now to be doubtful whether we shall have a war with Affghanistan or not; plenty of preparations are making, but the Affghans have not decided whether they will attempt to stand against us; I think they would win. The Indian army is in a poor condition, especially the Bengal part of it, which would be sent. The Sepoys say they cannot go into the field without their *hookahs*.

I very much fear I shall never see the letters you sent last. A ship was wrecked the other day off Cape l'Aguillas – all lives saved, but most of the cargo lost: I am afraid two or three of my letters were in it. As is usual in shipwrecks, it was commanded by a young Captain making his first voyage: those young Captains almost always try some clever experiment, and lose their first ship.

November 19th, 1838 – Hindered till now by divers fellow-creatures. The other day we had a visit from a very intelligent native, a friend of Rammohun Roy's: he came to ask A— to subscribe to a book he is going to publish. He told us he had three daughters and a son, and that he was determined not to be influenced by the Hindoo prejudices against female education, so he had taught his daughters to read and write their own language, English, and Sanscrit, and that he found they learnt just as well as their brother; but he had met with a great deal of trouble and opposition from his relations on account of his innovation – especially from his wife, who for a long time allowed no peace or quiet in the house. He says the natives much wish to see some of Rammohun Roy's suggestions adopted by the Government, and think them very useful and well adapted to their end. You could tell Mr G— this: Rammohun Roy's ideas were laid before Parliament, and Mr G— will know what they were. There is great distress in

LETTER TWENTY-TWO

our neighbourhood now, owing to the failure of the Monsoon. Whole gangs of robbers are going about, armed with sticks, waylaying the grain-merchants and breaking open the stores. A— is raising a subscription to buy grain and give it to those who will *work* for it – every man to have enough for himself, and his wife, and two children; and he intends that the workers shall dig a well, or deepen a tank, or do something of that kind which will be a benefit to the people. We have also sent for a quantity of potatoes, in hopes of introducing their cultivation: the cultivators are willing to try them now, in this time of scarcity, and I hope they may succeed. I am to give the potatoes, and A— is to give a reward to the man who raises the best crop. Potatoes would be very good to cultivate here, because they require so little water. The tanks are all dried up, and people are beginning to grudge the trouble of drawing water from the wells for their bullocks. One man said to me, "Two pots water, whole family drink quite 'nough; and two pots water one bullock arl own hisself drink up: too much trouble that bullock!"

A— is just returned from Samulcottah (the Military station), whither he went on occasion of a public dinner. Major C— is very much given to drawing, and good-naturedly sent me two portfolios filled with his performances to look at: they are very clever and well done; but, like most amateur drawings, they have every merit except *beauty*. I do not know how it is we all contrive to avoid that!

I am just now deep in the *surface* of geology. Mantell speaks of fine fossils in India, so I sent hunting about for some. One man brought word that he had found in the bed of the river a number of the *"bone-stones"* my honour desired: this put me in great glee; but when I came to see the "bone-stones" myself, they were nothing but common white flints, somewhat the colour and shape of bones.

Our school goes on but slowly, though we work a great deal at it. It requires time and patience to clear out their heads of nonsense. The old English school-books you have sent will be most valuable. We find the only way to teach these natives is by question and answer: they cannot take in anything of a prose, so we compose dialogues for them on what we want them to learn. The Narsapoor Missionaries go on zealously and sensibly, and I hope do the *beginning* of a little good. Bowden and his wife are here just now, that she may be under the Doctor's care during her confinement.

January 9th, 1839 – We had lately a long visit from poor Penny-Whistle. He came to tell us all his trouble on the loss of his wife. He said he was going to make a pilgrimage to Tripetty, a very holy pagoda some hundred miles off, and to give many hundred rupees to the Swamy. It was an excellent opportunity for giving him a Christian exhortation, so A— discoursed a good deal to him, and he seemed to understand a little, and said they were "words of great wisdom"; but the difficulty of talking to natives is, that, instead of attending, they are all the time on the look-out for any loophole to insinuate some of their absurd provoking compliments, and one can never ascertain whether they really take in what is said to them. I gave him two of the Gospels bound in red satin with yellow flowers, and he seemed pleased, and promised to read them. Among other questions, he asked *where* our God was, that we could worship Him without making pilgrimages. He complained of being very dull for want of something to do, so A— advised him to set up a school in his town, and look to his estate, and employ people in cultivating the waste lands, which are all utterly neglected for miles around him.

We are now writing dialogues for the natives – to be printed in parallel columns of English, Tamul, and Teloogoo – on different subjects, just to give them a *soupçon* of sense. Mr Binning has made us a very good one on Grammar; A— is *doing* Ancient History; the Doctor is doing Anatomy; I am to do different ones. The school continues full, but does not

LETTER TWENTY-TWO

advance much: the two first classes come to us every Saturday to read St Luke's Gospel and repeat Scripture questions – I mean, questions and answers on Scripture History, which we prepare and they learn by heart. This they seem to like and enter into; but we are only as far as Abraham yet. If we really get through the Scripture History we mean to publish it, as we think it might be useful.

Baby is very well and very intelligent. Every now and then she learns to pronounce some new word, which she thinks is very clever; but I intend, as much as possible, to prevent her learning the native languages: though it is rather difficult – most English children do learn them, and all sorts of mischief with them, and grow like little Hindoos. If my child were to stay long in the country, it would be worth while to send for an English nurse; but, as it is, I hope to bring her home before it becomes of any consequence, and meanwhile I keep her as much as possible with me. The native "system" of managing a child is to make it cry for everything. If "Missy", as they call her, asks for anything, Ayah is too lazy to give it, but argues, and tries to persuade her to do without it: then Missy whines – Ayah does not care for that, she whines too: then Missy roars – then, whether right or wrong, good or bad, Ayah gives her whatever she wants. She has nothing to do but to roar long enough and loud enough, and she is sure to get her own way – anything may be done by means of naughtiness.

Notes

the Bishop: George Trevor Spencer (1799-1866) succeeded Corrie (see notes to Letter Six) as Bishop of Madras. He stayed in India for twelve years. In that time he published two Journals of visitation tours he made in the Presidency, and established three training colleges for native converts.

so screwed by taxes: is Julia referring to taxation by the British? Or by local Zemindars, who after all were raising sums they owed the British? Board of Revenue records for the time show that there was very little the British did not succeed in taxing – essentials to cooking such as the spice turmeric, onions and garlic, and tobacco, ganjah, bang, betel and, of course, salt.

JANUARY 1839

Colonel B—y: Julia had already asked her mother if she knew of Colonel Burney in her letter of 29 January 1838. 'Do you know whether the Col. Burney so much talked about in the Indian Newspapers is one of our black Burneys? If so, he must have been very clever to raise himself as he has done – for in this country the dislike of his Half-Caste birth is far stronger than at home, and yet he is quite a grand man. Ships named after him, and all his proceedings mentioned in every newspaper – he belongs to Bengal, not to Madras.'

Col. Henry Burney (1792-1845) was Fanny D'Arblay's nephew, son of her half-brother Richard Thomas Burney who left for India aged 19, never to return. Col. Burney began as a cadet in the East India Company in 1807, was a major by 1828, and a Lt.-Col. by 1834. In 1825 he was sent as Political Agent to the Siamese States, and in 1829 as Resident to the Court of Ava in Upper Burma. Col. Burney was on leave in England from 1838 and was with his aunt Fanny D'Arblay when she died on 6 January 1840.

Rammohun Roy (1772?-1833), the great Hindu reformer, born in Bengal. In 1828 he founded his own association, the Brahmo Samaj which promoted a monotheistic Hinduism. He condemned image worship, revived Vedic studies, published Upanishads (spiritual treatises), and in 1818 issued his first Bengali book against *sati*. Roy was in England as ambassador of the Mughal emperor, and died in England. He was buried in Bristol. His statue stands in front of the Central Library on College Green and was unveiled on 20 November 1997, the fiftieth anniversary of Indian Independence.

Mr G: Mr Garrett.

Major C—: Major McCurdy.

Mantell: Gideon Algernon Mantell (1790-1852), geologist. Mantell practised as a surgeon in Lewes but lost no opportunity to indulge in his interest in natural history and geology. He had a noted collection of fossils which he eventually sold to the British Museum. He was a prolific and popular writer and Julia was probably familiar with his *Fossils of the South Downs: or Illustrations of the Geology of Sussex* (1822), since she knew the area well.

pilgrimage to Tripetty: now Tirupathi, about 150 kilometers north-east of Madras and famous for its temple to Lord Venkatesa on the nearby hill of Tirumala. This is one of the most frequented pilgrimage centres in India as Lord Venkatesa is supposed to grant any wish made in front of the idol at Tirumala.

Letter the Twenty-Third

Rajahmundry, January 19th, 1839

The famine is decreasing now, but there has been much distress. A— collected about fifty pounds among the three or four English here, the Court writers, and Rajahs; and the Government gave him fifty pounds more; with which he has fed daily about two hundred and fifty or three hundred people, giving them grain in payment for their work. The old sergeant gives out the tickets to the labourers, and superintends them, but he is somewhat slow, and cannot make them mind him. One day we asked him how he managed: he said, "Pretty well, sir, along with the men – they are pretty quiet; but the *women*, ma'am !" (turning to me with a very coy look) – "they are dreadful bad to be sure! I can't get on along with them at all!" Next day A— went himself to see how they got on: there he found the poor sergeant with the tickets tied up in the corner of his pocket-handkerchief, and about fifty able-bodied women, all fighting, pulling, and dragging at him; and as many more shut up in a sort of pen of prickly-pear, fighting, scratching, and tearing each other, till A— thought there would really be some serious mischief done, and some of the babies in arms killed; but the sergeant took it all very quietly:- "Lawk, sir, never mind 'em! they won't hurt themselves!" A— goes now every morning to give the tickets away himself, and there is no trouble at all, but all the fighting ladies as quiet as mice. The women help to work as well as the men, but of course they only do a little of the easy part. They are all repairing the tanks and the roads, and the native subscribers are now much pleased with the plan of making the people work for their food. They are beginning to see the sense of it; but at first they tried hard to persuade A— to give it away in

JANUARY 1839

a sort of scramble to those that cried the loudest, which is the native way of giving charity.

We are just now very busy about a new plan, viz., to set up a native reading-room in the bazaar. A— thinks the people would often be induced to come and sit there and read, instead of spending all the day in gossiping and chewing betel in the bazaar. He has consulted one or two of the most sensible of our native visitors, who like the thoughts of it very much, and say it would be sure to succeed. We mean to hire a good room in the middle of the bazaar, have it whitewashed and matted, and ornamented with some of the penny pictures which are coming from you, and which will be great attractions; and keep always there a supply of all the Gentoo books and tracts that are to be had, all the easy English ones we can muster, a Gentoo and an English newspaper. There is a Gentoo newspaper published at Madras, and A— takes it, in order to please some of the Court servants by lending it to them. It is very quaint: sometimes there are articles translated from the English papers, always the most uninteresting and frivolous that can possibly be selected: for instance, a description of the Queen's bed, with the very unexpected assertion that she always sleeps on a hard mat, with nothing over her! In the last number there was an account of a ball given by the Governor of Madras, to which many of the natives were invited. They say, "the Nabob entered with a grand *suwarree* (attendance) of a hundred guards, and a hundred lanterns all in one line, and appeared like a man of penetration. The English danced together pleasantly after their fashion, shaking each other's hands, and then proceeded to make their supper, when the respectable natives all retired." Of course, the "respectable natives" of caste could not remain to partake of our Pariah food! They always despise us very much for dancing to amuse ourselves; the proper grand thing would be to sit still, solemn and sleepy, smoking, or chewing betel, and have dancing-girls to dance to us.

LETTER TWENTY-THREE

That poor Mr B— I told you about, who was helping us to concoct dialogues, is going home ill. He had set up a native school at Cocanada with forty boys; it was going on very nicely, but I am afraid nobody will keep it up now. A Rajah who called here the other day promised to take it in hand, and pay the master, and keep it up himself; but I am afraid his promises will not come to much. He was rather a clever, intelligent man, and came to tell us of a book he is writing on revenue and judicial matters. Some of his notions and schemes were very good, and A— thought they really might be useful; but probably the performance will be so queer and rigmarole that nobody will read it. He wanted A— to write a public official letter to Government requesting that attention might he paid to the book: I think Government would be rather surprised.

Our Narsapoor Missionaries are now engaged in travelling through the district, preaching as they go along. It is a very good plan for exciting attention, and that is the chief benefit that is to be hoped for at present. These poor natives are a long time before they can even be roused from their apathy: as for their *opposition,* they are scarcely equal to making any – it is like the opposition of dormice. I believe they could sleep through a battle.

March 6th – The reading-room is established and much approved. The doors are opened before six in the morning, but there are always people waiting outside, ready for the first moment they can get in. Always twenty or thirty at a time sit reading there, and about a hundred come in the course of the day. The wall is hung with divers of your penny pictures, which are much admired, especially that of the Queen on horseback. We have found plenty of suitable books, in English, Hindostanee, Tamul, and Gentoo; and I think it seems to be a very pretty invention, and likely to give great satisfaction.

The case of goods by the 'Argyle' arrived a little while ago, and we immediately selected a batch of rewards to give to our boys. There are sixty-five now in the school, but we only gave grand Europe presents to the twenty-four best, not to make them too cheap; and by way of a slight treat to the younger fry, they came to "point" at the presents, and scramble for *pice*. The penknives were more admired than anything; next the slates. We take a great deal of pains, but they learn very little; however, they just get the beginnings of notions.

The other day a Sunnyassee, or Hindoo devotee, came to pray in the middle of the river, and, being a wonderful saint, a number of people made a subscription of fifty rupees that he might pray for them — *that* being the price he set upon his prayers. The Doctor happened to see the crowd in the middle of the river, and asked a boy what they were doing: the boy said they were going to be prayed for by a great saint like Jesus Christ. The Doctor asked where he had heard of Jesus Christ. He said at the Feringhees' (Englishmen's) school, and that he thought Jesus Christ was a great saint, and that His prayers for any one would be granted. Miss L——'s idea, which you mention, of translating 'Watts on Prejudices' for the Hindoos, is just a hundred years in advance — they would not understand it. What they want is, 'des Catéchismes de six sous,' like Massillon's little infidel.

At the Translation Committee at Madras, some innocent Missionary sent in a proposal to translate Butler's 'Analogy' into Tamul. One shrewd old German said, very quietly, "Perhaps he will first give us the Tamul word for *Analogy*"; and that was all the notice taken of the proposition.

We lately received a petition, signed by the principal people, chiefly Mussulmans, in several of the surrounding villages, begging us to supply them with books of the same kind as those in our reading-room, mentioning the names of several that they particularly wish to have, and saying that they will thankfully pay for them, if we will only procure them. Therefore we have now a sort of circulating library in the district. We consign a packet of books to the head man in

LETTER TWENTY-THREE

one village, and he passes them on to the rest, and when they are all read, we send out a fresh supply.

Notes

chewing betel: pan is a combination of areca nut, lime and other ingredients, wrapped in a betel leaf. It was and is used both as a form of cerimonial hospitality and for more everyday consumption.

Mr. B—: the same Mr Binning referred to in the last letter.

a *Sunnyassee*, or Hindoo devotee: the fourth stage in a Brahmin's life is *Sunnyas*, the renunciation of all worldly interests and reponsibilities. The word *sunnyasi* or *sannyasi* is also applied to wandering ascetics.

pice: a copper coin of little value.

Miss L—: Mary Elliot, probably one of the Brighton congregation. There were two Reverend Elliots at Julia's wedding and Elliots are mentioned in a Diary attributed to Richard Barrett describing religious and educational activities taking place in Brighton in the 1830s.

Watts on Prejudice: Isaac Watts (1674-1748), the non-conformist hymn-writer. Watts also wrote on logic and in *Logic: or, the right use of reason in the enquiry after truth*, first published in 1725, he wrote on the nature and causes of prejudice. It ran into many editions.

Massillon's little infidel: from the sermons of Jean-Baptiste Massillon (1663-1742), French Oratorian preacher. One of the foremost preachers of a great generation, much respected even by leaders of the Enlightenment.

Butler's 'Analogy': Joseph Butler (1692-1752), bishop of Durham. *The Analogy of Religion, Natural and Revealed, to the Constitution and Course of Nature* (1763), attempts to show that as man reveals a supreme conscience, so nature shows a moral governor revealed through conscience. Considered the greatest theological work of its time, and, by some, one of the most original of any time.

Translation Committee at Madras: Julia complained in an earlier letter that 'all the Institutions in Madras are Committee ridden, which I look on as the next step to being bedridden!'

we lately received a petition: this may be similar, though probably on a smaller scale, to a petition which can still be seen in the Asia, Pacific and Africa Collections of the British Library and which can be read in Appendix II. This was certainly a common and accepted method of approaching authority on any issue.

Letter the Twenty-Fourth

Samuldavy, March 30th, 1839

Here we arrived this morning, and are enjoying ourselves, spreading our sails, and cooling delightfully. Rajahmundry was growing very hot, but this place is charming. Last night it was downright cold, and the colder and more uncomfortable it was the better I liked it. The babies and I shall stay here the next four months, and A— will come to us once a-week as before, if the Governor does not find it out; and in May he will have a lawful holiday. I had a little fever before I came away, and Henrietta was grown pale and pining; but the sea-breeze has cleared my fever away in this one morning, and I dare say in a few days I shall see a great change in her too. We have built a new room here, which is very comfortable, and we are to pay no rent until we have repaid ourselves the expense of it, after which it is to belong to the landlord. This makes it a good bargain both for him and for us, and it only cost thirty pounds altogether.

I believe there is a Missionary coming to Rajahmundry at last — a Dissenter; but if the Church Mission can do nothing for all this immense district, of course we can only be glad that the Dissenters should take it up. He is a Mr Johnston, seemingly a very quiet, humble person; and I wish he may come, but it is not yet quite settled.

Before we came away we exhibited the astronomical magic lantern to the schoolboys. We sent for them unexpectedly, on a leisure evening, so all who were not at school were "caught out", and lost the show. They were enchanted with it, and understood it very prettily, considering they would not have been capable a year ago of understanding any one of the slides. They particularly admired the moon: I heard some whispering, "*Oh nulla chendroodoo!*" — "Oh good moon!" whenever it appeared. Mr G. thinks our school is come on very nicely, and is much better than any of the others he has seen since he has been away: this pleases us, for we had been uneasy, thinking they learned nothing. One of the schools at which he has been teaching is an endowed school at Masulipatam, with a committee and a great deal of money; but very little really done, though much trouble taken in the committee-room: they think it necessary to write and ask the Archdeacon (of Madras) permission for every book, and he allows of none but the English national-school books, which are quite useless to the natives, so they do not get on at all. Mr Hamilton is going to have a *Pariah* school at Rajahmundry, by way of a companion to ours, as we do not admit Pariahs.

The "reading-room" also answers very well, and is always full. Mr H. went to see it one morning early, and found people waiting for the doors to open.

Here is a story for you, but it did not happen lately. There was a goddess carried in procession to one of the pagodas, and the Collector, as usual, had to supply the money: after the procession had advanced some way, the Bramins came and told the Collector that it had stopped because the goddess would not travel any farther with only twenty bullocks: the Collector gave ten more, and the Swamy went on another hundred yards; when the Bramins came back again and said she was still discontented and wanted more. This put the Collector in a passion: he said she was a "greedy devil", and various other little *politesses*; and if she could not be satisfied with thirty bullocks he would *chop her up*. So he sent his Peons to fetch her out of her car, and ordered them to chop her up on the spot: the Peons were afraid, and ran away: then he sent for the cook-boy, and made him chop her up before his eyes — and the Bramins just took it all quietly and went home. I believe this is quite true; and the moral of it is — that the people would not be so very ready to raise rebellions as is pretended on any deficiency of attention to the Swamies. The Collector was a very passionate man, but rather a favourite with the natives because he did not oppress them in money matters, which they care for much more than for Swamy. I must add, however, that A— says my story of the Collector chopping up the Swamy happened twenty years ago; and that no Collector in his senses would do such a thing now.

Our clerical friend, Mr —, is always in some scrape about christenings: he refuses to admit any sponsors who are not regular communicants, and consequently many children under his jurisdiction are not christened at all. A little while ago he was absent from his station for three days, and D—, who is Judge there, took the opportunity to christen, himself, all the children Mr – had refused; so when he returned he found it all done and registered, with the obnoxious godfathers and godmothers. Also, Master D— took upon himself to marry an English soldier to a Heathen woman, together with various other *scappate* of less importance, but very provoking. Poor – felt himself uncommonly hurt, as he often does, and appealed to the Bishop. He showed us the Bishop's answer, which was really beautiful; condemning all D—'s misdemeanors, and at the same time giving – such good and wise advice about his own vagaries, and yet so kindly and delicately expressed, and the whole tone of the letter so humble and Christianlike, that it was quite a pattern. All the young hands are quite wild about these new ideas concerning baptism. A— asked young B—, a slip of eighteen, to stand *proxy* for one of the godfathers at our baby's christening: B— said he could not possibly do it, because, if he were a proxy, he should feel called upon to remonstrate with the parents concerning their way of bringing up the child. A— explained that we by no means wished him to be godfather, and asked whether he knew the difference between that and proxy. No, he did not, but still "felt sure it must be wrong." Fancy a young chap like that thinking he *must* know best about

LETTER TWENTY-FOUR

education, and that his "remonstrances" would inevitably be wanted! He is a good lad too, only somewhat pragmatical and solemn. H— did not think it wrong to be proxy, but discoursed considerably on a variety of duties of a godfather, which being quite new to me, I ventured to inquire whether he found them in the Bible or the Prayer Book. "Why, neither," said he, "but I am sure they must be *somewhere!*"

April 16th – Do you know that Government has abolished the pilgrim-tax? It is a very good step towards leaving off their encouragement of idolatry. Mr Hamilton received a letter from a Missionary who lives at one of the "Holy Shrines", giving an account of the last festival since the tax; and the compulsory attendance of the natives to drag the cars has been done away with. That part of his letter is so curious that I will copy it for you.

I have just returned from a large Heathen festival held at the famous *Beejanuggur*. It is pleasing to find that the Company have remitted the tax this year to visitors, and I hear they have had nothing to do with the usual expenses of decoration of the car, &c. No military were present as is usual; notwithstanding, the attendance was unprecedentedly small: I do not suppose there were above fifteen thousand persons present, when last year there were seventy thousand; the year before, near one hundred thousand; and when Mr Hands, twenty-five years ago, attended, the usual number was about two hundred thousand. This is a pleasing indication of the decline of idolatry. The scarcity of provisions and water, and the fear of cholera, no doubt kept many away; but the decrease of interest in the superstitions of the country, I hope, a larger number. I do hope that three or four years will shut up the festivities of Beejanuggur for ever. The Anagoondy Rajah brought all his people, and used all his influence; but the large car could only be drawn a few yards on the first day, and, on the next day, instead of taking it to the end of the street, from which, had they conveyed it there, they never could have got it back, they brought it home to its place within about three yards, when, being quite exhausted, they left it there.

April 19th – I have received a message from a Bramin, who sends word that he keeps a school in the village, but has no books, and would be very glad "if Mistress please to give some books to teach the boys." You see that is a very good thing, because we can introduce Christian books instead of the histories of their gods. The misfortune is, there are not above six or eight books published in Gentoo, and those are religious tracts and disquisitions that children cannot possibly understand. Nobody knows how much elementary books for the natives are wanted. There was once a School-book Society, but it has dwindled to nothing; and once there was a sort of Native College at Madras for educating Moonshees, and Government was thinking of establishing schools up the country. Several were established; and though they were not Christian schools, they were much better than nothing; but they are all done away with now: there are neither schools nor college. Still, if every civilian up the country were to have a poor little school like ours, it would do something in time; but numbers of them disapprove, as they say, of everything of the kind. Mr L— set up a school at Cocanada: he had fifty boys and a capital master, much better than ours; but he was not here when we took ours, and now we do not like to turn ours away, as he does his best. L—'s school was going on very nicely when he was obliged to return to England on sick certificate: he asked the Collector to keep up his school, but the Collector thought the natives were better without education, and refused: so the school is broken up, for which I am very sorry.

The boys in our school take the trouble to copy for themselves all the question-and-answer lessons on Scripture History, &c., which we compose for them. A— and I write the English, Moonshee translates it, and the boys learn by heart and transcribe both the English and the Gentoo.

LETTER TWENTY-FOUR

A— and I had been lamenting very much the breaking up of Mr L—'s school, and if ever we leave Rajahmundry very likely our own will share the same fate: it depends entirely upon our successor. While we were thinking so much on the subject, A— made me write a letter to one of the Madras newspapers, with the results of our cogitations and calculations; and I will copy it for you, as I know you like to hear all our schemes and plans.

NATIVE EDUCATION
To the Editor of 'The Spectator'

SIR, – Your paper is so well known as a willing medium for the communication of any suggestions tending to the benefit of the native population, that I venture to request the insertion of a few remarks upon a plan for the more general diffusion of native education. At present all attempts for the improvement of the natives of this Presidency are confined to private, I might almost say to individual, exertions, which of course are capable of but very partial success. What is required is national education, a boon far exceeding the limited means of a few individuals to bestow. Government only can confer it; but government can, and ought. I doubt not that there exists in the mind of our rulers the wish to improve by education the condition of their native subjects, if it could be accomplished without risk to our dominion, or too heavy an expenditure of public money.

The "auld warld" prejudice of "risk to our dominion" is, I suppose, exploded amongst all who are really acquainted with the native character. It still holds its sway among those whose knowledge of India is limited to the Presidency, and whose native acquaintance extends only to a few writers in government offices; but really experienced Europeans, who have been long *in* the country and *up* the country – who are conversant with the native languages, customs, habits of thought, wishes, and prejudices – know, beyond the possibility of doubt or mistake, how eager the natives are for education, and how grateful for its being in any way facilitated. A European in the provinces has but to open a school of any description in his district, and it is immediately filled beyond the power of one master to superintend. Even with regard to the books used, it is altogether a *presidency prejudice* that the natives are averse to being taught from books of our selecting. They never even consider the matter, but receive, without an idea of hesitating, whatever we may choose to direct. Their difficulties and objections have, I fully

APRIL 1839

believe, been mainly elicited and encouraged by Europeans themselves. I can confidently appeal, for the accuracy of these statements, to any and every European who has himself fairly tried the establishment of native schools, in which truth should be taught, whether on religious subjects or on matters of general information.

Among some persons who are favourable in a general way to the establishment of schools, there still prevails the strange fallacy that we may venture to teach the natives truth on subjects of science, history, &c., but that we must use their own religious books in our schools, and, in fact, teach nothing but falsehood on matters connected with religion. Such arguers forget, or do not know, that what is physical science with us is religious doctrine with the Hindoos. We cannot teach them the most common known fact – such, for instance, as that the earth is suspended in space, instead of being perched upon an elephant, or that an eclipse is caused by a shadow instead of a snake – without overturning two or three dozen of their religious tenets: therefore, if we are to teach them nothing that is contrary to their own notions of religion, we must just leave them where they are on all other subjects; which procedure, or rather non-procedure, I believe few persons are quite prepared to advocate.

The expense of Government national education is, I conceive, greatly over-calculated, or rather over-estimated, for it is probably not calculated at all. A valuable and comprehensive Government general education might be given at a very moderate outlay, by the following plan.

Let there be four schools at Madras, one of which should be considered the central or model school; one at the principal station of every Zillah, and one in every Talook;* all, of course, free, unless it should be thought desirable to establish some payment at the Presidency central school, which might be rendered and considered superior to the rest, and would be chiefly attended by boys of the higher and richer classes. At the Presidency and station schools English should be taught, and a good substantial education given. In the Talook schools English would be unnecessary, but education should be carried on in the native languages to whatever extent the books published in those languages render possible. The Madras schools should be under the superintendence and direction of a Board of Education, and the provincial schools under that of the principal European residents at their respective stations. There should be a certain number of books authorized by government, and a fixed general plan, upon which all the schools should be conducted; but it appears to me expedient not to lay unnecessary restrictions upon the European

---

* A smaller division of the district.

superintendents' occasionally introducing additional hooks or trifling modifications of the system, according to their judgment. If they be too much fettered and restricted, they will naturally take less interest in the work, and their superintendence will be proportionably inefficient.

Now, let us calculate the expense. I believe one lac of rupees* per annum would amply cover the whole. There are twenty districts in the Madras Presidency, and altogether about two hundred and forty Talooks. Native teachers up the country may be engaged at from five to ten rupees per month. Houses in the villages may be bought, built, or hired for a few rupees per annum; and certainly the whole cost of the Talook schools, including cadjan, paper, pens, books, and sundries, need never exceed twenty rupees per month. This may even, in most cases, be reduced by the schoolmaster being paid by the grant of a small piece of land, free of taxes; and this land might be considered as an endowment, and always be the property of the school-master for the time being. The expense of the station schools, where English should be taught, would be about fifty rupees per month; of the Madras three minor schools, one hundred and fifty rupees per month; and of the superior one, to which the scholars might contribute, three hundred and fifty rupees per month.

Now, let us sum up the whole: -

	Rupees
240 schools, at 20 rupees per month	4800
40, viz., 2 in each district – one under the collector and one under the Judge, at 50 rupees per month	2000
3 at Madras, at 150 rupees per month	450
1 do., at 350 rupees per month	350
Total	7600

or ninety-one thousand two hundred rupees per annum; and allowing the overplus for sundries and unforeseen expenses, I think there can be no doubt that education might be diffused over the Madras Presidency for the sum of one hundred thousand rupees per annum, even allowing for all being paid in hard money, which need not be the case if the system were adopted of attaching a piece of land to the situation of schoolmaster.

I am, Sir,
    Yours obediently,
        MATTER OF FACT

---

* Ten thousand pounds.

MAY 1839

May 7th – The scarcity is over now. Government gave a great deal of money to spend among the poor. Our Collector gave A— fifty pounds of it, all of which he laid out in grain for the workers, both men and women. They have made several miles of beautiful high road, deepened tanks, and dug a well – the well is a very great acquisition to this place; you may suppose, in such a climate, how glad the people always are of additional water. A— was so pleased with his well that he sent all the way to it, a mile off, for water to christen our new baby!

Samuldavy, May 10th – The Bombay monsoon has just set in, so there will probably be the same delay in the steamers as there was last year; wherefore I intend this letter to go by an old ship. It is very hot now – land-wind all day – very bad. However, I do not suppose it will last many days; and then, whatever sea-breeze there is we shall have in full perfection.

In your last you ask how our potato plan answered during the famine: we were unable even to try it, for, owing to the difficulties of carriage in India, the potatoes did not arrive at Rajahmundry till the season for planting them was completely over. There were contrary winds, which prevented ships from coming quickly, and there are no roads in our district – nor, indeed, scarcely anywhere to the north of Madras. People say that, if Government would spend money sufficient to make good roads, it would be repaid over and over again in the increased trade and traffic; but there are very few who care about the matter, so it dawdles on. Rich people travel four miles an hour on men's shoulders; poor people walk; and luggage waits for an opportunity by sea.

May 14th – We are going to set up a school at Samuldavy for Gentoo only; we could not manage an English school here. The Missionary Beer came the other day, dined with me, and went to preach in the topes. A Bramin brought the tracts I had given, and asked Beer to explain them, as he said they were very fine, but nobody could understand them. He requested Beer to establish a school here, and said there

LETTER TWENTY-FOUR

would be plenty of boys glad to attend. So we are going to set one up, and Beer is to come now and then from Narsapoor to superintend it when we are at Rajahmundry. The head man of the village has offered to build a school-house himself — you know their houses are only sheds.

We have just had a long visit from a young Rajah, whose ambition is to engraft the character of an English dandy on that of a native don; and the result is, a sort of king of twelfth-cake. He goes about in an English palanquin with native penny flags by its side; and adds to his national muslin gown, and gold Rajah's cap, a pair of satin trousers, and a green satin waistcoat, embroidered with pearls. He wanted to show A— some papers, so one of his attendants brought in an English leather writing-desk, and Twelfth-Cake proceeded to twiddle at the lock, turning the key round the wrong way, clicking the bolt, and fumbling and fidgeting for full five minutes before he could get it open. By and by he produced an enormous silver watch, like a prize-turnip, with six chains, and begged to set it by our watches. He made a great fuss with the seal and key, but contrived it at last, and sat down again, looking as proud as an infant schoolboy — and almost as clever. He professed a wish to make his name famous, so A— advised him to educate the people in his Zemindary, and especially to be the first to establish a girls' school. He promised that he would set up both a girls' and a boys' school; and looked at spelling-books, asked directions about building a school-house, and really seemed in earnest. I wish he may keep in the same mind, for he is a person of sufficient consequence to make the innovation, and to carry it through; but I fear it will all end in buying shaving-glasses and penny prints to stick up in his house.

Our last papers bring an account of a society in England for protecting the natives of India, with a very clever and true speech from a Mr Thompson — who is he? He puts a few tigers and boa constrictors into his speech, just to keep up

MAY 1839

attention, I suppose; but it is a capital speech; and his accounts of the shameful taxation, &c., &c., are not in the least exaggerated.

The troops have been short of food and water, owing to the bad arrangements of the Commissariat, and altogether the war is said to be grievously ill-managed.

There is now an opportunity for sending letters *viâ* Beyrout, so I shall despatch this, as there is no ship now in the roads; but ten to one the Arabs or their dromedaries will eat up my letter.

"No more news to report, but I beg always to keep much regard upon me ; – excuse me." That is the proper Native manner of ending a letter politely.

Notes
The babies and I: Julia gave birth to a son on 3 February 1839, 'what I always wished for.' She had what she describes as a very easy confinement of four and a half hours; 'my son is a most superb baby....my stupendous son.' From this point, Julia refers to her eldest child by name in her letters, rather than as 'Baby'. She is sensitive to her mother being reminded of her dead daughter (see note to Letter One): 'If it is painful for you to hear our baby called Etta, we can call her by her second name. It was one of my reasons for giving her two names.' Julia's son was christened James Cambridge Thomas by the Rev. Shortland. The child's sponsors were Archdeacon Cambridge, Elizabeth Jenyns and a favourite cousin to James Thomas, Philip Secretan. Julia wrote of Etta at this time: 'She is a curious little mimic and actress, making most intelligible signs for everything that she cannot say' (1 April 1839). And Etta gradually overcame her jealousy of her little brother: 'The other night I was surprised to see the Ayah come home in the tonjon with the baby on her lap and Etta sitting cramped up on the seat, sucking her thumb, and holding on by Ayah's ear, as good as gold. I asked the old woman how she had contrived such an arrangement, but she said "Missy self make order" and now everyday she "makes order" the same, and will not get into the tonjon till she sees the "Baba" first settled in it.' James she went on to describe as 'a fine sturdy fellow, very fat and strong and somewhat passionate' (10 April 1839).

magic lantern: Julia and her husband had first tried this out themselves. 'We are both enchanted with it – it is the prettiest invention I ever saw – we mean to show it to all our Europe ladies and gentlemen for a treat at our dinner parties' (9 March 1839).

LETTER TWENTY-FOUR

Mr. G, Mr Hamilton, Mr.H: all Jellicoe.

our clerical friend, D——, B——: the Reverend Shortland, Dowdeswell, young Boswell,.

pilgrim-tax: the *Bombay Courier* complained in an article in May 1839, 'Every cruel penance, every religious station, every heathen procession, every absurd devotion, every ablution, every offering, every prostration in India, was taxed for the benefits of the honourable company, and their honourable servants.'

the famous Beejanuggur:Vijayanagar was the capital of the Hindu Vijayanagar empire, at its height in the early sixteenth century and covering all India south of the Kistna river. It is now visited as the ruin Hampi.

School-book Society...Native College: by October Julia is writing that her husband and Walter Elliot were interested in reviving the School Book Society. James Thomas had renewed his subscription to the Native Education School in September of the previous year when news had arrived that a Mr Green from Cambridge had been sent as Master. *The Fort St. George Gazette* reported in August 1838, 'The Committee of the Native Education Society have the satisfaction of stating that a Gentleman has arrived from England to take charge of their seminary – Mr Green, B.A., a graduate of the University of Cambridge.' Experience of four years has shown that 'the superior classes' of the Native community are 'sending their youth to them to be educated.' The Committee points out that the school needs further funding and are soliciting subscriptions – hoping to get these from 'those interested in the advancement of liberal education among the higher order of Natives.' The curriculum was in Grammar, Maths, Scriptures.

Mr L——: Binning.

The Spectator is listed in the *Madras Almanac* as a twice weekly paper published by C. Sooboo Moodelly. No surviving copies of the paper were available for consultation.

topes: a grove of trees, often mango.

a society in England: George Thompson (1804-78), anti-slavery advocate, took part in forming the British India Association.

Letter the Twenty-Fifth

Samuldavy, June 10th, 1839

The day before yesterday was Etta's birth day – two years old; so we had a feast in her honour. Feasts are cheap enough among these poor creatures; ours cost a guinea and a half and fed five hundred people. We gave them rice, which is equivalent to roast beef and plum-pudding in England. They live on a cheaper sort of grain; and many of them cannot even get that, but live on such herbs and roots as they can pick up.

One cannot cook their dinners for them, and see them eat it, as one would at an English feast; but each person had a portion given to him enough for two meals, and took it home. They all sat down near the house, in rows; and Master, and servants, and Peons, measured out the rice, while Etta and I sat and looked on; but *she* soon grew tired of it. I noticed one old squinny man, with a long white beard, who sat a great way off from the rest, very solemn and dignified; a most grand grub, with his old wife at a respectable distance behind him. We found he was a decayed Rajah, who was thankful to come and receive his share of rice with the beggars! They were all very much pleased with their feast, and next morning many of them came back, to pick up, grain by grain, what little had been scattered on the ground in measuring it out.

A— has established a school here, at Samuldavy; and the schoolmaster is willing to teach with our books, so he and his boys have begun with St Matthew. They read, transcribe, and learn it by heart, and come once a-week to A— to be examined; the greatest difficulty in schools is, the want of schoolbooks in the native languages.

A little while ago two young Parsees were baptized at Bombay, and there is every reason to suppose they were real

LETTER TWENTY-FIVE

converts: their countrymen were furious, and assembled in crowds around them, as they left the church, using most violent menaces; and there were great apprehensions of a serious uproar, but the two young Christians were rescued. The Government have taken measures to protect them and keep the peace, and all is quiet again. I believe it never was anything more than the bluster of a mob, but the poor boys might have been hurt.

There is just a chance of a move for us soon: two appointments are vacant, to either of which A— has the first claim – *Sta a vedere*.

What you say about Governors giving appointments, and people fitting themselves for them afterwards, is very true in England, but it is not the case here. There is a regular rule, established by Act of Parliament, that people of a certain standing are entitled to certain appointments, and the Governor has no right to act contrary to it. He may very well choose among those of the *requisite standing,* and give the appointment to whichever may be his favourite; but he has no right to make "the lag of the school captain". *That* is the innovation complained of here: the natives say, "Lord E— is fond of doing justice, but does not know how."

Masulipatam, July 4th – "A change came o'er the spirit of my dream!" I *now* look upon Lord E— as a most excellent Governor, and W— E— as an admirable Private Secretary. A great many things have happened since I wrote last. A— is appointed "Acting First Judge of Circuit in the Centre Division," and with every prospect of being confirmed permanently, either as First or Second Judge, at the end of the year; the real holder of the appointment being expected to go home in January. It is not *quite* certain that we shall remain there, but very probable; and if we do, we can have nothing more to wish. It is a most capital appointment – high rank, high pay, good climate, and pretty country; at all events, we shall never return to Rajahmundry, and are now *en route* to

JULY 1839

our new station. The only drawback is, that A— is obliged to go on circuit directly, and to begin by two very hot places, Cuddapah and Bellary, to which he does not like to take the babies and me. We are therefore to stay at Madras with his brother, till he has finished all the Cuddapah and Bellary business; then we shall join him, and go the rest of the circuit with him, to Chingleput and Cuddalore, which are both of them cool and pleasant. The name of the place we are to live at when stationary is Chittoor. It is said to be healthy and pretty, with fine gardens and plenty of grapes; hot in summer; but there is a beautiful place, called Palmanair, within twenty miles of it, very high and quite cool – a most delightful climate. We shall also be within two hundred miles of the Neilgherries, so we *can* go thither if necesssary, and within one hundred and twenty miles of Cuddalore, a good sea-coast.

We are both of us exceedingly pleased, and "quite content".

July 6th – We are now fairly on our road.

Besides all our own attendants, in number a hundred and fifty, there are divers "camp followers", such as Amah's husband, Ayah's grub, &c., &c. We proceed, on an average, about twenty-five miles a-night, and rest every day, and on Sunday night, and any other night if we are fatigued. Masulipatam was an ugly place; a swamp, two miles broad, between the town and the sea; nothing to be seen but wide sandy roads, with prickly-pear hedges, enclosing black-looking Palmyra-trees, and red-tiled houses peeping (no, not *peeping,* they are not coquette enough for that – *staring*) out from among them; altogether, a most *vapid* sort of place. The Twelfth-cake Rajah paid us a visit there, to ask all particulars about our school, as he thinks of keeping it up. We had plenty of curious farewell letters from the natives at Rajahmundry; one of them says "he depends entirely upon the protection of A—'s sublime feet, and Mistress Mama!"

LETTER TWENTY-FIVE

Ramiahpatam, July 15th – We have been halting here for two or three days, and were met by the best of all company, viz., nearly a dozen English letters brought by the two steamers of April and May, which arrived within three days of each other.

Madras, July 31st – We arrived here, babies and I, on the 23rd, and A— on the same day at his destination, Cuddapah. He was able to come with us to within two nights' run of Madras; and we had Servants and Peons, and made the rest of our journey without any difficulty. We are living about six or seven miles from Madras, on the very beach, and enjoy the sea-air much: this situation is cooler and drier than Samuldavy.

Miss T— is very busy now with a school for half-caste young ladies, which seems likely to be very useful. Those half-caste girls are in the depths of ignorance, indolence, and worthlessness, and utterly neglected; they have no ideas but of dress and making love – one girl brought forty gowns to school! Our schoolmaster's sister at Rajahmundry (who was a half-caste) came very seldom to church; but, when she did, she used to be dressed in white shoes, gold chains, earrings, two or three brooches, and all such rubbish.

The poor Female Orphan Asylum is as bad as ever: Lady N—, the present Commander-in-Chief's lady, takes an interest in it, and is very sensible in her propositions, such as the teaching them washing, plain work, &c., &c., but the other ladies do not co-operate with her. If I come to live at Madras, I do not think I shall be likely to take a part in it, because A— has a great objection to the institution itself, though he would let me help if I wished to do so. But it is very bad – professedly for orphans of European soldiers, while scarcely any of them really are orphans; and the half-caste young left-handed ladies look down upon the poor little honestly-born Europeans, and boast of being "gentlemen's children;" and they go out visiting their relatives without shame or ceremony.

There is always something doing in the way of schools, and certainly an increasing desire among the natives for instruction, and an increasing willingness to receive our books. Towards the south they are more bigoted, and their bigotry is greatly encouraged by timid or ungodly Europeans, who really put objections into their heads; but at Rajahmundry, where they had never heard of hesitations and difficulties, we used to receive applications for books from distant villages, and especially for any portions of Scripture; and the people used to sit in our reading-room for hours, copying our books on their own little cadjan-leaves. It is very remarkable that here, at Madras, people are declining to help the schools in which the Bible is taught, under the old pretence of its being "a dangerous interference with Native feelings", &c.; while, not two streets from the English school, which is dwindling away for want of support, there is a common native Braminee school, in which the Bramin master uses the Bible as a school-book, of his own accord, because he happens to like it; and no idea of difficulty enters his mind or those of his scholars, though they are all Heathens of a high and prejudiced caste. The Missionaries publish many tracts, of which some are very good, but the greater number are not sufficiently simple, and the natives cannot understand them; and the tracts which come from England are altogether *un-Indian,* and unfit to translate. We want an Indian Hannah More.

I wish I could tell you anything satisfactory about the Tanjore Mission; there is much talk of pruning and purifying it. The church at Tinnevelly will very soon be begun; the plan and site are settled, and all is in progress.

You ask what news I can give you of the "caste question". It is all as undecided as ever. People, even religious people, take such very different views of the matter, that the discussions are never ended. A——, and his brother, and many others, look upon caste as a mixed usage, partly civil and partly religious; and they think it will only be broken down

LETTER TWENTY-FIVE

by education, and that many of the native Christians who still adhere to it are among the most satisfactory of the converts; but they think that those who do so should only be employed as schoolmasters or catechists, and not be considered fit for *Ordination*. The Bishop, however, looks upon caste as entirely a distinction of rank, and has lately ordained a native Christian who will not give it up – others insist upon its being altogether a religious distinction, and will not even acknowledge as Christians those who do not renounce it. Mr T— was wishing lately to have a series of meetings for freely discussing the subject – the principal native Christians to take part in it, besides the English gentlemen who differ so much in their views. I, in my ignorance, thought it a very pretty plan and likely to be useful; but the wiser heads thought it would do no good, and I believe it is given up.

August 9th – A— is still on duty at Cuddapah, a place noted for fever, which can only be kept off by violent exercise. This *he* is able to take, so that his health does not suffer: he tells me he is quite well, notwithstanding very hard work. He is employed on criminal trials, most of them for life or death; and he says the incessant falsehood to which he is obliged to listen is most painful and wearing, – witnesses by scores coming forward to swear away the life of another, and often the only motive some petty spite, – and no shame or disgrace felt, even when detected! Certainly, the first characteristic of Heathenism is *lying!* A— has met with a good painstaking Dissenting Missionary there – a Mr Howell, whom he is helping in his books, schools, &c., &c. Old civilians, like him and J—, generally know much more of the people, and the languages and customs, than the Missionaries do, and can be of great use to them.

Have you heard yet in England of the horrors that took place at the funeral of that wretched old RUNJEET SINGH? *Four* wives and *seven* slave-girls were burnt with him; and not a word even of remonstrance from the British Government!

AUGUST 1839

J— says there cannot be a doubt that a word of disapprobation from the British Resident would have stopped it at once, for the whole power of the Punjaub depends on our will, and they profess to follow our wishes in everything. Is it not shocking? The four Ranees burnt themselves at their own desire, from pride of family and caste; but the poor slave-girls could have had no such motives, and must have been burnt by the wretches around them. One Grandee *man* pretended he meant to burn himself too, and could scarcely be persuaded against it; but I believe his was all sham: he knew very well they would not let him, because he was useful to the country. When poor old Runjeet Singh was dying, he gave away in charities and offerings to the Bramins, in order to propitiate the gods, treasure worth a million sterling. He was enormously rich, having never hesitated to steal anything he could lay his hands on. He wanted to give the immense diamond he stole from Shah Soojah, but his courtiers persuaded him not.

Here is another disgraceful story of English ungodliness. When Shah Soojah arrived at his capital, Candahar, he and all his Mussulmans went directly to pay their devotions to a rag of Mohammed's shirt, which is kept there as a precious relic. Of course, all the Mussulmans had a right to do so, and no one would think of preventing them; but think of *our Envoy* and the British troops and authorities all accompanying him in state on such an errand! I could scarcely believe it, but it is really true.

August 14th – Preparations are making for a Burmese war, and the Indian newspapers are full of Colonel Burney's wisdom, and wishing they had followed his advice long ago. There has been a *"petite drôlerie"* in the way of treason, headed by the Nizam's brother, but it was found out and stopped long before it came to anything. The old experienced hands quiz it like the *"petits spectacles"* in Paris, but some of the younger Collectors, who were not accustomed to such matters, were rather frightened, and one Collectress told me very solemnly

LETTER TWENTY-FIVE

that she understood it had been distinctly announced in the mosques that all the English ladies were to be seized and made slaves of. If you hear any frightful stories, *non pensi,* for it is all fudge. There is another little Rajah trying at a little rebellion fifty miles from the place at which A— now is; and a couple of regiments are sent to settle his mind. J— says as soon as he sees the red-coats and Sepoys he will give in; but, poor man! I am rather sorry for him – he has been four or five years collecting arms and ammunition and concocting his little rebellion, and of course his property will be confiscated, and his independent kingdom, such as it is, done away – and, after all, we shall only have *"conquered a green blight,"* like Frank when he was a little boy.

I am very glad those insects I sent were so curious, and that you gave the new specimens to the British Museum. No doubt I shall be able to send you plenty more: I do not at all recollect which they were, but in future I will keep numbered duplicates, that I may learn their names. Pray, ask Mr Samouelle what names were given to the five new species, and let me know.

I really believe the Madras ladies spend all their time in writing notes – *"chits",* as they are called. I do not know ten people now, and yet there never passes a day without my having one or two "chits" to answer – what with writing them, composing them, finding my penknife, mending my pen, hunting for proper note-paper, which is always hidden in some scribbled foolscap beginnings of tracts, or such-like, all my morning is hindered; – and their chits are generally only to say "how sorry they are they have not been able to call lately, that I must have wondered at it, and *thought,*" &c., &c. Now, I never *think* about it, – "*les absens*", &c., – and I would always rather they did not call, because I must sit all day with my hair dressed and my best clothes on, waiting for them; and remember the thermometer is at 92°. I am going to-morrow to Mrs W—E—. I have not been able to call on her

AUGUST 1839

yet, because we live so far off that I quite dread going out for a *morning* visit according to this horrid Madras fashion. If I see her I shall say that I cannot come in the morning, and beg her to come to me in the evening; but for the first visit there is no help: – just now the weather is cloudy; so I shall take advantage of it before it clears up.

Notes

two young Parsees were baptised: the case of the two young Parsees, Dhunjeebhoy and Hormasjee, was reported by the *Bombay Courier* in May. Some in the Parsee community believed the young men had been forcibly converted. A British show of force at the court house, where a decision was to be made as to the nature of the conversions, inflamed the Parsee community which saw it as an 'attempt on the part of the Government to uphold the cause of the religion professed by its leading functionaries.' Many Parsees were said to have withdrawn their children from the Mission Schools.

the wig of the school captain: she added, 'that is his system. I call Ld Elph, Walter Elliot's Cypher, as he sets his seal to whatever Walter Elliot chuses – However there is this to be said for them both – they do no real mischief, there is no wickedness in any of their arrangements' (10 June 1839).

Walter Elliot had been in India since 1821. From 1837 he was Private Secretary to the Governor and Third Member of the Board of Revenue.

"A change came o'er the spirit of my dream!": she quotes from Byron's poem, 'The Dream'.

Miss T— is very busy: Miss Tucker.

Lady N—: Lady Nicholls, wife of Sir Jaspar Nicholls, Sir Peregrine's replacement.

Tanjore: Thanjavur was the ancient capital of the Chola kingdom, at its most powerful between the 9th and 13th centuries. The town is dominated by the Brihadeshwara Temple, a masterpiece of Chola temple architecture.

Hannah More (1745-1833), religious writer. Julia refers to the plain talking of Hannah More's tracts; she may also have been interested in her services to education.

Mr T—: the letter is missing but this is probably Mr Tucker.

J— John Thomas, her brother-in-law. His wife Diana had died in May, and Julia received the news when she was in Samuldavee, 'she was a most kind and affectionate and sisterly friend to me....Poor John can scarcely yet "realise it" Mr Tucker says; it was so completely unexpected' (1 June 1839).

old Runjeet Singh (1780-1839), the Sikh ruler, the Maharajah of Lahore, 'this faithful and highly valued Ally' as the *Fort St. George Gazette* described him. Ranjit Singh had united the Punjab and under his rule had made it a prosperous state. Ten years of rivalry, confusion and war over the succession led to the forced annexation of the Punjab in 1849. Dalip Singh, Ranjit Singh's youngest son, was forced, for himself and his successors, to give up all rights to the sovereignty of the Punjab. The immense diamond Julia mentions is, of course, the Koh-i-nor, which Dalip Singh was forced to surrender to Queen Victoria after the annexation by the British of the Sikh kingdom in 1849.

Shah Soojah: the early stages of the Afghan war. Shah Shuja was returned to Afghanistan by the British and installed as ruler of Afghanistan. See note to Letter Twenty-One.

a Burmese war: this is a false alarm.

Nizam's brother....another little Rajah: see note on Kurnool, Letter Twenty-Seven.

new specimens: the Natural History Museum has a record of Julia's entomological specimens under Zoological donations (Entomology was part of Zoology until 1913), '1839 June 8 Fine specimens of Coleoptera from Madras. Presented by Mrs Barrett.' The Entomology department can no longer find specimens to correspond with this. Julia described what she sent as 'one or two beetles – there is one which looks to me very like a [Bapristi Pisana?] – It was found on a fig tree in the compound – we have all hunted well but couldn't find another' (21 December 1837).

Mrs W—E—: Mrs Walter Elliot.

"Les absens," &c, &c: A footnote in 1843 reads: 'Alluding to the recorded speeech of a French lady, who exclaimed, "Je ne sais d'ou cela vient, mais les absens me passent toujours de l'âme!"'

Julia was now occupied over the summer by a new writing project. 'I am busy with a new concoction – Pharaoh and I have got a doing of a Pocket-book for Indian Ladies – in imitation of Chte Elliots – only mine is to be composed of extracts from books which the ladies ought to read and don't – Pharaoh is to publish it at his own expense, and I am to prepare it for nothing the first time' (13 June 1839).

Letter the Twenty-Sixth

Madras, September 24th, 1839

Here is the steamer going, and almost gone, and my letter for it not begun, though I have a whole steamer-load of things to say, and scarcely know where to begin; but I have been hindered by an attack of Indian fever, and the baby also has been ill, and the doctors talk very seriously of the desirableness of my sending her home. That is the grand Indian sorrow – the necessity of parting with one's children. However, she is still so young that we hope change of air may possibly be sufficient for her; and therefore A— will fetch us, and leave us at Bangalore, a cool place in the table-land above the ghauts, while he continues his circuit to Bellary, which he thinks too hot for us.

September 30*th* – I have been paying a round of visits to all my Madras acquaintances: they seem just in the same state in which I left them, with nothing in this world to do. You can scarcely imagine such a life of inanity. A thorough Madras lady, in the course of the day, goes about a good deal to shops and auctions; buys a great many things she does not want, without inquiring the price; has plenty of books, but seldom reads – it is too hot, or she has not time – *liking to "have her time her own",* I suppose, like old Lady Q—; receives a number of morning visitors; takes up a little worsted work; goes to tiffin with Mrs C., unless Miss D. comes to tiffin with her; and writes some dozen of "*chits.*" Every inquiry after an acquaintance must be made in writing, as the servants can never understand or deliver a message, and would turn every "politesse" into an insult. These incessant *chits* are an immense trouble and interruption; but the ladies seem to like them, and sit at their desks with more zeal and perseverance than their

LETTER TWENTY-SIX

husbands in their cutcherries. But when it comes to any really interesting occupation, it is pitiable to see the torpor of every faculty – worse than torpor: their minds seem to evaporate under this Indian sun, never to be condensed or concentrated again. The seven-years' sleep of the Beauty in the fairy-tale was nothing to the seven-years' lethargy of a beauty's residence in Madras, for the fairy lady awoke to her former energies, which I should think they never can.

Chittoor, October 8*th* – Here we are on our travels again in our way to Bangalore. This Chittoor is a very pretty place, with beautiful views all around, but the houses and gardens are so choked up with trees, that we can see nothing – I should like to cut down half of them. Our road lies through the most picturesque country I have yet seen in India, and I enjoy the scenery in the evenings and early mornings when I am not asleep. We are obliged to outrun all the servants, except the ayahs, who travel in palanquins like ourselves, so we manage rather, as Mr Wilberforce used to say, "in the wild-beast way" in the daytime, but very comfortably notwithstanding. We have a towel for a table-cloth, plantain-leaves when dishes are not forthcoming, and we put the palanquin-cushions on the floor for sofas. Travelling by night, lying down in a palanquin, is much less fatiguing to me than sitting upright all day in an English carriage.

Bangalore, October 12*th* – We arrived here yesterday safe and well, after a *pretty considerable* journey – seven nights travelling, with a rest of two days and nights half-way. We always stop on Sundays, but last Sunday night our rest did not do us much good, for in the middle of the night another travelling lady arrived at the bungalow. We had spread ourselves over all the rooms, thinking nobody else was likely to come at that time, and were very comfortably asleep, when I had to rise and scuffle my things out into the other half of the building, through the verandah, in a heavy rain, which was not at all pleasant; after which, some thieves came and ran away with a bundle of the bearers' clothes, so they were making an uproar, howling and yelling the whole night.

October 16th – I am charmed with Bangalore, and hope it will do us all a great deal of good. The climate at this time of the year is delightful, equal to any in Europe. For the first two or three days there was a good deal of fog, but it has now cleared away, and all is so cool, clear, and bright, that it is quite a pleasure to feel oneself breathing. The early mornings especially are as pleasant as anything I can imagine: they have all the sweetness and freshness of an English summer. The air smells of hay and flowers, instead of ditches, dust, fried oil, curry, and onions, which are the *best* of the Madras smells. There are superb dahlias growing in the gardens, and today I saw a real staring full-blown hollyhock, which was like meeting an old friend from England, instead of the tuberoses, pomegranates, &c., I have been accustomed to see for the last two years. We have apples, pears, and peaches, and I really should know them one from the other, though it must be confessed there is a considerable family likeness, strongly reminding us of a potato; still they look like English fruit: and the boys bring baskets of raspberries for sale, which are very like blackberries indeed. The English children are quite fat and rosy, and wear shoes and stockings.

There are fire-places in most of the houses, and no punkahs in any of them. It is altogether very pleasant, but a queer place – a sort of cross-breed between the watering-places of every country in the world. Ladies going about dressed to every pitch of distraction they can invent, with long curls which the heat would not allow for an hour elsewhere, and warm close bonnets with flowers hanging in and out of them like queens of the May; black niggers, naked or not, as suits their taste; an English church, a Heathen pagoda, botanical garden, public ball-rooms, Dissenting meeting-house, circulating library, English shops, and Parsee merchants, all within sight of each other; elephants and horses walking together in pleasant company over a great green plain in front of our house, where the soldiers exercise; European soldiers and Sepoys meeting at every step; an evening promenade, where people take good brisk walks at an English pace, and chirp like English sparrows, while a band of blackies play "God save the Queen" and call it the "General Salute." There is a fine old fort here – Tippoo's stronghold; a most curious place, adjoining the old native town, surrounded with mud walls *to be strong!* The Pettah it is called. The English ladies told me this Pettah was "a horrid place – quite native!" and advised me never to go into it; so I went next day, of course, and found it most curious – really *"quite native"*. It is *crammed* with inhabitants, and they bustle and hum like bees in a beehive. At first I thought my bearers would scarcely be able to make their way through the crowd of men, women, children, and monkeys, which thronged the street. The ground was covered with shops all spread out in the dirt; the monkeys were scrambling about in all directions, jumping, chattering, and climbing all over the roofs of the houses, and up and down the door-posts – hundreds of them; the children quarrelling, screaming, laughing, and rolling in the dust – hundreds of *them* too – in good imitation of the monkeys; the men smoking, quarrelling, chatting, and bargaining; the women covered with jewels, gossiping at their doors, with screams at each other that set my teeth on edge, and one or two that were very industrious, painting their door-steps instead of sweeping them; and native music to crown the whole. Such confusion was never seen! Landing at Naples is nothing to it. As I came out of the gate I met some young Moorish dandies on horseback; one of them was evidently a "crack rider", and began to show off – as great a fool as Count P—. He reined up his ragged horse, facing me and dancing about till I had passed; then he dashed past me at full gallop, wheeled round and charged my tonjon, bending down to his saddle-bow, and pretending to throw a lance, showing his teeth, and uttering a

OCTOBER 1839

loud quack! That quack was really too killing. I am busy now making a drawing of a very uncommon pagoda inside the fort. It is a mixture of Hindoo and Moorish architecture, very grotesque and curious indeed. I perceive there are regular styles and orders in the Hindoo architecture. Wild and confused as it seems, it is as determinate in its way as Grecian or Gothic. A— thinks it is all derived from Jewish or Egyptian traditions, and there is as much of *corruption* as of *invention* in their idolatry. Many of the stories in their mythology are most curiously like the Talmud, and one sees numbers of idolatrous imitations of the Temple-service in every Indian pagoda. There are outer courts, and a Holy place, an altar of sacrifice, brazen bulls, &c. The Hindoos look upon both snakes and monkeys as sacred, but more like demons than gods; and do not you remember Adam Clarke's notion among the quaint fancies of the world, that Satan tempted Eve in the form of a monkey?

In your last you ask whether there is any truth in the account of the conversion of a whole tribe of Hindoos in Bengal. I believe there *is* truth in it. I asked Mr T—, and he said he had heard nothing to throw discredit on the story, but I could not learn any more details or particulars than what you seem to have heard already. One grows sadly suspicious here of all such histories. My mind is, as you say yours is, rather "poisoned"; still I believe it is poison, and must not be allowed to work. I do not think the failures, or even the faults, of the present Missionary system any reason at all for lessening exertion – quite the contrary; the less that has been done, the more remains to be done: but what we want are workmen – *schoolmasters* especially. I do not see any use in making the collections you mention for the *converts* – better not, unless it is to pay Missionaries or schoolmasters for them.

Notes
Indian fever: there was a lot of illness in the family between June and September. First her husband at Samuldavee in June: 'Poor Master has

LETTER TWENTY-SIX

been very ill indeed – He is better but still keeps his bed – It was a most severe attack. He came as usual for his Saturday and Sunday last week and was very feverish and bilious – the rains have been very heavy, and the roads were so bad that he was 18 hours on his journey, and of course several of them in the sun. He took 5 grains of calomel and then went creeping about outside the house in the middle of the night, in cold rainy weather – so he caught a violent cold and fever on the calomel and was very ill indeed for several days, and no Doctor within reach.' Dr Thomson in Masulipatam assisted by letter but was unable to leave his station, and our own worthy scamp of a Dr at Rajahmundry is away pleasuring without leave, a hundred miles off' (21 June 1839). In July Julia complained of her teeth: 'I had dreadful toothache after that beastly Doctor's calomel at Rajahmundry and he had the impudence to tell me that it was impossible ... the back teeth are all going' (31 July). In Madras her attack of fever meant she was 'obliged to have leeches on my head.' But her major concern was, of course, for Etta, 'Lane says she has an enlargement of the liver which will not get well in this country, and advises our sending her home soon – so – she is to go with John when he goes' (21 September). If Etta were to stay, Lane reported that she would have to take so much calomel that her constitution would be ruined.

Lady Q, Mrs C, Miss D: all unidentifiable as this section does not survive. One gets the idea anyway.

bungalow: rules required travellers to make space for each other in these Travellers' Bungalows. See notes to Letter Ten.

Tippoo's stronghold: Tipu Sultan of Mysore, killed at Seringapatam in 1799. His death effectively ended Mysore resistance to the British.

painting their doorsteps: very fine decorative work is done by women in India, on the ground before their homes and on the walls of their homes. This is done generally with a flour and water paste, with or without colour added.

Adam Clarke (1762?-1832), Wesleyan preacher, commentator and theological writer. Between 1810 and 1826 Clarke published his commentary on the Scriptures, in eight volumes. It is in these, despite an overall orthodox evangelical approach, that Clarke maintained that the serpent that tempted Eve was in fact a baboon.

Letter the Twenty-Seventh

Bangalore, November 1st, 1839

This place is not quite perfect as to climate, I see, pleasant as it is. I went a few days ago to call on some friends who live in a rather lower ground, in a very pretty English-looking house, with the compound sloping down towards a tank, to look like a villa on the banks of the Thames: very pretty, but rather deadly – "horribly beautiful!" They walked me round their charming damp garden, and into their sweet shady walks, which all smelt of ague, till my feet were as cold as stones, and I felt myself inhaling fever with every breath I drew. I hurried home as soon as I civilly could, but I had a sharp fit of fever in the night, and was prevented from getting my letter ready for the last steamer.

The Europeans here are chiefly military, and the ladies are different from any I have seen yet. The climate does not tempt them to the dawdling kind of idleness, so they ride about in habits made according to the uniform of their husbands' regiments, and do various spirited things of that sort. Then there is another set – good-natured, housekeeper-like bodies, who talk only of ayahs and amahs, and bad nights and babies, and the advantages of Hodgson's ale while they are nursing, and that sort of thing; seeming, in short, devoted to "suckling fools and chronicling small beer!" However, there are some of a very superior class – almost always the ladies of the colonels or principal officers in the European regiments. These seem never to become Indianized, and have the power of being exceedingly useful. Some of them keep up schools for the English soldiers' children, girls especially – superintend them, watch over the soldiers' wives, try to keep and encourage them in good ways, and are quite a blessing to their poor countrywomen.

LETTER TWENTY-SEVEN

We hear there has been a great deal of fighting at Kurnool. Colonel D— had the command of our troops, and has taken the country. The Rajah of Kurnool himself was an insignificant creature, but it turns out that he was in the pay of some higher power, supposed to be the Nizam's brother, who is trying to organize a conspiracy all over the country, but it is always discovered before it comes to anything. The Rajah of Kurnool, being unnoticed and out of the way, was chosen to collect and receive all the arms and ammunition; and when the English took his fort an enormous arsenal was found, and quantities of gunpowder kept in open chatties, under sheds made of dried leaves, and such queer contrivances, that it is a wonder the fort and the plot were not both blown up together long ago.

November 4th – We have just heard news from Rajahmundry that has vexed us very much. Mr X—, who was appointed as A—'s temporary substitute, has taken the opportunity to turn out, by hook and by crook, under one pretence or another, a number of the native Court servants, writers, &c., just in order to put in his own dependants from another district. It is a shameful proceeding, for the poor people who are thus disgraced and deprived of their livelihood have committed no fault at all, and are among the most respectable and clever servants of the Court.

November 5th – More bad news from poor Rajahmundry. A short time ago a violent storm – such a storm as only occurs in the tropics – raged all along the coast from Narsapoor to Vizagapatam, and as far inland as Rajahmundry and Samulcottah. It must have been most awful. There was an irruption of the sea which drove all the shipping on shore, some of it four miles inland, and sloops are still fixed in gentlemen's gardens. It is computed that ten thousand people have been killed. All the little native huts at Samulcottah were blown down; all the European houses except two unroofed; our house at Rajahmundry all unroofed except one room; all

X—'s furniture destroyed. We cannot be sufficiently thankful to the kind Providence which removed us before it took place, for with our two babies there is no saying what dreadful mischief might have happened. Neither we ourselves nor the children ever occupied the only room that remained safe, and the storm rose so suddenly in the night, that there would not have been time to escape from one part of the house to the other. The destruction of property has been enormous: all the goods in the merchants' storehouses at Coringa and Ingeram ruined; the crops destroyed; the tanks filled with salt water – till the irruption of the sea subsided, no fresh water was to be procured all along the coast. It has been a most fearful visitation. I am very sorry indeed for the poor people, already so impoverished by two years' scarcity and constant heavy taxation. The Collectors are chiefly bent upon keeping up the revenue, whatever may happen; and the people suffer terribly when they have any additional drawback. A "crack Collector", as the phrase goes, is one who makes a point of keeping up the usual revenue in defiance of impossibilities. There may be a famine, a hurricane; half the cultivators may take refuge in another district in despair; there may seem no possible means of obtaining the money: but still the Collector bullies, tyrannizes, starves the people – does what he pleases, in short – and contrives to send in the usual sum to the Board of Revenue, and is said to be a "crack Collector."

December 12th – All the fighting at Kurnool is now over. Colonel D— had the command of it. There were some European corps, dragoons and others, in the force. The fort which they went to besiege was given up to them directly, and they found it full of arms and gunpowder. But after they thought the whole affair was over, and that they had settled the matter without a shot, a party of Patans seized the Rajah, and our force was obliged to attack them. There was sharp fighting, and many killed; but it is all settled now. Colonel D—'s native regiment behaved so well, that, after the charge,

LETTER TWENTY-SEVEN

the English dragoons went up and shook hands with them, and said they were as good soldiers as Englishmen, or "words to that effect." I saw the party of dragoons come home; poor things! they had lost the most men of any. Their band went out to meet them, with a large party of officers and civilians to welcome them home. The band had been practising the "Conquering Hero" for a week, and they all marched in in great state and looking very grand. Then there was a break in the procession, and the led horses of the men who had been killed followed; and after that the widows, with their palanquins and bullock-carriages covered with black cloth. I think it was the most melancholy sight I ever saw, from the extreme contrast of all the music and gaiety preceding, and such a mournful change. A few days afterwards we saw Colonel D— come in at the head of his Sepoys, very grand and proud, with all the colours and trophies they had taken. There seems no doubt but that there really *has* been a combination against us between all the Mohammedans in India; but, now they are put down, I suppose we are stronger than ever. It was remarkable that no Moormen came out to see the show of the regiments' return. In general they take such excessive delight in any military spectacle, that they will come from far and near to see it. This conspiracy seems like a last rise of the Mohammedan power: it is crumbling away everywhere. The English have now opened Affghanistan, and all that country will be under our orders. The Madras army is preparing for a Chinese war, and expecting to be ordered to China very soon.

Vellore, December 18*th* – We are again on our road to Madras, and all our plans changed. This is the last letter you will receive from me, for I hope to be "over the surf" and on my way home to you all in another fortnight. We have been so strongly advised not to keep little Etta any longer in India, that we have at last made up our minds on the subject. A— has applied for leave of absence, and will accompany her and

DECEMBER 1839

me as far as the Cape, which he can do without losing his appointment; and I am then to proceed to England with her Our passages are taken, and we expect to sail early next month.

Notes
fighting at Kurnool: following defeat of Tipu this district fell to the share of the Nizam. He ceded it in 1800 to the British, in payment for a subsidiary force to be stationed in his territories. But the Nawab of Kurnool was left in possession of his *jagir* [hereditary portion of land], subject to a tribute of a lakh of rupees. Munavar Khan was succeeded in 1823 by his brother Ghulam Rasul Khan, the last of the Nawabs. In 1838 this latter was found to be engaged in 'treasonable preparations on an extensive scale' and in the next year he was sent to Trichonopoly, where he was subsequently murdered by his own servant. His territories were annexed.

Mr X—: Dowdeswell.

a violent storm: *The Fort St George Gazette* in 1840 summarised the storm of November 1839: 'A dreadful hurricane occurred on the coast to the Northward of Madras – at Coringa, Samulcottah and parts adjacent, but most severely felt at Coringa. The sea rushed with much violence within a mile into the country, and several villages were inundated and swept away. In many houses it rose to upwards of 8 feet. Above 130 vessels from 50 to 500 tons either driven ashore or sunk at sea, and others driven for miles into the country. A great number of houses were unroofed. Nearly 10,000 persons perished and property to the amount of 7 lacs of rupees was destroyed and lost.'

Wight and his wife (see note to Letters Seventeen and Nineteen) lost their lives in the storm and were buried in the Rajahmundry Cemetery near the old Civil Court: '1839, 8 November, Alexander Wight, Asstt. Surgeon, Madras Establishment, aged 32 years; and Mary Anne, his wife, aged 31 years, who were drowned in the Godavari. This tomb is erected by their brothers'(Le Fanu, who also notes 'Surgeon Wight, a botanist of repute, author of *Icones Plantarum Indiae Orientalis*, founded the Madras Horticultural Society in 1835').

Chinese War: the first Opium War with China began in November 1839.

Appendix 1

The response of the Company authorities to the building of a church in Black Town

The following case, taken from the Madras Public Proceedings (APAC) and taking place while Julia was in Madras, is a good example of the changing attitude of Government to religious issues.

A group of Hindus petitioned Government more than once over the building of a school and chapel in Salay Street, 'one of the principal streets occupied exclusively by the Hindoos.' It appears that a Mr Drew was suspected of having 'clandestinely' bought land in Salay Street in 1834, 'with a view to interfering with our religious observances.' The petitioners are now sure he is building a church. They refer to an 1817 case when the Rev. Mr Thompson was stopped by the then Governor in the building of a church. If the church is built, they say they would rather move, 'preferring [that] to running the risk of losing our religion and customs, in the observance of which we have been duly protected by the British Government ever since their settlement in this country being about 200 ye rs.' The building of a church, 'will embitter the feelings of the whole community' and the result could be 'serious and dangerous.' Drew is reported to have made the following statement, 'with the Divine blessing he believes that residence in such a place is admirably calculated to accomplish the great purposes of Mission labour.' The ruling of the Governor goes against the petitioners: 'his residence there situated, as it is, in the heart of the town, will facilitate in no ordinary degree his communication with all classes of people, and the preaching of the Gospel, in that neighbourhood. We are inclined to consider this an important experience in Missionary operations, and we therefore earnestly recommend it as an object worthy of general support.'

Appendix 2

Petition for Native Education

The text of this unwieldy object in the Asia, Pacific and African Collections of the British Library appears first in English and is then reproduced in two native languages, Tamil and Telugu. There follow yards of signatures, written in Roman and local scripts. It is too delicate to be completely unwound.

The tone of this petition would have pleased Macaulay. The petitioners express a strong desire for a 'British' education (literature and science) as a route to participation in the Administration. They support a system in which the 'upper classes' are educated first, and the knowledge acquired passed on to the 'inferior classes'. The petitioners note that any education that interferes with their religious practice would not be acceptable.

The sentiments expressed in the Petition match so well with those of some branches of contemporary British and Company feeling that one suspects leading petitioners may well have been already involved in the Administration in some way, or have had strong links with those who were.

To the Right Honourable Lord Elphinstone, G. C. H. Governor of Fort St George.

My Lord,
We, the undersigned Native Inhabitants of the Territories under the Government of Fort St George, approach to address your Lordship in the name and behalf of our whole Native Community upon a subject which unspeakably concerns our best and dearest Interests.

APPENDIX 2

We have learnt with feelings which this address can but weakly display, that your Lordship in Council contemplates some effective and liberal measures for the establishment of an improved system of National Education in this Presidency. It is our hope that these, the united sentiments of all classes, which such an announcement has instantly called forth, will at least prove to your Lordship the gratitude of a whole people.

We have had occasion to learn the inestimable advantages of Education. The natural effects of useful knowledge are fully open to our comprehension. We see in the intellectual advancement of the people the true foundation of a Nation's prosperity.

My Lord, we are *the people* of this country – inheriting this land for thousands of generations. From our industry its wealth is supplied. By our arms it is defended from foreign foes. By our loyal obedience to the established Government its peace and its safety is maintained. If the diffusion of Education be among the highest benefits and duties of a Government (to the conviction of which we have been led) we the People petition for our share. We ask advancement through those means which we believe will best enable us, in common with our fellow subjects, to promote the general interests of our native land. We ask it only in proportion to our long proved attachment to the British Government and to its enlightened institutions.

My Lord, we look around and see what has been done, and is doing, in other parts of the Indian Empire, for the mental improvement of the Natives – and we turn to contemplate our own condition. We descend from the oldest Native subjects of the British Power in India; but we are the last who have been considered in the Political endowments devoted to this liberal object. To the voluntary labor of personal friends, and to the charitable contribution of the kindly disposed, has been hitherto confided almost the whole task of ameliorating the intellectual progress of the many millions of our population.

The benevolent intentions of the Court of Directors (often recorded) towards us we have learnt and we acknowledge. But where can their effects be traced? Where are the Natives whose minds have been enlightened through the only means by which advancement in political station and in the higher walks in life is to be gained? Where amongst us, are the Collegiate Institutions which, founded for these generous objects, adorn the two Sister Presidencies. Such Institutions have shed a light over those Presidencies, and rendered illustrious the names of the Founders among a grateful community – who tell of their benefactions, and point at their statues. We have had no such benefactors to commemorate. We cannot share in their just pride.

APPENDIX 2

If the generous dispositions of the Court of Directors have been heretofore thwarted by considerations connected with our attachment to the religion of our Fathers, or by those connected with the present depressed condition of the Native Community of this Presidency generally, we entreat with earnest warmth that your Lordship and your government will no longer allow these considerations to defeat our present hopes. It may be true, that any scheme for National Education, founded on a real design, whether avowed or not, or interfering with the religious faith or sentiment of the people, may prove abortive through our common aversion or opposition to such designs. It may also be true, that the superior classes, and probably the bulk of the people at large, would be indifferent to any such plan, in which no Natives whatever of any quality, should be considered entitled to any co-operation or share. But we encourage a confidence that your Lordship will believe that for Government to act no longer on these principles would be unjust.

We, my Lord, who can sensibly feel the infinite benefits which [tear] the diffusion of useful knowledge, anxiously look that the rising generation may attain instruction in European Literature, Science and Philosophy, as well as our own Native learning and languages; and tha[tear] may study the liberal arts of life, and the Laws of their Country. We believe that they will thereby raise themselves in every relation, both Civil and Social, and we believe that they will at the same time advance the prosperity of this Country, and the attachment of the people to the British Government. But we can never be persuaded that no instruction whatever for these objects can be imparted, except through an interference with our religion. We pray that your Lordship will not impose as a condition for any measure of National Education that the people should act as if they renounced the religious faith in which they have been brought up. It is no toleration of the religion of a people to visit it with the pains of ignorance.

My Lord, we pray too, that we, the Native people, should have some voice and share in the great measure you contemplate: that you will not disdain their co-operation, without which that measure can have no life. We seek not Education which depends on charity. We shall take a pride in contributing according to our means to so noble a work. We look to the mental improvement of the upper classes of the Native Community, who have the leisure and means to pursue the higher branches of study; and from them it may be most reasonably hoped, that the blessings of knowledge will be gradually spread abroad amongst the inferior classes of our native fellow-subjects.

The people of this Presidency are not without their claims on the promoters of the cause of National Education throughout Europe, and

APPENDIX 2

especially on those of the English Nation. The Madras Native system of Education has given its name to a method of instruction which we are told, has contributed to benefit mankind. It will not accord with the justice of a civilized nation to be reminded of this in vain.

We, my Lord, approach as humble Suitors, praying that your generous intentions towards us may not be put aside, or fail of effect. But your Lordship will not be unmindful that on the voice and love of the Native people must depend the greatest glory of your Government. The atchievements [sic] of the English nation in India though we can contemplate with admiration – yet we cannot regard them with the feelings of Englishmen. We trust it may appear a higher glory to accomplish the intellectual advancement of a Country than to subdue it by arms.

That you, my Lord, may emulate the labours of illustrious men in the other Presidencies, and attain by measures as you now propose the fame which is most permanent, because best founded – namely, that which arises from the united sense of a benefited, an intelligent, and a grateful people, is the hope and prayer of the undersigned subscribers to this Address.

Madras, 11th November 1839.

Sources and References

Abbreviation
APAC: Asia, Pacific and Africa Collections of the British Library, previously the Oriental and India Office Collections.

Unpublished sources
Barrett: The Barrett Collection in the British Library Eg3708, Eg3707, Eg3705, Eg3704B, Eg3700A, Eg3702A, Eg3706F

Berg: The Burney Archive in the Berg Collection of the New York Public Library: Letters and other material written by Julia Maitland, letters written by Fanny Burney D'Arblay, Charlotte Francis Broome, Charlotte Francis Barrett, Charles David Maitland, Henry Barrett, Sarah Harriet Burney.

Madras Proceedings: various volumes from the 1830s of the Public Proceedings, Judicial Proceedings, Board of Revenue Proceedings. APAC

Rajahmundry Survey, 1821-24. APAC

Primary sources
Bombay Courier, issues for 1839

East India Register and Directory, London, editions from 1830 to 1842

The Fort St George Gazette, Madras, issues from 1836

The Madras Almanac and Compendium of Intelligence, Madras, editions from 1830 to 1842

A Handbook for India, London, 1859

Bacon, Thomas : *First Impressions and Studies from Nature in Hindostan,* London, 1837

Eastlake, Elizabeth: 'Lady Travellers' in *Quarterly Review,* cli, London, 1845

Eden, Emily: *Up the Country,* London, 1866

Graham, Maria: *Journal of a Residence in India,* Edinburgh, 1812

Hemingway, F.R.: *Madras District Gazeteers: Godavari.* Madras, 1907

Le Fanu, H.: *List of the European Tombs in the Godaveri District, with inscriptions thereon,* Cocanada, 1895

Parkes, Fanny: *Wanderings of a Pilgrim in search of the Picturesque,* London, 1850

SOURCES AND REFERENCES

Prinsep, C.C. : *Record of services of the honourable East India Company's civil servants in the Madras presidency, from 1741 to 1858,* London,1885

Shore, J.F.: *Notes on Indian Affairs* London, 1837

Secondary sources

Dictionary of National Biography

Bayly, C.A. (ed.), *The Raj: India and the British*, 1600-1947 London, 1990

Clark, Lorna J., *The Letters of Sarah Harriet Burney,* University of Georgia Press, 1997

Danvers, F.C. et al, *Memorials of Old Haileybury College,* London, 1894

Dodwell, Henry, *The Nabobs of Madras,* London, 1926

Dyson, K.K., *A Various Universe,* Oxford, 1978

Ghose, Indira, *Women Travellers in Colonial India,* Oxford, 1998

Hemlow, Joyce (ed.) and others, *The Journals and Letters of Fanny Burney (Madame d'Arblay)*, Oxford: Vol VIII, 1815, edited by Peter Hughes with Joyce Hemlow, Althea Douglas and Patricia Hawkins (1980); Vol IX, 1815-17, edited by Warren Derry (1982); Vol XI, 1818-24, edited by Joyce Hemlow with Althea Douglas and Patricia Hawkins (1984); Vol XII, 1825-40, edited by Joyce Hemlow with Althea Douglas and Patricia Hawkins (1984)

Love, Henry D., *Vestiges of Old Madras,* London, 1913

Robinson, Jane, *Wayward Women: a guide to women travellers,* Oxford, 1990

Stokes, Eric, *The English Utilitarians in India,* Oxford, 1959

Thomas, Timothy, *Indians Overseas: a guide to source materials in the India Office Records for the study of Indian Emigration, 1830-1950*, The British Library, 1985

Woodruff, Philip, *The Men who ruled India*, Vol.I, London, 1953

Acknowledgements

Extracts from the Barrett Collection are reproduced by permission of the British Library.

Extracts from the Berg Collection, together with the plates and the letter printed as an endpaper, are reproduced by permission of the Berg Collection of English and American Literature, The New York Public Library, Astor, Lenox and Tilden Foundations.

Extracts of documents in APAC (Asia, Pacific and Africa Collections of the British Library, previously the Oriental and India Office Collections) are reproduced by permission of the British Library.

Extracts from Joyce Hemlow's edition of Fanny Burney's *Journals and Letters* are reprinted by permission of Oxford University Press.

Thanks to:

Julia's descendants Michael Wauchope and his son Piers Wauchope, who provided me with family information and generously allowed me to reproduce the sketch of Julia with her guitar.
Virginia Murray for the information she provided from the John Murray Archive.
Staff at the Berg Collection in the New York Public Library.
Staff at the Asia, Pacific and Africa Collections (the Oriental and India Office Collections) of the British Library.
Harold J. Cook, Professor and Director of the Wellcome Trust Centre for the History of Medicine.
Professor Francis Robinson, Vice-Principal of Royal Holloway College, for a very helpful reading of the typescript.
Polly Smith, Assistant Archivist at the Natural History Museum, London.
Paul Beel, for the maps.
Lee Foust, Alessandra Marchi and Jay Wolke for their contributions.

A.P.